RADIO FREE STEIN

RADIO FREE STEIN

GERTRUDE STEIN'S PARLOR PLAYS

ADAM J. FRANK
with Samuel Vriezen (and many more)

Northwestern University Press
Evanston, Illinois

For Lewis and Merle

Northwestern University Press
www.nupress.northwestern.edu

Copyright © 2025 by Northwestern University.
Published 2025 by Northwestern University Press.
All rights reserved.

Printed in the United States of America

10 9 8 7 6 5 4 3 2 1

Library of Congress Cataloging-in-Publication Data

Names: Frank, Adam J., author. | Vriezen, Samuel, 1973– author.
Title: Radio Free Stein : Gertrude Stein's parlor plays / Adam J Frank with Samuel Vriezen (and many more).
Description: Evanston : Northwestern University Press, 2024. | Includes bibliographical references and index.
Identifiers: LCCN 2024021275 | ISBN 9780810148062 (paperback) | ISBN 9780810148079 (cloth) | ISBN 9780810148086 (ebook)
Subjects: LCSH: Stein, Gertrude, 1874–1946—Criticism and interpretation. | Stein, Gertrude, 1874–1946—Audio adaptations. | Stein, Gertrude, 1874–1946—Dramatic works.
Classification: LCC PS3537.T323 Z5897 2024 | DDC 812.52—dc23/eng/20240507
LC record available at https://lccn.loc.gov/2024021275

CONTENTS

Prologue. The Radio Free Stein Project 6

Essay 1. Gertrude Stein's Radio Audience 22

Interlude 1: *What Happened | Plays*—a radio script 56

Essay 2. Speech, Acts, Parlor Plays: Stein with Austin 92

Interlude 2: *What Happened | Plays*—a score (Samuel Vriezen) 122

Essay 3. Composing *What Happened* (Samuel Vriezen) 150

Acknowledgments 161

Appendix: Recording and Performance Notes 164

Notes 172

Bibliography 179

Index 185

PROLOGUE

THE RADIO FREE STEIN PROJECT

For the past few years I have been producing radio and music theater renderings of Gertrude Stein's early, lesser-known plays for a project called *Radio Free Stein*. Working primarily with composers, but also with directors, musicians, opera divas, actors, sound engineers, poets, and other literary critics (divas all, in our own way), I have created nine recordings, some of which have been broadcast on radio and others staged in live performance. Our main goal has been to develop enjoyable and persuasive sonic interpretations of these plays. At the same time, and from the beginning, the Radio Free Stein project has been motivated by a set of critical questions: What might a Stein reader be able to think and say about her plays after undergoing the process of staging them as radio theater? What new affordances for understanding and criticism would emerge from this experience? These questions, and a handful of others, have guided me both in producing the sound recordings available on the project website and in preparing the essays assembled in this book. The website (radiofreestein.com) and book are meant to accompany one another as a digital boxed set.[1]

While I hope that the project's critical and theatrical energies have vitalized one another, they have also, at times, antagonized one another. I have tried to capture the intimate, unpredictable, lively yet dangerous relations between theatrical and critical approaches by describing the process as *rendering* Stein's plays (rather than *adapting* them, a more neutralizing term about which much has been written). This ungainly word suits the project for a number of reasons. First, it retains the French form (*rendre*) in English and accords well with Stein's famously expatriated situation in Paris (other examples of such words include *tender* and *gender*, crucial for both Stein and her critics). Clearly the word's primary meaning, "to give in return," describes this project's efforts to exchange recorded performance for printed page. But any attempt to perform Stein's plays immediately brings in the second meaning of render, "to give up, surrender, or relinquish." By making choices that give up elements on the page, the service we have rendered Stein's writing in performance is, necessarily, a disservice. Here the word's third meaning, "to change state (to cause to be of a certain nature)," becomes relevant: these plays have been rendered as radio/music theater, recorded voice, music, and sound, mediums that are substantially different from both printed text and live theater, although they participate in both. Finally, the chemical definition ("to obtain or extract by melting, to clarify") suits Stein's compositional poetics, in which confusion plays a significant role. As she puts it in one of her lectures, "there is really no difference between clarity and confusion, just think of any life that is alive, is there really any difference between clarity and confusion."[2] Any lively attempt to render or clarify Stein's plays will create its own compositional, possibly fatal confusions.

This prologue describes the rendering process, the steps I have taken in various groups to move from a given Stein play text to a recording or staged performance: from brainstorming workshop, to script preparation, to music composition, to performance rehearsals, and finally to the recording studio or theater stage. I would like the reader to be aware of these group experiences in production and the people involved in this many-handed and many-headed task, and to understand both the rationales for and the contingency of our choices. Group experience is utterly integral to Stein's plays and theater poetics as I understand them. The project's conceptual approach to groups is closely linked to my earlier work on Stein that reads her compositional poetics and the peculiar theatricality of her writing by way of several theories of affect, emotion, and object relations. I will try to connect the dots between this previous conceptual approach and its more practical applications here. This prologue also lays out, in preliminary form, several backgrounds or contexts for the Radio Free Stein project, interpretive and performance contexts as well as theoretical and historical ones. The three essays in this book take these up in more detail as they grapple with Stein's plays from various angles, including modernist media studies and radio history, affect theory and linguistic performativity, scholarship on Stein's theater, and musical composition.

One word about this book's unusual arrangement and its guiding conceit, the boxed set. This idea appeals to me, not simply for reasons of nostalgia, but for the image it offers (at least, to someone whose habit of acquiring actual boxed sets dates to the late 1990s/early 2000s) of a loose assemblage of materially different objects and mediums: sound recordings (compact discs) plus printed book (often substantial) plus miscellany (cards, stickers, kitschy *objets*). A listener can handle these distinct artifacts, combine and recombine them to activate a highly textured, near-scholarly participation in some specific musical scene or history. In other words, a boxed set appeals to the obsessive fan or (what may come to the same thing) a listener looking to situate what they hear. This book with its accompanying website includes sound recordings and critical essays, as well as a variety of archival materials: excerpts from musical scores, scripts or scenarios based on Stein's plays, the play texts themselves, photographs, posters, performance reviews, composers' remarks. Some of these materials appear in separate interludes or the appendix, some appear as illustrative figures, but in all cases they speak for themselves. The book-and-website's arrangement aims to offer a reader qua listener the experience of opening up a boxed set and choosing their own adventure as they become acquainted with the project. While the looseness of this assemblage and the project's commitment to collaboration stretch the conventions of the scholarly monograph, they also convey key qualities of Stein's theater, its poetics of loose coordination and epistemology of group portraiture, qualities that will be unfolded in the pages that follow.

GERTRUDE STEIN, THAT QUEER, American, woman, Jewish, punk-modernist writer, composed around a hundred plays and theatrical works.[3] A few have received substantive critical treatment, the same ones that have entered the performance repertoire: *Doctor Faustus Lights the Lights* (1938) and the two operas *Four Saints in Three Acts* (1927) and *The Mother of Us All* (1945). A few more have been performed professionally or used as material for adaptation in a variety of mediums, including music, dance, and television.[4] But Stein is not primarily known as a playwright, in part because she threw most conventions of written drama out the window. Her plays are not legible in naturalist performance traditions and continue to pose challenges to experimental and avant-garde theater as well as to criticism. They are not obviously mimetic: only rarely and sporadically can you read Stein's plays for plot; they may or may not include characters or settings; and they tend not to distinguish between formal dramatic elements such as dialogue and stage direction. In other words, her plays reject Aristotelian mimesis and the hierarchy of theatrical elements in which plot (*mythos*) and character (*ethos*) take precedence over speech, song, and spectacle. And yet, as we will see, her plays do re-create something.

The many challenges of Stein's plays could simply be chalked up to the infamous, oft-attributed "difficulty" of her writing in general. From press reviews of her first publications in the 1910s, to the publicity surrounding her rise to celebrity following the best-selling success of *The Autobiography of Alice B. Toklas* (1933), to critical as well as popular treatments of her work from mid-century to the present, Stein's writing and person have provoked at least as much shoulder-shrugging perplexity and resentment as wonder, admiration, and genuine curiosity. There are complex reasons for the negative responses, homophobia, misogyny, and antisemitism not least among them, as well as anxious, moralizing debates about her politics and writing.[5] The Radio Free Stein project, in focusing on Stein's early parlor plays (those written during the 1910s that foreground speech in domestic settings) as well as her encounter with radio in the mid-1930s, does not primarily engage with reception history or historiography. Its goals and methods are more speculative and interpretive than genealogical. Ever since Stein's work entered the literary canon, largely through the efforts of feminist critics of the 1970s and '80s, and partly in the context of theoretical approaches informed by French feminism, her writing's prestige and her iconic status as a queer transmedial modernist has grown.

And yet journalists still feel entitled to wonder whether Stein's writing makes any sense or to represent her writing as unendurable. For a critic and teacher of Stein this journalistic uptake is frustrating, but it points to something meaningful. Reading Stein does require that we endure it in the specific sense that we undergo or suffer it as writing. As a post-Romantic writer in the Emersonian tradition and a student of William James, Stein inherited and transformed a key category for so much nineteenth-century American thinking: experience. Steven Meyer has offered the most comprehensive account of Stein's relation to James and the Emersonian tradition.[6] Reading Stein, Meyer suggests, involves us in an acute phenomenological exercise, a close cousin to what James called radical empiricism: we are invited to become aware that reading consists of experiences of words, sentences, paragraphs, punctuation marks, sounds, tones, images, concepts, feelings, associations, and the multiple, compositional relations among all of these and more. If it is difficult to read Stein, it is because the practices of awareness that her writing cultivates in us interfere with our basic literacy, our ingrained habits of skilled reading. Unlike the experience (I hope) you are having of reading this sentence, reading one of Stein's sentences can be a process of trial and error that involves considerable intonational, rhythmic, and grammatical guesswork. I begin, say, with one idea of its grammar, then encounter a knot or obstacle that requires me to start over and discover a different structure or intonation that makes some kind of sense. Reading Stein's sentences refocuses my attention on the process of reading itself and the attempt to find or make meaning. In this way, her modernist reflexivity emerges, not from a concern with literary form and allusion, but from a practical, pragmatic obsession with the way writing (in English) works—its rhythms, structures, and forces. A movement between levels of awareness is custom-built into every sentence and leads to the near-physiological opacity of our reading experience. I will be returning to these aspects of Stein's writing throughout this book.

Stein's plays require yet more and different kinds of endurance and trial-and-error than her other writing. Any attempt to read or stage them (and Stein's plays make less of the difference between reading and staging than most, as we'll see) involves an elaborated version of the iterative reading practice I have just described. A reader of a Stein play—a group of readers, this project proposes—must attend not only to the grammatical and intonational senses of her sentences but also to the dramatic and theatrical senses of the dialogue, scenes, and acts. Reading any Stein play involves reflexively posing and reposing the question: How could this possibly be played? According to some critics, the obvious answer to this question is that it's not possible, Stein's plays (with just a few exceptions) are not meant to be performed. A commonplace in the criticism casts her plays, especially the early plays, as linguistic experiments intended for the page rather than the stage. For example, Martin Puchner describes them as closet dramas, a phrase that contradicts Stein's emphatic wish, expressed in a letter to Carl Van Vechten, to see them performed in front of audiences ("No decidedly not, I do *not* want the plays published. They are to be kept to be *played*") and that does not suit the outness of her queer theater.[7] Even Sarah Bay-Cheng, who criticizes Puchner and seeks to take into account discourses of turn-of-the-century homosexual identity, deems the early plays "not terribly stage-worthy (though numerous productions have been attempted)."[8] But as Julia Jarcho points out in one of the relatively few approaches that rejects this critical commonplace, "I am not sure how one might distinguish an 'attempted' production from, say, a fully accomplished one."[9] No accident that Jarcho is herself a playwright who sees Stein's plays as "uniquely appropriate to theater as a collaborative medium," an approach congenial to my own.[10]

In fact, avant-garde and other non-naturalist theater artists have been interpreting Stein's work for the stage at least since *Four Saints in Three Acts* (with music by Virgil Thomson, directed by John Houseman) opened in Hartford, Connecticut, in 1934 with its all-Black cast and cellophane sets. The remarkable success of this production (it was, in its moment, the longest-running opera on Broadway), the publication of her lecture "Plays" in *Lectures in America* (1935), and earlier and later publications of various collections, including *Geography and Plays* (1922), *Operas and Plays* (1932), and *Last Operas and Plays* (1949), made Stein's theater and ideas about theater available to many readers. Mid-century directors, performers, and choreographers brought Stein's plays into performance venues especially in New York City of the 1950s and '60s. One theater historian remarks that his working title for a book on the Off-Off-Broadway movement was *What Happened*, the name of Stein's first play, because of this work's key role in the independent New York theater that emerged after the war.[11] In the past two or three decades theater scholars have given Stein pride of place in genealogies of alternative theater. Elinor Fuchs and Una Chaudhuri credit Stein with the role of visionary in initiating landscape as a new spatial paradigm for theater in the twentieth century, while Hans-Thies Lehmann has argued for Stein's significance for what he has influentially termed postdramatic theater.[12] Others have made similar claims.[13] Stein's theater poetics have exerted a powerful gravitational pull on postwar non-naturalist theater.

And yet, for all this influence, until very recently only a handful of Stein's many plays have been written about critically in any depth, and the theatricality they propose remains difficult to understand or conceptualize. The most significant and thoroughgoing account of Stein's theater is still Jane Palatini Bowers's study of her "metadrama," a book published thirty years ago. Bowers argues that Stein's plays are fundamentally antagonistic to the basic conditions of theatrical performance insofar as they foreground language and writing themselves: "language represents nothing other than itself. Words are the things that are exhibited during the performance of a Stein play. The text-making activity of the poet and her language become a theatrical event."[14] Bowers's insights owe much to theater semiotics and, more generally, to theoretical frameworks in which meaning emerges largely from systems of linguistic signification. (Essay 2 returns to her argument in more detail and makes clear my debt to this approach.)

My work has consistently aimed to supplement such linguistic frameworks with theories of affect and an accompanying orientation toward transferential movements across and between bodies, texts, and minds. This orientation sparked the Radio Free Stein project in the first place and prompts its close attention to experiences of reading and staging Stein's plays. Kleinian and post-Kleinian affect and object relations theory have led me to query the roles for subjective states of feeling in techniques that tend toward both theatrical performance and critical interpretation. The essays in this book, in different ways, are attempts to make good on these techniques.

They are committed to the idea that affect and phantasy subtend speech and writing to create densities of meaning, and they acknowledge the difficult, confusing back-and-forth temporalities that accompany transference. In her lecture "Plays," Stein analyzes these movements of affect, in particular those between audience and stage. I turn to this writing now to locate and unfold my theoretical orientation and her theater poetics.

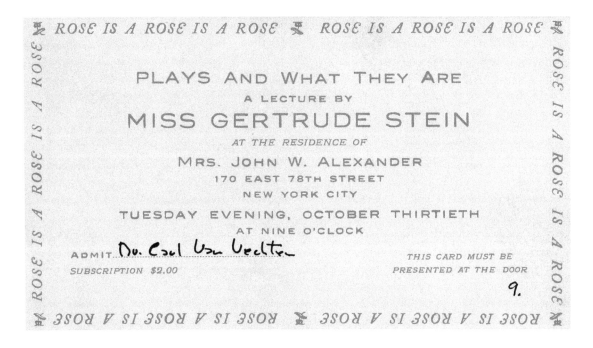

Figure 1. "Plays and What They Are" (1935), invitation card. Gertrude Stein and Alice B. Toklas Papers, Yale Collection of American Literature. Beinecke Rare Book and Manuscript Library. Estate of Gertrude Stein.

PROLOGUE · 11

STEIN THOUGHT VERY CAREFULLY, and often, about the relations between feeling and writing. For example, "Plays" begins with what she calls "a discovery which I considered fundamental, that sentences are not emotional and that paragraphs are."[15] Stein does not explore this insight here (see Essay 2 for more on this). Rather, it serves to introduce the topic of her lecture, a related discovery of the emotional syncopation between audience and events on the stage which, she says, "makes anybody nervous" (95), and which she analogizes to jazz performance "which made of this thing an end in itself" (95). Stein's lecture consists of a sustained meditation on the experience of emotional syncopation in three parts: a comparative phenomenology of different kinds of excitement; a biographical account of her theater experiences as a child (in San Francisco in the 1880s) and adult (in Paris after the turn of the century); and an explanation of her own playwriting as it turns away from narrative ("I concluded that anything that was not a story could be a play" [119]) and toward landscape, which, she claims, resolves the problem of emotional syncopation at the theater ("I felt that if a play was exactly like a landscape then there would be no difficulty about the emotion of the person looking on at the play" [122]).

Many Stein critics have offered interpretations of this lecture, and I, too, have offered an extended, somewhat technical reading.[16] Because the Radio Free Stein project builds on this previous work, I will briefly summarize relevant aspects here. For Stein, the familiar nervous excitement that characterizes theater-going—the excitement of waiting for the curtain to rise, of encountering sudden plot twists and character developments, of moving back and forth between program and stage—these anticipatory excitements and efforts to keep pace with the events on stage interfere with her knowledge practices. Excitement plays a key role in these practices, as this description of her portraiture method in the lecture "Portraits and Repetition" suggests: "I had to find out inside every one what was in them that was intrinsically exciting and I had to find out not by what they said not by what they did not by how much or how little they resembled any other one but I had to find it out by the intensity of movement that there was inside in any one of them" (*Lectures*, 183). Stein's method involves paying attention to her own feeling as a gauge, her excitement an index to her subject's ("I must find out what is moving inside them that makes them them, and I must find out how I by the thing moving excitedly inside in me can make a portrait of them" [183]). Clearly, for Stein, learning about other people is a function of an emotional or affective coordination or transference. In the context of such a method, the syncopated excitements of plot-driven drama interfere with and confuse the coordination she requires for understanding.

Such strong epistemological commitments to affect and feeling emerge everywhere in Stein's writing, as in the question that guides the lecture "Plays": "What happens on the stage and how and how does one feel about it. That is the thing to know, to know and to tell it as so" (101). In her comparative phenomenology of varieties of excitement she contrasts theater-going with "an actual violent scene" (96) in which one takes part. She observes that the movements back and forth at the theater, those that lead to a climax in the plot, culminate in a "relief" from excitement. But in an exciting lived scene in which one participates, these movements lead to what she calls a "completion" of excitement, a "new proportion" (108) rather than a return to some previous emotional equilibrium. This feeling of completion, for Stein, is the sign that a genuinely new emotional ratio has emerged, that a change has led to new knowledge. Think of the difference between, say, the relief you are supposed to experience at the end of a classic Hollywood action movie when the villain is finally defeated and everything goes back to normal (the social order is restored) versus the completion experienced at the end of a difficult quarrel with a loved one, a resolution (if there is one) that signals that some new state of affairs has been achieved—the norm itself may have changed. Stein's concern is that theater can only ever offer relief, whereas she wishes for it to be the occasion for norm-altering new knowledge.

Whatever one thinks of Stein's modernist claim that narrative theater never alters norms or occasions experiences of new knowledge, her treatment of what she considers the problem of emotional syncopation aims to address fundamental questions about the ethics and politics of theater. Her lecture, in my reading, is not as far from Jean-Jacques Rousseau's complex, ambivalent polemic against theater in *Lettre a d'Alembert sur les spectacles* (1758) as it would initially seem, nor are her concerns so different from Bertolt Brecht's in his much more explicitly political epic theater. Stein's particular contribution to these theatrical debates is to locate the ethical and political problems of theater in their affective and epistemological contexts. These are two different but related contexts: one, the role of affect or emotion in experiences of coming to knowledge, and two, the status of theater as group experience. Stein's approach to plays is fundamentally political, in the broadest sense, because of her understanding of the literary form:

I had before I began writing plays written many portraits. I had been enormously interested all my life in finding out what made each one that one and so I had written a great many portraits.

I came to think that since each one is that one and that there are a number of them each one being that one, the only way to express this thing each one being that one and there being a number of them knowing each other was in a play. (119)

For Stein, literary forms can be charged with different epistemological tasks, that is, they let us know different kinds of things. Portraits are for knowing individuals, while plays, as Stein understands them, are for knowing aggregates of individuals: they are group portraits.[17] (And if we think about the history of European painting, a portrait configuration generally depicts one person, sometimes two, while a landscape's horizontality can be used to depict historical groupings of several or many persons.) For Stein, plays depict or explore the dynamics of a number of individuals in epistemological relation, and this aggregate includes, necessarily, the performers of the play as well as the audience attending the play. Her plays are, in a sense, reflexive experiments in audience and group psychology.

I have found the work of the psychoanalyst Wilfred Bion very helpful for conceptualizing group dynamics as well as the intimate relation between feeling and thinking. Bion (Samuel Beckett's analyst in the late 1930s, already significant, somehow, for the history of post/modernist theater) was a member of the group of object relations theorists, those analysts who followed Melanie Klein in her unorthodox departures from classical Freudian theory. Bion coined the term *group therapy* to mean, not the therapy of the individual in a group, but the therapy of the group as such. His approach (published in a series of essays collected in *Experiences in Groups* [1961]) took up Klein's thinking about infantile experience and, in particular, what she called projective identification, a primitive defense in which an unwanted part of the self is aggressively projected outward and located elsewhere. Bion's early work on groups evolved through the 1950s and '60s, especially in the context of his clinical encounters with schizophrenia, into an exploration of thinking itself. In several books—*Learning from Experience* (1962), *Second Thoughts* (1967), and *Attention and Interpretation* (1970)—Bion developed an innovative account of thinking as a phenomenon emergent from the infant-mother dyad. Thinking, in this account, involves a constant to-and-fro of projective and introjective identification, a transference of emotional elements that involves a modification (rather than evasion) of fear and frustration. Bion eventually redescribed his theory of thinking in terms of a reversible container-contained relation that plays out, not only between mother and infant, but also between group and individual, thinker and thought, or word and idea. Its reversibility means that, for Bion, a group may contain an individual, but so may an individual contain a group; similarly, a word (or other aesthetic form) may contain a meaning, but so may a meaning (such as a dream, a feeling, a perception) contain words (and other aesthetic forms). Crucially, and with potentially significant consequences, containment almost inevitably fails. (I take up what Bion calls "catastrophic change" in Essay 2.)[18]

With Bion's work in mind, we can begin to see an affective and conceptual link between Stein's approach to plays as reflexive explorations of groups, on the one hand, and her compositional goal of writing plays that can afford experiences of thinking, on the other. Stein seeks to compose plays as reversible containers that permit thinking to become possible both for audience members and for players on the stage. The problem of naturalist theater, as Stein understands it, stems from its failure to accommodate the to-and-fro of emotional coordination that leads to completion; it leads, instead, to relief from the nervousness of emotional syncopation. If Stein begins in the early 1920s to model her plays on landscapes, it is because these permit "a movement in and out with which anybody looking on can keep in time" (*Lectures*, 131), a loose coordination that she sees as necessary for occasioning the experience of new emotional ratios and new knowledge. By contrast with Aristotelian drama, in which the portrayal of individuals in relation requires story (plot and character become functions of one another), Stein seeks to portray intersubjective dynamics without the help of narrative: "in my early plays I tried to tell what happened without telling stories so that the essence of what happened would be like the essence of the portraits, what made what happened be what it was" (121–22). She does not mean that there is no story to tell; rather, "the story is only of importance if you like to tell or like to hear a story but the relation is there anyway" (125). Stein's plays seek to re-create intersubjective relations without stories.[19]

APPROACHING STEIN'S PLAYS by way of Bion's work offered the Radio Free Stein project a set of guiding premises for production. While affect and object relations theory may appear occasionally in my readings of the plays, more often this material lurks in the background and prompts questions: How do Stein's plays seek to know and re-create group relations? What affect dynamics are being portrayed or explored, and how can we think about these? The first, crucial step toward answering these questions for any given play involves holding a brainstorming workshop with a number of readers, as if it takes a group to arrive at a sense of the play's group (a kind of group transference). I invite the composer who has agreed to work with me on a given play, and a handful of good, available Stein readers (colleagues, critics, poets, translators), as well as one or two graduate students who are studying modernism, theater, affect theory, or sound studies. I prepare for a workshop by reading through any relevant criticism and performance history (bibliographies are usually assembled by a project research assistant, usually one of the graduate students) and request that the other participants simply read the play in advance. Almost entirely unstructured, workshops become opportunities to think with the meanings and non-meanings that emerge from airing Stein's words. They begin in disorientation and disarray with a handful of desultory observations (often in answer to the leading question, What's it like to read this play?). Two hours later, the group arrives at tentative answers to questions such as: How many voices are there? What is the structure? What are the emotional arcs or moods? Is there a theatrical situation or setting?

The experience of being almost comically mystified before arriving at some more stable sense of Stein's work has been typical of the nine workshops I have held for the Radio Free Stein project. The process has been surprisingly, gratifyingly reliable. Not that participants always agree about how to answer these questions, nor even whether there needs to be an answer—the disagreements have been, at times, significant. As Bion explains, groups are inevitably frustrating for the individuals they comprise (in part, because they are a result of regressive phantasy). At the same time, groups are necessary for some tasks to get done (and he makes clear that a group gathered together for work must have some task). One premise of this project is that understanding a Stein play is a group task of this kind. Part of the success of the workshop depends on making our task clear at the start: by the end of our time together I would like to be equipped to transcribe Stein's play text into a script, scenario, or libretto that the composer can use for the purposes of composing the music. In principle, anyone participating in the workshop could create their own transcription of Stein's play, or use the experience effectively for some other purpose. (Indeed, if each participant created their own transcription, these could be performed successively to explore the radical openness of Stein's texts.)

My term for this initial transcription has varied over the course of the project. The term *libretto* naturally emerged to describe the preparatory work for one of the Radio Free Stein productions, Daniel Thomas Davis's chamber opera *SIX. TWENTY. OUTRAGEOUS*. The more operatic a given composer's musical intentions, the more likely we are to describe the post-workshop transcription as a libretto. Initially, however, I called these *scenarios*, the word Maurice Grosser used to describe his work on Stein's *Four Saints in Three Acts* and *The Mother of Us All*.[20] My transcriptions of Stein's plays are not scenarios in the operatic sense but full scripts. The term is inflected by film, where a scenario names a script with detailed annotations about direction, set design, lighting, and so on. Grosser wrote such a film script (*Ladies Voices and What Happened*) based on two early Stein plays and listed the credits this way: "Text by Gertrude Stein / Story by Maurice Grosser." This is closer to my use of the term, although rather than story, my radio scripts offer a means for realizing Stein's play texts as sound recordings. Of course, I agree with Grosser's assertion that "Without doubt other solutions to the problem of staging could be found which would serve equally well."[21]

The post-workshop script or scenario serves as the first rendering of a given Stein play. (See Interlude 1 for the radio script I prepared based on Stein's play *What Happened*.) Drafting the scenario involves extensive discussion with the composer. Together we tackle ongoing interpretive and conceptual issues, and address key practical and financial considerations: intrumentation, vocal range and style, choice of performers or ensembles, musical direction, recording venues. All of these questions, practical, conceptual, and interpretive, have consequences for the scenario, which remains open to redrafting throughout the process. When the composer begins the work of actual composition, yet more fine-tuning of the scenario takes place, as it does even once the music has been composed and we begin performance workshops. It has been interesting to observe which elements of our interpretation of a given Stein play remain stable, and which remain ambiguous or uncertain until very late in the process. For example, each of the three performances of the chamber opera *SIX. TWENTY. OUTRAGEOUS.* was slightly different from the others as Doug Fitch, the director, continued playing with staging ideas on the fly and redistributed lines of dialogue among the players. The performance fell together even if, at times, it seemed like it might fall apart. This genuine quality of not-knowing, of not being able to predict how or whether an interpretation or performance choice will work in advance, is central to experiences of reading Stein. I am gratified when this uncertainty manifests in performance (despite the accompanying risks to reception).

No doubt, such uncertainty is inevitable in, and makes for much of the excitement of, live performance in general. But it is also true that, at least historically, such uncertainty has not been easily accommodated in most European classical music and theater. There are musical traditions in which varieties of uncertainty, with respect to both composition and performance, are part of the music itself. Improvisation can play a structural role in jazz performance, as well as in the work of John Cage and his mid-century contemporaries, themselves influenced by hot jazz.[22] Stein's writing was important for Cage, who composed some of his earliest pieces as musical settings for her work—the now lost *Three Songs for Voice and Piano* (1933), also *Living Room Music* (1940). Cage repeatedly mentions Stein in his writing, as does Morton Feldman, whose early piano compositions and graphic scores required players to make conscious choices of notes or chords during performance. While it is well known that Stein's writing has appealed to twentieth-century composers—Cage, Thomson, Gerald Berners, Al Carmines, Ned Rorem, Robert Winslow, and others through the postwar period and into the present—only recently have scholars begun to explore the underexamined role that Stein's process-oriented writing and poetics have played in postwar North American music.[23] Several of the Radio Free Stein musical settings, especially those by Olive (Dave) Chokroun and Sam Shalabi, are informed by the blending of jazz and other popular performance with the American post-Cage tradition. There is much more to say about Stein's poetics, popular song, Black musical performance, and the epistemology of groups in relation to free jazz and "out" performance more generally.[24]

I often describe our renderings of Stein's plays as radio melodramas. My use of the term *melodrama* refers, in the first instance, to an eighteenth-century composite genre that integrates the performance of spoken words with musical accompaniment in a manner that nevertheless keeps them separate (the words are not sung). Rousseau's *Pygmalion* is often considered the first of these works in which music prepares for or subtends speech. While this form makes an appearance in classical European opera (such as Beethoven's *Fidelio*), it takes distinctive shape in modernist opera and music theater in the technique of *sprechstimme* as differently used by Arnold Schoenberg, Alban Berg, and Kurt Weill. In the United States, Robert Ashley has gone furthest in exploring this form: Ashley's textually dense work uses complex notation to mark pitch and tempo, at the same time that it encourages and investigates the speaker's own speech styles and patterns of intonation. Radio Free Stein's commitment to forms of melodrama is a consequence of its focus on Stein's language: we have insisted on intelligibility in the delivery of speech and language, even when, for example, operatic singing or contrapuntal layering might otherwise threaten it. If, in classical melodrama music plays a supporting role for declamation, in modernist settings we may hear more reciprocal, mutually implicating relations between speech and music: music contains (and fails to contain) speech, speech contains (and fails to contain) music, while composition explores and deconstructs such relations of affective containment and catastrophe.

It is for this reason that, at least in this project, I have not pursued Stein's wish expressed in *Everybody's Autobiography*: "As yet they have not done any of mine without music to help them. They could though and it would be interesting."[25] Why is there such a prevalence of musical interpretations of Stein's plays? Samuel Vriezen will offer one approach to this question in Essay 3 in his discussion of Stein's meditations on time. I can hint at the issues involved by invoking Virgil Thomson's observation that Stein's poetry "need[s] musical reinforcement," which he immediately corrects: "I do not mean that her writing *lacks* music; I mean that it *likes* music."[26] This formulation implies several claims at the same time: that Stein's writing is somehow helped by music; that it is somehow like music (Thomson suggests that "Much of it, in fact, lies closer to musical timings than to speech timings")[27]; and, finally, that Stein's writing is not the same as music. Some of the kinds of sense Stein's writing makes are musical, a musicality related to the intonational contours that give her sentences meaning. Steven Meyer has suggested that intonation "provides a compositional landscape for grammar, and thereby provides grammatical constructions with determinate significance," one of a number of critics who have attended to the crucial role for intonation in reading Stein.[28] If I have enlisted composers in this project, it is precisely because musicality helps us understand Stein's writing in its affective movement between linguistic and intonational sense-making.[29]

The composers who have participated in this project, each influenced by distinct musical styles, have been keen to explore Stein's writing for their own compositional purposes of bringing words and music together. Samuel Vriezen's game-like setting of *What Happened* is more explicitly after Cage than the others (see Interlude 2), but each composer engages with questions of postmodern composition in his or her own way. As Olive (Dave) Chokroun explains in their composer's note (included in the appendix), the musical setting for *He Said It* is completely scored but incorporates indeterminate sections, gestures that are written out but arranged and repeated ad lib by the performer. Informed by Cage's idea that music is a container of time, Chokroun describes the setting as serial-ish rather than serialist: "I spent a lot of time speaking the text and trying to absorb the cadence of the spoken words—not for the purpose of transcription but to try to capture the affect of the text." In our rendering, we wanted the piano to restate aspects of Stein's play text, and for the vocal performers to read the play with the piano music in mind. Her words circulate through music and speech.

Dorothy Chang chose a Stravinsky-ish, neoclassical style for her setting of *For the Country Entirely*, clean lines and structures that become distorted over the course of the play, eventually interrupted by a series of miniatures consisting of quiet tone clusters and pitch bends.[30] Very different is her setting for *White Wines*, the musical language of which is largely modal, and which treats the text in many ways: as natural speech, contrapuntal layers of speech, rhythmic speech, recitative, chanting, and song. Daniel Thomas Davis's gorgeous operatic settings for *Photograph*, *Captain Walter Arnold*, and *The Psychology of Nations* are in conversation with American new opera traditions (see figure 2), while Sam Shalabi's setting for *Short Sentences* offers Zappa-esque pop melodies that approach show tunes, with electronics, rock percussion, and a medley of jazz, folk, and punk influences. Finally, Dan Warner offers an electronic treatment of *An Exercise in Analysis* that calls to mind Laurie Anderson's work from the 1980s. Readers interested in these composers' perspectives on the project will find links to discussions with them (a YouTube broadcast called RADIO FREE RADIO) in the appendix.

WITH THE SCENARIO OR LIBRETTO prepared and the music composed, we are ready to move, in the final stages of the rendering process, toward performance workshops and rehearsals, then recording, editing, and mixing the audio. Radio Free Stein was initially conceived as a recording project, and although some of our productions have been performed live, I have consistently imagined radio to be its primary medium and guiding technological apparatus. By radio I mean, quite generally, the dissemination of sound either via broadcasting or digital media. There are substantial differences between radio broadcasting in its historical forms, realized in different institutional and national contexts, and contemporary audio forms such as podcasting and streaming distribution of mp3 or other digital files. But I am using the umbrella term *radio* to capture the practice of recording, editing, and distributing performance in the medium of sound (often at no financial cost to the auditor), and pursuing the continuities between radio in its historical and contemporary forms by focusing on the studio, whether home or professional, as a site of performance. Essay 1 unfolds the appropriateness of radio for interpreting Stein's plays in some detail.

Figure 2. Daniel Thomas Davis, *SIX. TWENTY. OUTRAGEOUS. Three Gertrude Stein Plays in the Shape of an Opera* (2018), score excerpt. Copyright © Daniel Thomas Davis.

I am not the only reader of Stein's parlor plays to suggest that they work well on radio. Donald Sutherland, who wrote the first book-length critical study of her work, remarks that "most of the plays of the first period are, I think, literary and not for the stage, though they might be very interesting on the radio" since "the text in itself [is] the play."[31] Alongside the familiar commonplace that opposes the literary to the theatrical, radio appears here as a third term. For Sutherland, radio can give us Stein's words without distracting us with visible referents on stage. My approach emphasizes, not this subtractive quality of radio, but its additive quality. For radio gives us something that audiences do not directly encounter in most live theater: the material script. When we listen to a play written and performed for radio, we are (almost always) hearing actors reading—they are, as theatrical jargon puts it, on book (like musicans who perform from a score). Radio plays are literally readings of a text that is phenomenologically present to the players in performance. This convention of radio performance suits Stein's theater well because the words remain in the picture, as it were, such that listeners can experience an auditory performance of reading.

Stein's writing remains in the picture when we hear her plays because, like musical notes written on a stave, written words are images capable of being both seen (and read silently) and heard (when read aloud). For Stein, the commingling of this audiovisual quality is more keen or acute in plays than other forms: "In the poetry of plays words are more lively words than in any other kind of poetry."[32] This gives rise to a paradox that Stein, in one explanation of her approach to playwriting, puts this way: "Whenever I write a play it is a play because it is a thing I do not see but it is a thing somebody can see that is what makes a play to me."[33] If a theater is a place for viewing or beholding (from Greek, *theatron*), it is a place that Stein declines to occupy even while she leaves it open for "somebody" else: a reader. While this formulation seems to invite a director's theater approach, one often taken in twentieth-century presentations of Stein's plays (notably those by Lawrence Kornfeld and Robert Wilson), Radio Free Stein orients Stein's plays back toward the reader qua reader rather than director. Listeners to the streaming Radio Free Stein audio files are encouraged to read Stein's play texts at the same time in order to "see" her plays as sound, a theater of the mind's ear.

I PURSUE QUESTIONS ABOUT RADIO, and about the mixed sensory experience that Stein understands as fundamental to theater, in Essay 1. There I unfold the various ironies of the project's title *Radio Free Stein* in the context of recent work on modernism, media, and propaganda. The essay takes up Stein's 1934 interview on NBC radio and its surrounding historical archive to unfold a powerful phantasy about *radio audience* as it simultaneously connects Stein to a new mass audience and frees her from it. It then turns to Theodor Adorno's writing of the 1930s on "radio physiognomics" to analyze the interiorization of the microphone and the studio in production and reception. In its final section, the essay reads Stein's play *Photograph* and its treatment of technological reproduction by way of the twin, a figure for biological and psychological splitting. In a discussion of Radio Free Stein's rendering of *Photograph* and *The Psychology of Nations*, the essay argues that the acousmatic theatricality associated with Stein's early plays indexes a phenomenology of studio recording and gives us access to the psychic and social realities of sound reproduction.

Essay 2 moves from the spatiality of the radio studio to a different, related interiority, the hollowness associated with J. L. Austin's theory of performative utterances. I argue that Stein's early plays offer traction on the specific role of affect in assessing linguistic force. The essay reads Austin's citations of ancient Greek theater to unfold the structural hollowness of both theatrical performance and the performative utterance, a reading that attends to what I call performativity's scenic aspect. The essay then brings this form of attention to readings of Stein's plays *He Said It*, *What Happened*, and *White Wines* to track a variety of forces (illocutionary and perlocutionary) in these parlor plays. The essay analyzes the ongoing tension in Stein's work between theatrical conventions (or norms) and motives (or affect), and argues for the constitutive, reciprocal relation between theater and domesticity. Reading these early Stein plays permits me to develop a distinctive, broadly Wittgensteinian understanding of performativity rather than an exclusively deconstructive one.

Samuel Vriezen composed the musical setting for the Radio Free Stein production of *What Happened | Plays*. An Amsterdam-based composer, pianist, essayist, and poet, Vriezen unfolds his approach to transforming Stein's sentences and scenes into sounds and musical structures in Essay 3. This essay offers a brilliant deep dive into Stein's thinking about varieties of time by way of her meditation in *What Happened* on the difference between a *cut* and a *slice*, which Vriezen reads in terms of "the frequency domain" and "the time domain." These terms offer a way to move through a series of "transforms" between speech and song, melody and harmony, memory and lived experience, pitch and resonance. Vriezen describes our collaboration and offers context for choices made in composition and production, thus supplementing a reader's encounter with the script (in Interlude 1) and excerpts from the score (in Interlude 2), as well as a listener's experience of the sound recording (available via the project website). The book's appendix includes links to all the recordings, full credits, and selected composers' notes on musical settings, as well as visual archival material associated with the project.

To conclude this prologue to the Radio Free Stein project, and as a segue to the essay on radio, I refer, as so many other Stein readers have done before me, to her famous response to the NBC radio interviewer William Lundell. In reply to his bemused question about the greater intelligibility of her speech relative to her writing, Stein insists that "being intelligible is not what it seems. . . . You mean by understanding that you can talk about it in the way that you have a habit of talking, putting it in other words, but I mean by understanding enjoyment. . . . If you enjoy it, you understand it."[34] This radio interview serves as a metonym for my project as a whole, and I have tried to take seriously Stein's gesture toward the role of enjoyment in reading and writing about her work. Whatever else it does, Stein's writing utterly disables the masterly habit of paraphrase, explication, or "putting it in other words," a particular challenge to those of us who inhabit literary critical contexts where readers often feel that they have so much to lose in giving up the fantasy of mastery that accompanies skilled reading itself. Simply put, Stein's writing invites us to invent other modes of critical reading, thinking, and feeling—what this project has tried to do.

ESSAY 1

GERTRUDE STEIN'S RADIO AUDIENCE

To begin with a brief meditation on this project's title *Radio Free Stein*, which resonates politically, ironically in ways I cannot control but that are entirely appropriate to its subject and our contemporary moment: The *radio free* moniker refers in its first historical instance to a major CIA initiative to disseminate American free market ideologies to Cold War Europe and beyond. Founded in 1949, Radio Free Europe quickly became a model for similarly named CIA-sponsored stations elsewhere, and since the 1970s, under the umbrella Radio Liberty network, it continues to participate in global strategies to support the (oh-so-slowly waning) American empire. My project title suits Gertrude Stein's embarrassingly unabashed patriotism, her proleptic embrace of the so-called American century as it expresses and realizes the modern. At the same time, *radio free* has been taken up by liberationist efforts from all over the political spectrum, from civil rights to Scottish nationalism to religious pirate radio, and broadly signifies a rejection of any authority that restricts the communication of ideas. This, too, suits Stein's legacy, for whatever her nonradical economic politics may have been (I'm thinking of her staunch fiscal conservatism), her distinctly radical writing and poetics continue to give readers, especially queer and feminist readers, fundamental permission in the Emersonian mode to unburden ourselves of linguistic traditions and the authority of literary and cultural histories.

The irony of my project's title is a consequence of what happens when the word *free*, with its intricate, near-impossible meanings, cozies up to *radio* to form a prefix that evokes, fairly precisely, ideas of propagation and propaganda. Radio Free Stein, in using the audio medium quite literally to propagate Stein's early plays, serves as propaganda in its pre-twentieth-century sense ("an organization, scheme, or movement for the propagation of a particular doctrine, practice, etc." [*OED*]). But this term's more tendentious meanings are unavoidable. Propaganda, as Mark Wollaeger has helped us to understand it, is crucially part of the twentieth-century information-media matrix in which modernist literature, in its concern with the autonomy of the aesthetic, should be understood. Wollaeger's study of British literature between 1900 and 1940 suggests that propaganda's current meanings emerged most powerfully in the global context of two world wars and the multiple means for disseminating deceptive information in the service of state-sponsored political causes. This period, which precisely spans Stein's career, saw the emergence of wireless radio as a mass medium, one of the primary means for disseminating information in a variety of related, propaganda-like modes including advertising, boosterism, promotion, and public relations. As we will see, Stein's experiences with radio and its role in promoting her celebrity in the mid-1930s fully support Wollaeger's unfolding of the symbiotic relations between modernist literature and propaganda: "Neither uniformly antithetical nor identical, modernism and propaganda were sometimes agonistic, sometimes allied, and sometimes nearly indistinguishable."[1]

Inexpensive digital means for recording, editing, mixing, and disseminating sound have made independent audio productions like the Radio Free Stein project possible. But why not call it *The Stein Theater Podcast* to avoid unseemly associations? Precisely because these associations speak to the historical rootedness and political connotations of the term *radio*. To my ears, podcasting's celebrity orientation and commitment to intimate lyrical style embrace the social ideals that Theodor Adorno has analyzed and criticized in his writing on radio that I will be discussing here. That is, podcasting permits listeners far too easily to set aside the institutional factors in the reception of sound and supports the myth that peer-to-peer digital networks bypass institutional mediations. Radio, by contrast, is more explicit and offers a historical rubric for thinking about information flow and the near-structural role for promotion, bias, and agenda in the propagation of ideas. I would hazard a guess that podcasting and other radio-style practices have recently reemerged in the face of our contemporary (oh-so-late) modernist need to find sources of reliable information, trustworthy voices, and ways to assess what we hear. To insist on the term *radio* in the project's title is to foreground these questions and the layered historical remediations that accompany all so-called new media.

We experience these remediations constantly, now that all the major twentieth-century mediums—radio, film, and television—are located on a single twenty-first-century device that we carry around in our pockets or handbags. This astonishing intensification and convergence of institutional media structure and integrate perception, feeling, politics, and everyday life to create the conditions for what has emerged as a near-consensus in modernist literary studies. Most contemporary scholars who study literature around and after 1900 consider it, among other things, to register, respond to, and be transformed by the accelerating relations among technologies of recording and transmission. That is, they approach a broad media ecology in (more or less) materialist terms that supplement an earlier emphasis on print and publishing institutions (the little magazines, say) with attention to multiple media. Conceptually, they are frequently informed by the media theory of Friedrich Kittler or, somewhat differently, by Marxist media studies, whether that of the Frankfurt School or of Raymond Williams.[2] Wollaeger's work on modernism and propaganda participates in this consensus (although it turns to Jacques Ellul, interestingly), as does the subfield of radio studies.[3]

My project also participates in this consensus, but in two somewhat unusual ways. First, where scholarship on Stein and modernist media has, until recently, focused largely on cinema and celebrity, I address her theater poetics vis-à-vis sound and radio studies.[4] Second, as this essay's complementary and contrastive use of the terms fantasy (with-an-*f*) and phantasy (with-a-*ph*) throughout indicates, its theoretical approach is by way of Kleinian and post-Kleinian object relations theory, more specifically, Wilfred Bion's understanding of dynamic, reciprocal relations of psychic containment (the prologue addresses the relevance of this approach for interpreting Stein's theater poetics). Bion's work permits me to pose a series of guiding questions: How do Stein's theater poetics contain radio and its expressive techniques? How might radio interpretations of her plays contain (and fail to contain) Stein's poetics? And what might Stein's writing tell us about those f/phantasies that accompany the ubiquitous technological reproduction of sound images in the ongoing modernist moment?

This essay pursues answers to these questions in three main sections. The first attends to materials associated with Stein's 1934 NBC radio interview: a recording, a script prepared in advance of the broadcast, and a popular magazine article for *Cosmopolitan* that Stein wrote at the time of her interview. Stein articulates a powerful fantasy of *radio audience* that connects her to a new audience and simultaneously frees her from it via the protective space of the studio. In other words, and to add to the layers of meanings accruing to the project title, radio frees Stein from the audience precisely because radio frees Stein to audience as the act of hearing itself. This section moves from an interpretation of Stein's phenomenology of radio audience to a more general phantasy that, I suggest, belongs to radio: a speaker introjects the microphone-and-studio to create an interiorized space of audience. The second section builds on this phantasy associated with radio transmission to supplement Adorno's writing on the radio voice and the situation of reception. Adorno brings social, technical, and aesthetic considerations together in pursuit of what he calls radio physiognomics, an approach I find helpful especially in its effort to separate radio's technical possibilities from its institutional, social ideals.

While the first two sections address radio as a medium of public relations and propaganda, the third approaches radio as a medium of interpretation. Phantasies of audience continue to play a role insofar as hearing speaking voices, according to Stein, poses epistemic problems for her portrait writing, a confusion of tongues that results from temporal lag and affective disjunction and that becomes the subject of her plays of the 1910s. Stein's parlor plays are fundamentally acousmatic, that is, they explore sound without identifiable source, and in that sense are well suited for interpretation via radio. This section offers readings of Stein's *Photograph* and *The Psychology of Nations*, works that my collaborators and I have rendered as part of the chamber opera *SIX. TWENTY. OUTRAGEOUS.* In our staging, Stein's plays address the acousmatics of phonograph and radio in a manner that brings together sociopolitical, aesthetic, and psychical considerations. Related concepts in these works (the twin, the brother) allow Stein to take up questions of biological and psychological splitting and the estranging dissociations that accompany (audio and visual) image reproduction. Stein works through the psychic and social consequences of these ubiquitous reproductions, their dissociative or disjunctive qualities, by way of family relations.

If the Radio Free Stein project has embraced the task of propagating Stein's theater, it is with a Spinozist cheerfulness, an ironic awareness that her theater is, to cite Walter Benjamin's famous phrase with a slight twist, utterly useless for the purposes of propaganda (for better and for worse). Unlike propaganda's efforts to overwhelm and confuse or to deceptively clarify, or both, Stein's plays offer opportunities for thinking about the intimate relations between clarity and confusion. Put differently, as I suggested in the prologue, Stein's writing attends to the epistemic value of feeling. To prioritize feeling is not at all to subordinate thinking, not in the pragmatist tradition to which Stein belongs.[5] Rather, Stein's theater amplifies the corporeality of thinking and what John Durham Peters has identified as the erotic uncanniness of those tele-technologies that communicate at a distance: "Not the ghost in the machine, but the body in the medium is the central dilemma of modern communication."[6] This is also the central concern of writing as such, at least from the perspective of Stein's radically empiricist and transferential poetics. My approach here shares with Peters's a sense of the theoretical stakes of communication, as he puts it in his overview of philosophical thinking on the topic in the 1920s and '30s: "The task today is to renounce the dream of communication while retaining the goods it invokes . . . to find an account of communication that erases neither the curious fact of otherness at its core nor the possibility of doing things with words," an account he seeks by way of "a pragmatism open to both the uncanny and the practical."[7] This is the approach that Stein appears to take in her radio interview. I turn to that broadcast now.

THE EVENING OF NOVEMBER 12, 1934, the NBC reporter William Lundell conducted an interview with Gertrude Stein in a New York radio studio that was broadcast live and distributed coast to coast.[8] Both Stein and Lundell read from a script they had prepared a day or two earlier and, it appears, revised just prior to the broadcast.[9] While the seasoned broadcaster improvised lightly to create the effect of spontaneity (adding "Well" or "Miss Stein" here and there), Stein kept close to the script. Until, that is, about halfway through the interview when she began, like Lundell, to play a little more freely with the words on the page and to engage with the emotional dynamics of the interview situation. Lundell, the director of special events progams at NBC ("the first man to do an interview from earth to airplane in 1929"),[10] was friendly but reserved, and combined an ironic appreciation of Stein's remarkable celebrity at the start of her U.S. lecture tour with a genuine curiosity about her writing as well as skepticism about its reception. When he assumes the

Figure 3. "I write for myself and strangers and this is what broadcasting is." William Lundell and Gertrude Stein (1934). Photograph by Ray Lee Jackson. Gertrude Stein and Alice B. Toklas Papers, Yale Collection of American Literature. Beinecke Rare Book and Manuscript Library. Estate of Gertrude Stein.

journalist's mantle and becomes more confrontational, Stein goes ever-so-slightly off-script to address the interviewer directly in her best bluff, patronizing manner ("Well, you see Lundell"). Energized by the tension and Stein's wish to get her ideas across, the interview warms up and sounds more like conversation. While both remain on-script, they do seem to be listening to one another.

In preparing a written script and then improvising from it, Lundell and Stein were pursuing standard radio practice of the time. As the early theorist of radio Rudolf Arnheim explained in the 1930s, "In broadcasting to-day it is customary to read from a paper what one wants to say to the listener."[11] Arnheim assesses this practice in a chapter with the (Stein-like) title "The Art of Speaking to Everybody" in which he moves through a set of dialectics (direct and indirect address, composition in speech and in writing) while exploring how best to deliver expert knowledge. Given the "double function of language" as medium of information and expression, the nature of listener attention, and the intimidating need to deliver high-quality broadcasting to a large radio audience, Arnheim ultimately commends the practice of preparing a script and then formulating expression as if for the first time: "So, when one is drafting out a wireless talk, one must consciously include in the script the personal tone of voice and way of speaking, quite indifferent as to whether the resultant 'score' of the talk makes at the same time a good piece of printed literature or not."[12] By analogy with the performance of scored music, Arnheim implies, radio should be carefully composed for the ear and performed with attentive spontaneity.

Lundell and his colleagues knew what they were doing and Stein could not have been more pleased. Having stepped off the boat from Paris (the SS *Champlain*) just three weeks before, Stein and Toklas had already been filmed in a Pathé newsreel and flown to Chicago to attend the opening night of *Four Saints in Three Acts*, and Stein had given the first lectures of her six-month lecture tour. But as she put it in a piece for *Hearst's International-Cosmopolitan Magazine* (see figure 4) that describes her radio experience, "of all the things that I never did before, perhaps I like this the best."[13] Stein liked radio broadcasting for a number of related reasons, first and foremost because it cultivated a powerful feeling that "everybody was listening."[14] Stein's long-standing wish for a large American audience, gratified as a result of the best-selling success of *The Autobiography of Alice B. Toklas* (1933) and the lecture tour that followed, intersected with radio in a distinctive way. Where her lecture audiences were physically present to her and capped at five hundred (at Stein's insistence), the radio audience was largely conjectural and potentially infinite. In this respect, radio broadcasting shares a situational structure with the activity of writing itself when it takes place within a private, enclosed space (a study or *studio*) and conjures endless numbers of imaginary readers. This analogy between radio broadcasting and writing, we shall see, is the other main reason that Stein takes such delight in her radio experience. But in broacasting it is not only the audience that is conjectural. Stein experienced herself as becoming conjectural in the context of the U.S. tour, radio one among several of the powerful publicity machines that helped to create the emerging public persona, Gertrude Stein the celebrated author, an entity not altogether familiar to Gertrude Stein the writer. That is, Stein was experiencing a strange dissociation of writer from author-function that at once gratified her wish for fame and posed new problems for her writing.[15]

The *Cosmopolitan* article was Stein's first published attempt to think through the whirlwind of exciting and unsettling experiences that accompanied her emergence, at the age of sixty, as a successful author on the American scene. As its unusually breathless tone attests, she had not yet brought to these experiences the careful, sustained, remarkable attention that characterizes her more usual meditative writing. She appears to have completed the article the night of the broadcast ("Tonight I did the last thing that I never did before"), the article itself part of the whirl she describes.[16] Illustrated with photographs captioned by Stein's aperçus, the article is a primer on the technologies and media of modernism: sound film, airplanes, American urban space (streets, skyscrapers, traffic lights), and radio. Stein emphasizes the novelty and strangeness of her encounters with new mediums even while she addresses them in more familiar terms. For example, she compares airplane flight with boat travel ("why did nobody tell me before I got on that the air is solid. Of course it is solid, it is just as solid as water" [168]) and compares the experience of being recognized by strangers in New York to village life in rural France ("It is just like living in the country where I live and there are very few people and where I know anybody and everybody knows me" [167]). Some of the article's content overlaps with that of the radio interview where Stein is more forthright about her fear ("I who am easily frightened by anything unexpected find this spontaneous considerate contact with all and any New York touching and pleasing").[17] But in both article and interview she emphasizes "the gentle pleasant unreality of it" (167),

of her experiences of streets, buildings, people, a variety of mediums in which she is newly immersed, and in particular, the estranging-yet-familiarizing meta-medium of publicity. She puts it this way toward the end of the article: "The unreal is natural, so natural that it makes of unreality the most natural of anything natural. That is what America does, and that is what America is" (168). Both interview and article identify publicity in modern America as a variety of "natural" "unreality," which is to say, utterly phantasmatic.[18]

Stein is deeply ambivalent about what she sees as the naturalizing of unreality that accompanies American publicity. She compares seeing herself in the short Pathé newsreel to "unexpectedly seeing one's name in print" (167) with its "slightly mixed-up feeling, are you or are you not one" (167). This dissociative feeling is significantly amplified by film: "Imagine what is that compared to never having heard anybody's voice speaking while a picture is doing something, and that voice and that person is yourself, if you could really and truly be that one. It upset me very much when that happened to me" (167). In observing sound film's capacity to reproduce images of the voice and body or face ("person"), Stein registers a further disturbance to perception (as Roland Barthes famously describes photography) that accompanies cinematographic technologies, the novelty of hearing and seeing oneself speaking and moving from the outside, from the uncanny perspective of another. The very same publicity machines that, on her lecture tour, created a much-sought-after celebrity also disturbed Stein's perceptual self-orientation and threatened her carefully calibrated separation of inside from outside. These confusions would preoccupy Stein for years and troubled her compositional agency (she suffered

Figure 4. Gertrude Stein, "I Came and Here I Am," *Hearst's International-Cosmopolitan Magazine* (February 1935). Estate of Gertrude Stein.

from writer's block for six months after returning from the U.S. tour to France).

But radio was different. Stein compares her broadcasting experience, not to the disturbing and desired publicity of print, but to the practice of writing itself. Rather than confuse inside and outside as film did, radio permitted her to maintain a distinction that she believed to be crucial to her writing: "I write for myself and strangers and this is what broadcasting is. I write for myself and strangers" (168). This formulation, a refrain from her long novel *The Making of Americans* completed almost twenty-five years before and published (in abridged form) in spring 1934, identifies radio as the culmination of the long arc of Stein's career. Radio, it appeared to Stein, permitted her to maintain the difference between inside and outside, writing and print. It offered positive answers to her most pressing questions: Will there be an audience for my writing? What will it be like? How might I come to know, or become acquainted with, this audience? She had represented these worries to herself very clearly in a piece written in September just before leaving France, "Meditations on Being About to Visit My Native Land," in which she was concerned about the behavior of her imagined lecture audiences ("Will they ask me questions and will I ask them questions and which will ask the questions most and first, and will they listen to me and will I listen to them").[19] These concerns become crucial given Stein's commitment to lived experiences of writing and thinking, what she decribes elsewhere as "talking and listening at the same time," which is, she claims, the "essence of genius."[20]

In the context of these worries radio offered Stein clear comforts. The question-and-answer format of the radio interview and the fact that it was scripted in advance were reassuring ("And then we went into training. I liked that; I wrote out answers to questions and questions to answers and I liked that").[21] She notes with pleased surprise that what she reads aloud sounds, even to her, like improvised speech ("it was, it really was, as if you were saying what you were saying" [168]) and she is impressed by the efficient, exacting temporal coordination of a live broadcast ("they were going to time us and they did . . . they knew so well how to do this thing and no fuss was made about anything" [168]). What emerges from these experiences of broadcasting is a specific fantasy about radio audience:

> Then we sat down one on either side of the little thing that was between us and I said something and they said that is all, and then suddenly it was all going on. It was it was really all going on, and it was, it really was, as if you were saying what you were saying and you knew, you really knew, not by what you knew but by what you felt, that everybody was listening. It is a very wonderful thing to do, I almost stopped and said it, I was so filled with it. And then it was over and I never had liked anything as I had liked it. (168)

I wonder what would have happened had Stein interrupted her reading of the script to improvise, to communicate this "wonderful thing" and express her feeling that "everybody was listening." She didn't, and I suspect that some part of her understood that this feeling associated with radio's basic fantasy can only be communicated retrospectively (later in the article, not now on the radio). For this fantasy condenses two meanings that exist in some tension with one another: *the audience* in the more usual sense of an assembly or "a body of hearers, spectators" and *audience* in the somewhat less usual sense of "the action or scope of hearing" (*OED*). There was an assembly of people at the studio watching and listening to Stein and Lundell, a small studio audience (including Toklas; the publisher Bennett Cerf, who arranged the radio event; possibly the actor Miriam Hopkins; journalists and photographers, sound technicians, others), but Stein's attention is elsewhere ("and then I was taken into another room and there there were more people but by that time I was not noticing much of anything" [168]). In her excitement and fear she concentrates on reading from the script, on talking and reflexively listening to her own speech and Lundell's. Audience took place regardless of whether anyone other than Stein was actually listening.

To put this another way, radio freed Stein from *the audience* (outside) by making *audience* available as a feeling (inside) ("you really knew, not by what you knew but by what you felt, that everybody was listening"). This is a fantasy in Freud's sense, an affective expression of a writerly wish for the greatest possible number of listeners. But it is also a phantasy in Melanie Klein's sense, an unconscious idea of the inside of the (mother's) body, and relatedly, in Bion's sense, a reversible experience of container and contained. Consider that all the important locations in Stein's story about radio are interior: "There were so many rooms and all the rooms were empty rooms, that was all right; and then all of a sudden we were in a little room . . . and then I was taken into another room" (168). In the studio the little (phallic?) thing that acts like an ear and that gave her a wonderful feeling of being "so filled with it" lets Stein introject (in phantasy) the microphone-and-studio as audience. This feeling of audience is both container and contained, and its dynamic reversibility means that audience can eventually become available for thinking, meditation, and a resource for writing, as it does in later writing such as *A Play Called Not and Now* (1936), *Everybody's Autobiography* (1937), and *Ida: A Novel* (1941).

To be clear, I am not reading the microphone and the studio simply as static symbols, thereby identifying Stein's feeling of audience as a phantasy of penetration and enacting critical (heterosexual, classical Freudian) mastery over her. Rather, from a queer object relations perspective the microphone, that little (clitoral or nipple?) thing, is a part-object introjected to enable vocal transmission and aural reception. (Robert Ashley's 1964 composition *The Wolfman*, for performer, microphone, and amplification system, offers a noisy, sonic literalization of this introjective phantasy.) Moving between an analysis of (conscious) fantasy and (unconscious) phantasy, I am trying to understand the affective conditions that mediate production and reception, both in the space of the studio and at home for the listener. In a sense, I am crossing methodological wires in radio studies where there has been a tendency to approach questions of reception from a phenomenological perspective and questions of production from a historicist one. I have been combining historical and phenomenological methods in arguing that fantasy and phantasy are necessarily present in both production and reception. The scene of Stein's radio interview leads me to wonder how the phenomenology of transmission (studio broadcasting, in this case) affects the receiver.[22]

So here's a more historical point: If in her radio broadcast Stein imagines that she is speaking to the audience of strangers that is not present, she is also, at the same time, speaking to those who are. And it helped that the studio audience enjoyed the performance. When Bennett Cerf, her publisher at Random House, introduced her to the audience this way—"I'm very proud to be your publisher, Miss Stein, but as I've always told you, I don't understand very much of what you're saying"—she immediately replied, "Well, I've always told you, Bennett, you're a very nice boy but you're rather stupid."[23] Banter with her publisher becomes entertainment for the studio audience who "let out a howl" (103) of laughter. In asserting that Stein "was the publicity hound of the world—simply great; she could have been a tremendous hit in show business" (102), Cerf was noticing Stein's wit, her ability to turn the tables on condescending interlocutors, and her laser-like address to specific others. Despite her oft-repeated claim to write for herself and for strangers, Stein was complexly dependent on people she knew and loved to form her readership. Early in her writing life she solicited her brother Leo as reader; for most of her career Alice Toklas was her primary emotional support (listener, reader, typist); and always Stein wrote for friends, acquaintances, and portrait subjects. In *Everybody's Autobiography* she describes a conversation with several Hollywood actors and directors this way: "They wanted to know how I had succeeded in getting so much publicity, I said by having a small audience."[24]

And here's a more phenomenological observation: Stein's nuanced play with address suits radio perfectly, for what accompanies its interiorizing phantasy of audience and universal access is its actual address to specific groups of listeners. In the 1930s, radio's movement across a range of spaces of address (between one and everyone) is conditioned by many things, including the listener's ethnic, racial, class, and linguistic status vis-à-vis the broadcaster, but also by her geographical proximity to the broadcasting source as well as spatial proximity to the radio set in its location in the home or elsewhere. But the situation of the performer in front of the microphone is at least as important as these other factors for what is often described as the intimacy of radio address. Insofar as the microphone in studio broadcasting is close to the sound source, a listener experiences radio vocalization as closer than voices in ordinary conversation (the visual analogy is a film close-up). A radio performer's physiology may be absent, but subtle traces of his or her breathing, the movements of breath or instrument, brush up against our eardrums, at once intimately proximate and entirely separated from us.

Adorno described this crucial aspect of radio as "the illusion of closeness" in his analysis of the physiognomics of the radio voice. Before turning to Adorno, I would like to summarize my argument so far. The U.S. lecture tour gratified Stein's desire to be celebrated, and while she clearly participated in efforts to promote her celebrity, she also discovered that the technologies and media of publicity disturbed her separation of inside and outside and her connection to lived experiences of writing and thinking, those affective circuits of "talking and listening at the same time" that helped her to make sense of any experience. Radio, a public relations machine that generated publicity (part of the "unreality" of America), nevertheless offered her a way to resolve this contradiction through the fantasy and phantasy of radio audience. Stein's exhilarated

Figure 5. "... by having a small audience." William Lundell, Alice B. Toklas, and Gertrude Stein (1934). Photograph by Ray Lee Jackson. Gertrude Stein and Alice B. Toklas Papers, Yale Collection of American Literature. Beinecke Rare Book and Manuscript Library. Estate of Gertrude Stein.

identification of broadcasting with writing (rather than print) evokes radio's phantasmatic structure of address as it gratifies a writerly wish: to enjoy communion with an audience while, at the same time, being alone and protected from it. This powerful wish could be realized at the microphone in the studio (etymologically, the artist's or scholar's workroom, a private space for reverie, a study) but only by disavowing the actual presence of a studio audience.[25]

Stein had good reason to find these protective aspects of radio helpful as she introduced her radically queer, reflexively experiential writing to skeptical, at times hostile audiences. There are several moments in the radio interview when Lundell questions Stein about the opacity and estranging materiality of her writing. I have already quoted (in the prologue) an excerpt from an exchange in which she replies to his question about the intelligibility of her opera *Four Saints in Three Acts*. Here is the fuller passage: "Look here, being intelligible is not what it seems. . . . After all when you say that they do not understand FOUR SAINTS what do you mean. You mean by understanding that you can talk about it in the way that you have a habit of talking . . . putting it in other words . . . but I mean by understanding enjoyment. If you enjoy it, you understand it, and lots of people have enjoyed it so lots of people have understood it."[26] Stein's insistence (like William Empson's) on enjoyment as a mark of understanding, here and elsewhere in the interview, is not simply defensive. It is her way of describing in highly compressed form her radically empiricist, transferential poetics. For Stein, as for William James, understanding is located in a reflexive, affective, near-physiological awareness of the present-tense nature of experience. She expresses these poetics most succinctly a couple of minutes later: "And you must not think that you do not understand because you cannot say it to yourself in other words. If you have something happen in you when you read these portraits you do understand no matter what you say to yourself and others about not understanding. Really and truly that is really and truly true" (05:18–05:33). Stein utters and insists, exemplifies and enacts the repetition-with-a-difference that plays such a key role in her poetics. The specific difference here, and what occasions this unusually clear insistence, is radio.

BUT WHY DOES RADIO ELICIT such a clear expression of Stein's poetics? What difference does radio make anyway? As Martin Harries and Lecia Rosenthal suggest, this is the question that guides Adorno's approach to radio: What difference does radio make to the situation of aesthetic reception?[27] So far I have been primarily pursuing radio from the perspective of production or transmission (Stein at the microphone). I have found Adorno's writings on radio helpful for thinking about the situation of reception, particularly in their emphasis on affect, expression, and the unconscious reach of the radio voice, which he describes this way: "Radio 'speaks to us' even when we are not listening to a speaker. It might grimace; it might shock us; it might even 'raise its eyes.'"[28] In this section I take up Adorno's work, both to contextualize my Kleinian/Bionian approach in the longer history of radio studies and to supplement his analysis of the situation of the listener or receiver. This situation, Stein's radio experience suggests, depends upon that of the broadcaster, the voice that reads aloud in front of the microphone (a voice that, in the 1930s, includes the phonograph). If the radio voice introjects the microphone-in-the-studio to form an interiorized and (as we will see) theatrical space of reading, then the difference radio makes to the situation of aesthetic reception is a function of this introjected audience. In the weird, reciprocating spaces of radio and their accompanying dynamics, the radio voice contains the conjectural listener whose ear contains the studio.

Adorno's writing on radio acknowledges his unusual, even perverse commitment to radio physiognomics ("*the study of the elements of expression of the 'radio voice'*" [49]) given the obsolete status of physiognomy in twentieth-century psychology. But he finds something valuable in this concept insofar as "the phenomena we are studying constitute a unity comparable to that of a human face" (44). In analyzing not a given singer's expression or a commentator's intonations but the voice of the radio itself, Adorno approaches the affective transference that takes place between the radio instrument and the listener, which he claims is comparable to that between persons spatially co-present: "To render it in psychological terms: in the experience of live voices and faces the phenomenon is not merely a superficial sign of whatever is behind it, replaceable by another sign. It constitutes a unity with the content that is its expression. The specific characteristics of the radio voice, such as the 'illusion of closeness,' tend in the same way to such an expression which is more than a contingent set of signs" (373). Adorno's physiognomic method seeks less to anthropomorphize radio than to estrange the media of affective communication ("live voices and faces"). By setting his analytic sights on the indexical expressiveness of the radio voice, Adorno hopes to discover the particular authenticity of the radio instrument.

I have been quoting from *Current of Music* (2009), a reconstruction of a volume that Adorno proposed but never published in his lifetime that consists of the writing he completed while working on the Princeton Radio Project ("Adorno's most extensive work in English" [4], according to the editor). Adorno had arrived in New York City in the winter of 1938 (four years after Stein, also on the SS *Champlain*) to join Max Horkheimer at the Institute for Social Research and to begin work on a study of American radio supported by the Rockefeller Foundation. The director of the project, Paul Lazarsfeld, a University of Vienna trained mathematician and psychologist, was quickly becoming an innovator in the new field of market research.[29] Lazarsfeld had immersed himself in American social psychology and brought university-based methods (large-scale sociological surveys and quantitative studies) to advertising and corporate communications research. Needless to say, Adorno's critical conceptual approach contrasted sharply with Lazarsfeld's narrow empiricism and demographic goals of determining what programs which people were listening to when. Adorno described these goals as concerned with the "what" elements of radio, whereas he pursued its "how" elements, ordinarily only of interest to radio engineers, technicians, and aesthetes. The specific qualities of radio sound, what Adorno insists on calling the *radio voice*, is his physiognomic topic of investigation.

Brian Kane has offered a careful reconstruction of the intellectual contexts for these radio writings. He observes the provenance of the *what*/*how* distinction in Edmund Husserl's phenomenology which Adorno had critiqued as idealist but nevertheless mobilized against the empiricism of the social psychologists, in particular that of his colleague at the Princeton Radio Project, Hadley Cantril. In *The Psychology of Radio* (1935) Cantril (with Gordon Allport) had developed a concept of the radio voice as the voice on the radio, but Kane explains that, for Adorno, this would become the uncanny voice of the radio itself. "In Adorno's use of the what and the how," Kane argues, "we see him pressing phenomenology into dialectical use," physiognomics the name of an immanently transformed phenomenology developed as a robust form of social critique, at once psychological, technical, and political.[30] I would add to Kane's analysis that Adorno's notion of physiognomics emerged from his encounters with psychoanalytic as well as phenomenological writings (indeed, Freud's relation to phenomenology, especially through the teaching and work of Franz Brentano, is a complicated story). Where Kane emphasizes Adorno's concept of phantasmagoria ("by exposing the phantasmagoric aspects of the radio voice, Adorno moves beyond the supposed immediacy of the radio voice toward the articulation of the radio phenomenon as an expression of social forces"),[31] I emphasize the somewhat different concept of phantasy. In my reading, Adorno never really "moves beyond" radio's immediacy or closeness in his analysis of social forces. Radio requires physiognomic analysis precisely because it elicits phantasmatic (psychical, somatic) responses which can be interpreted but (unlike phantasmagoria) not dispelled.

As Adorno understands it, radio's "illusion of closeness" (a phrase borrowed from studies of the role of radio in children's education) names the way the instrument appears to "speak for itself" despite the fact that "it merely distributes the voices of other speaking people."[32] Adorno believes that this illusion interferes with the listener's contact with reality because of the physical situation of the listener "who directly faces the apparatus instead of the man [*sic*] who is playing or speaking. Thus the visible tool becomes the bearer and the impersonation of the sound whose origin is invisible" (*Current*, 47). With reference to Orson Welles's infamous broadcast of *The War of the Worlds* (in October 1938) Adorno proposes that the illusion of closeness establishes the authority of the radio voice, making it seem "more objective and infallible than a live voice" (47), even reaching into "atavistic layers of our psychic life" (47). In a conceptual moment that participates in modernism's prosthetic logic and anticipates Marshall McLuhan's writing, Adorno observes the "analogy between the technical structure of the microphone and the ear" (48) and considers how "the radio mechanism is a sort of mechanization of human sense organs" (48) that offers substitutes for the voice and the ear. In this way Adorno seeks to justify physiognomics as a method for analyzing the mechanized, authoritative, intimate, and highly effective radio voice.

The radio voice's effectiveness is partly due to its unconscious reach. In a long footnote in his essay "The Radio Voice" (included in *Current of Music*), Adorno refers to the work of two psychoanalysts, Siegfried Bernfeld and Sandor Ferenczi, specifically to Bernfeld's explicit discussion of "the 'physiognomics' of individual organs of the human body" (372). Bernfeld, mostly known now for his work on education and Freud's scientific training, was drawn in the mid-1930s to Ferenczi's bioanalysis, that is, the proposal that bodily organs are invested with psychic meaning.[33] As Elizabeth Wilson has suggested, one significant aspect of Ferenczi's contribution, which led to conflicts between him and Freud, pertained to different kinds of biological commitments.[34] Where Freud the neuroanatomist emphasized the brain as the important location of whatever biological events underlie psychic phenomena, Ferenczi insisted that other bodily locations (peripheral, organic) act independently and can communicate without necessarily involving the central nervous system. We can see these ideas percolating when Adorno proposes this curious analogy: "In the case of an organ of society such as the radio, the idea of its appearing as something independent and self-styled and speaking for itself is certainly no less appropriate than in cases of biological functions" (372). His physiognomic approach appears to be indebted to a more Ferenczian, less brain-centered perspective.[35] Melanie Klein, whose first analysis was with Ferenczi, developed her difficult concept of unconscious phantasy out of this perspective. Like Ferenczi, she was oriented toward a speculative organic ground for psychical phenomena: "Unconscious phantasies underlie every mental process, and accompany all mental activity. They are the mental representation of those somatic events in the body which comprise the instincts, and are physical sensations interpreted as relationships with objects that cause those sensations."[36] This definition glimpses the Ferenczian possibility that "mental activity" need not only and always refer to brain activity. For Klein, to use a Steinian double negative, mind is *not* not organic body.

In a discussion of Adorno, John Mowitt observes that radio's illusion of closeness "is clearly more than proximity: it is about a feeling that sound, amplified noise, is penetrating, breaking into something or someone who can face a wireless."[37] But from the Kleinian perspective that I am unfolding here, the relevant phantasy is less the radio voice's penetration or projection than its introjection of and by the listener, a function of studio audience. To clarify this intervention, consider how Adorno's approach to radio physiognomics both resembles and departs from McLuhan's influential description, a couple of decades later, of technologies as externalizations of the sense organs, projections or "extensions of Man," as the subtitle of *Understanding Media* (1964) puts it. For McLuhan, electrical communication technologies such as radio and television extend the information-processing capacities of our central nervous systems in a prosthetic logic of substitution that reciprocally alters the human sensorium.[38] McLuhan's neurological high-modernist account fits well with some contemporary media theory (especially that of Kittler and his followers), but I prefer Adorno's physiognomic method that twines together the psychical, aesthetic, and political-institutional aspects of radio. In Adorno we encounter an attempt to unfold the psychic details of our encounter with radio machinery as an "organ of society" for which introjection and phantasy are as significant as projection, extension, and neurophysiology.

Adorno's most powerful analysis of the illusion of closeness takes place in the context of a discussion of broadcast music where he is concerned about the political authority that accompanies the interiorizing aspects of radio.[39] After describing the sound of a symphony broadcast over radio in physiognomic terms ("aggressive, barking and bellowing" [53]), Adorno characterizes it as "'bad' chamber music" (54), the scare quotes around "bad" qualifying this reductive aesthetic judgment. In fact, Adorno suggests that all broadcast music becomes chamber or parlor music, oriented toward private, interior spaces of reception in a manner that encourages "sensuous listening" over "structural listening" (64), an attention to musical texture, nuance, and detail rather than to compositional structure or form. This socio-technical quality of the musical radio voice leads Adorno to observe "something fundamental about radio itself, namely that a private person in a private room is privately addressed by a public voice to which he is forced to subordinate himself" (70). The authority of the radio voice derives from its chamber or parlor aspect: "When a private person in a private room is subjected to a public utility mediated by a loudspeaker, his response takes on aspects of a response to an authoritarian voice even if the content of that voice or the speaker to whom the individual is listening has no authoritarian features whatsoever" (70).

The political payoff of Adorno's physiognomic analysis finally arrives when he correlates radio's authority with its private address, a claim that culminates in a remarkable image of the listener's body and domestic objects as themselves sources of the radio voice: "The deeper this voice is involved within his own privacy, the more it appears to pour out of the cells of his most intimate life; the more he gets the impression that his own cupboard, his own phonograph, his own bedroom speaks to him in a personal way . . . the more perfectly he is ready to accept wholesale whatever he hears" (70). Ferenczian bioanalysis and Marxist critique combine in Adorno's understanding of radio as the perfect instrument of bourgeois governance, an ideal socio-affective guidance system (or, in Michel Foucault's phrase, a technology of the self) for a society that requires individuals to re-create themselves in the image of the standardized collective. Here the voice of Adorno that most of us recognize from *The Dialectic of Enlightenment* (written with Max Horkheimer just after the contract with Lazarsfeld ended and Adorno moved to Los Angeles) emerges with great clarity and conviction.

But it is interesting to note when Adorno sounds less programmatic and more like his colleague Walter Benjamin in these writings on radio music. In a discussion of "radio ubiquity" Adorno cites Benjamin to differentiate between the idea of the original in music and in the visual arts: "Every score is, in a way, only a system of prescriptions for possible reproduction, and nothing 'in itself'" (89). The uniqueness attributed to an original work of visual art (its aura, in Benjamin's famous description) is, in music, attributed to performance rather than exclusively to composition, a performance that necessarily involves technical reproduction (reading and playing from a score). Musical authenticity, realized in performance, does not oppose reproduction but depends upon it. For this reason Adorno rejects the idea that live or in-person presentation of music should be valued more than its radio reproduction, and proposes instead that "the stubborn condemnation of mechanically reproduced music would deprive it of possibilities which . . . should be developed and improved with the help of criticism instead of being rejected for the sake of the sanctity of the work of art" (59).

In effect, Adorno's writings offer a powerful, if ambivalent, analytic attempt to separate radio from what he describes as its social or cultural ideals. Radio can oppose "the remnants of the pre-technical concept of authenticity" (91) and the seeming privacy of the listener ("the ideal of imitating live music and the ideal of maintaining the privacy of public experience . . . if radio gives up these two 'ideals' some of the technical characteristics which we considered most problematic would be dropped" [72]). Examples from the 1930s of the ideals that Adorno would reject are not hard to find. Franklin Roosevelt's Fireside Chats used radio's intimate address to maintain the privacy of public experience as an instrument of governance, while the proliferation of programs that aimed to educate American listeners about European symphonic music promoted the imitation of live music in the service of so-called social uplift (as the editor's introduction to *Current of Music* makes clear). By contrast, we could think of forms of music emerging in the 1930s and '40s that began to forgo the ideal of imitating live music, whether by using electronic sounds or (a little later) magnetic tape, and performances that insisted on the publicity of radio listening. Some of John Cage's early pieces ("Imaginary Landscape No. 1" and his radio play with Kenneth Patchen *The City Wears a Slouch Hat*) fit these descriptions, as would the work of American composers after Cage such as Alvin Lucier and Robert Ashley.

If what Adorno identifies as radio's social or cultural ideals are its phantasmagorical aspects, it should be possible to distinguish these ideals from the introjective phantasies that are exploited and made to serve them. Adorno presents an analysis of the radio voice as an index to the aesthetic situation of the listener in the subordinated privacy of the home. But this phantasmagoric privacy depends on the radio voice's phantasized introjection of the microphone-and-studio: the privacy made available to the listener is, at the same time, the publicity of studio transmission. In other words, whatever authority radio has is less a condition of the listener's supposedly obtruded-upon privacy or isolation than of how they take in the cultural ideals and institutional authority of the broadcaster while participating in the inevitable introjections of audience. I wonder to what degree contemporary podcasting's lyrical address, often crafted in the home studio, is committed to maintaining the phantasmagoric privacy of the listener while obscuring institutional mediations.

In the American context, radio's institutional authority is less that of a state utility than that of commercial broadcasting, the somewhat state-regulated authority of supposedly free enterprise. Perhaps this is why Stein's very brief discussion of her radio experience in her autobiographical writing emphasizes money: "I talked over the radio once, they never seemed to want to pay you for doing that unless it is advertising, that seemed to us a very strange thing, so I talked once naturally nobody wanted to pay me for advertising" (*EA*, 198). In his memoir Bennett Cerf describes a brief argument after the broadcast when the actor Miriam Hopkins insisted that Stein should have been paid for her appearance: "'Bennett ought to be ashamed of himself,' she declared. 'Gertrude, don't you *ever* go on radio again unless you get at least five hundred dollars for it.'"[40] Cerf insists that radio offered Stein free publicity, but Stein sides with Hopkins's Hollywood-based understanding that performers should be paid for their time and talent, and is made uncomfortable by a compromised transaction that undermines her authority as producer. In other words, Stein came into conflict with the particular institutional authority of commercial radio which is definitely not free: advertisers pay for it, which means that we listeners pay with our time and attention, a variety of positive and negative affective responses, fantasies, and phantasies that conduce toward our subjectification. Benjamin insists that we can always turn the radio off, but Adorno thinks otherwise.[41]

IF THIS ESSAY HAS, so far, largely addressed radio as a medium of public relations and propaganda, whether from the perspective of transmission (Stein's interview) or that of reception (Adorno's phenomenology of the radio voice), this final section turns to radio as a medium of interpretation. The Radio Free Stein project has committed to the constraints and conventions of radio and sound recording in interpreting Stein's plays, a commitment that accords well with her theater poetics. As the prologue explains, these poetics aim to address and accommodate the temporal lags and affective disjunctions that Stein believes accompany audience experience. Her parlor plays, in seeking to resolve epistemic challenges, are fundamentally acousmatic in their explorations of sound without identifiable source.[42] This section begins by returning to these sensory, affective, and epistemological aspects of Stein's poetics, then offers an extended reading of *Photograph: A Play in Five Acts* as well as a much briefer discussion of *The Psychology of Nations, or What Are You Looking At*. The Radio Free Stein project rendered these works (both from 1920) as the first and last acts of *SIX. TWENTY. OUTRAGEOUS. Three Gertrude Stein Plays in the Shape of an Opera*. In performance these plays become meditations on the ubiquity of image reproduction by way of a set of related concepts (the twin, the brother) that thematize duplication via biological and psychological splitting.

Recall how, in the lecture "Plays," Stein describes theater's problem of emotional syncopation: "The scene as depicted on the stage is more often than not one might say it is almost always in syncopated time in relation to the emotion of anybody in the audience" (*Lectures*, 93). For Stein, the "nervousness" of live theater comes from a difficulty she has seeing, hearing, and feeling in time with the events on the stage, an experience of temporal lag that interferes with her enjoyment and understanding. In *Everybody's Autobiography* Stein revisits this problem of syncopated time in another context of performance, that of lectures and recitations: "I never really did care much about hearing any one lecture. My eyes always have told me more than my ears . . . speaking voices always go on at a different tempo than when you listen to them and that bothers me, things seen might too, but then you do not have to look at them, but things said have to be heard, and they always go on at the wrong tempo" (*EA*, 87). This contrast between sight and hearing, and Stein's particular difficulty listening to "speaking voices," suggests that hearing "things said" is the more threatening source of syncopation ("Sound can be a worry to any one particularly when it is the sound of the human voice" [87]).

Stein delves into personal memory (as she does in "Plays") to dredge up and analyze an exemplary scene of worrisome sound: the high school poetry recital. Listening to her brother Leo try to recall words or phrases in class was acutely embarrassing for young Gertrude ("Anybody with a brother or sister knows how that can come to matter" [88]), and the weekly Friday poetry recitations were "even much worse because then you had to stand on the platform alone and it was no longer your brother but some one who certainly could not remember and anyway what he had to say was so far away and more and more what you heard had no reality. What you say yes that was a picture but what you heard really did not matter" (88). Stein recollects a recital scene in which she appears to alternate between roles of speaker and hearer. What she speaks or recites "was a picture" but what she hears from her classmates "has no reality." If the vicarious shame of poor recall makes Stein uncomfortable at school poetry recitals, performances that empty words of their meanings are even more distressing. The distance between spoken words and affective reality ("what he had to say was so far away") creates an alienating gap between a poem's meanings and the emotional meanings being communicated by way of the speaker's voice.

Enforced school poetry recitals, lectures delivered in frozen monotone or with phony enthusiasm—these are some examples (and there could be many more nuanced ones) when a listener encounters the distance between a speaker's affective or emotional register and the verbal meanings associated with their speech. Such a gap between spoken words and the affective qualities of the voice itself, a problem that Stein casts as one of emotional syncopation, becomes more distinct in contexts of authority ("I suppose really that is the trouble with politics and school teaching, everybody hears too much with their ears and it never makes anything come together, something is always ahead of another or behind" [87]). These are the contexts in which Stein found herself on her lecture tour as she tried to establish her own authority in front of large audiences in museums, university halls, and on the radio. By various accounts Stein was fairly successful as a speaker, well able to negotiate what Arnheim, in his writing on radio, calls "the double function of language" as a medium of information and expression.[43] As one journalist attending her lectures put it, "To hear Miss Stein read her own work is to understand it—I speak for myself—for the first time. . . . You see how from sentence to sentence, which seem so much alike, she introduces differences of tone, or perhaps of accent. And then when you think she has been saying the same thing four or five times you suddenly know that she has carefully, link by link, been leading you to a new thing."[44]

Stein's success on the lecture circuit is due to her need or wish for her audience to see what she is saying. In *Everybody's Autobiography* Stein asserts that she has the capacity to "hear more pleasantly with the eyes than with the ears. This is true of me. I do" (87), even while acknowledging that this may be specific to her own capacities ("Well Alice B. Toklas would say that depends on who you are. Perhaps" [87]). In hearing with the eyes Stein can control the pace of word-images passing in attention. She continues to explain her poetics in terms that contrast and combine these sensory registers: "When you have been digging in the garden or been anywhere when you close your eyes you see what you have been seeing, but it is a peaceful thing that and is not a worry to one. On the other hand as I write the movement of the words spoken by some one whom lately I have been hearing sound like my writing feels to me as I am writing. That is what led me to portrait writing" (88). Hearing a voice in her head (the afterimage of a speaking voice) and writing out of this memory is fundamentally confusing for Stein: Is the voice and the movement of its words mine or someone else's? Does this movement become mine in the act of writing? Stein's portraits offer verbal re-creations of what she elsewhere calls "the rhythm of anyone's personality," those lilts of voice or subtle gestural styles that let us know an individual by way of sensory, affective, expressive, highly specific bodily movements and sonic textures.[45] In other words, Stein's portraits rely on a method by which her portrait subject's movements are transferred to her writing. She explains this in the radio interview:

> When I know anybody well they are all something to me each one is. That is natural but then there has to come a moment when I know all I can know about anyone and I know it all at once and then I try to put it down to put it down on paper all that I know of anyone their ways the sound of their voice the accent of their voice their other movements their character all what they do and to do it all at once is very difficult.[46]

Stein goes on: "After anybody has become very well known to me I have tried to make a portrait of them well I might almost say in order to get rid of them inside in me. Otherwise I would have got too full up inside me with what I had inside me of anyone. Do you see what I mean?"[47] Lundell's response is appropriately confused ("Well, maybe I do, but [nervous laugh] maybe I don't"), for here Stein is describing her need to clarify what she feels inside by putting words down on paper in an attempt to convert the echoing confusion of heard voices and sonic afterimages to the peaceful picture of words said and seen.

This confusion of tongues (as Ferenczi's famous essay calls it in the context of his analysis of childhood trauma), or the transference of a portrait subject's tongue (voice) by way of Stein's pen (writing), leads not only to portraits but to plays. For Stein, plays are group portraits, depictions of "a number of them knowing each other" (*Lectures*, 119), and she describes playwriting in *Everybody's Autobiography* using similar sensory terms: "whenever I write a play it is a play because it is a thing I do not see but it is a thing somebody can see that is what makes a play to me. . . . When I write other things not plays it is something that I can see and seeing it is inside of me but when I write a play then it is something that is inside of me but if I could see it then it would not be" (*EA*, 193). One difference between portraits and plays, for Stein, rests in how vision serves and fails to serve composition. Internal vision leads to portraits or works such as *Tender Buttons*, with discrete, visually clear poetic objects (an umbrella, a carafe, roast mutton, and so on), but it does not lead to playwriting. Group dynamics, exponentially more confusing than individual persons or objects, are resistant to the clarities of internal vision. These nonvisual, partly sound-based sensory and psychic materials—murky, ambiguous, acousmatic—are what her plays are made of, raw materials for her theater.

Photograph: A Play in Five Acts (1920) reflexively thematizes these mixed encounters between clarity and confusion, eye and ear, visual and sonic afterimages or memories, and combines murky recollections of Stein's life and aspects of her biography with more general perceptions about image reproduction. Collected in *Last Operas and Plays* (1949), this play has been interpreted for the stage a number of times.[48] In the Radio Free

Stein project it appears as the first act of *SIX. TWENTY. OUTRAGEOUS.* with musical setting by Daniel Thomas Davis (see the appendix for more information about this production). In our program notes we framed the play this way: "An oddball couple and their cousin/housekeeper try to stage a parlor play with a group of friends." The queer partners are named V (for Voice, the Stein-like character) and ME (the Toklas-like character); the cousin/housekeeper is named THREE (dressed as a French maid); and the group of friends are the musicians (a pianist and string quartet). The parlor-play-within-a-play is called "Photograph" and the evening is not entirely a success: the play is continuously interrupted and eventually dissolves into a different parlor game, a musical guessing game which fatigues the guests. In the pages that follow I begin with Stein's play text and move through the Radio Free Stein interpretation-in-performance which emerged by way of an intense set of collaborations in workshops, drafts of libretti, musical composition, rehearsal, stage design, and choreography.

Stein's relatively brief three-page play consists of five acts: an untitled first act followed by the much shorter Act Second, Act III, Act IV, and Act V (a reader may wish to consult the play text included on the project website). There is no list of characters and the lines of dialogue, usually quite short, are not assigned to distinct voices. The initial act, by far the longest, appears to be in two untitled sections: about twenty lines of dialogue that end with "Let me hear the story of the twin. So we begin" are followed by a new line with the centered word "Photograph." The libretto I drafted in collaboration with the composer interpreted the first section as a prologue that introduces the play's main topic and three main characters, and sets the stage with the arrival of the musicians-cum-guests who prepare to witness and participate in the play-within-the-play. The rest of this first act consists of more than forty lines, some of which rhyme, that thematize twins and twinning or list names (such as Mrs. Roberts, Mr. Andrew Reading, Miss Nuttall) and brief characterizations ("Miss Nuttall was born in America / Mrs. Roberts was also born there").[49] This act, which ends with a few lines of meta-commentary ("I can sigh for a play. / A play means more" [345]), is followed by four acts that are briefer, denser, and even more challenging to interpret in mimetic terms. Sequences of highly compressed poetic lines in Act Second ("Snails eat leaves. / Expression falters. / Wild flowers drink" [346]) contrast with witty, prosaic lines of reflexive dialogue in Act IV ("Did you intend to depress me. Certainly not I asked for a translation" [346]). The play alternates between expanded and compressed lines and refers several times to song and singing.

A handful of critics have offered commentary on *Photograph*, one of several plays Stein wrote in the postwar moment that mentions photography, but there are no sustained readings. In a brief passage in *Gertrude Stein: The Language that Rises* (2000) the great Stein editor Ulla Dydo observes that the play "raises the question of representation by exploring photographs as reproductions, copies, or twins" and speculates that Act III, the play's center (in Stein's plays the middle act is often a theatrical crux), "was provoked no doubt by a snapshot."[50] In the headnote for this play in *A Stein Reader* Dydo similarly suggests that "the occasion for *Photograph* appears to be a picture taken at a birthday party, perhaps for new twins" (343). Here is the entire act.

ESSAY 1 · 43

> A photograph. A photograph of a number of people if each one of them is reproduced if two have a baby if both the babies are boys what is the name of the street.
> Madame. (346)[51]

The road from photographic to biological reproduction seems to go through Stein's own family, as Dydo explains: "On rue Madame, a few steps from rue de Fleurus, lived Michael and Sarah Stein," Gertrude's oldest brother and his wife (who had one son).[52] Dydo points out, by way of glossing the first line of the next act ("We say we were warm. Guess McAdam"), that "Rue Madame was a paved, macadamized street" (17). In this reading strategy, where Stein's writing strips away associational context, Dydo's own text resupplies it. While such biographical and historical context may turn out to be relevant for interpretation, it does not by itself interpret the play. In the analytic reading strategy I develop here, biographical information becomes relevant for the specific purposes of unfolding phantasy.

Sarah Bay-Cheng in her commentary on the play argues for the more general significance of cinema for Stein's theater poetics. Bay-Cheng frames *Photograph* as a Benjaminian meditation that assimilates "mechanical duplication and human reproduction" by way of the figure of the twin.[53] But why does the play focus specifically on twinning, that unusual or exceptional form of biological reproduction ("if two have a baby if both the babies are boys" [*Stein Reader*, 346])? The play's concern with twins is presented in the (as-it-were) prologue ("Twins. / There is a prejudice about twins. / Twins are one. Does this mean as they separate as they are separate or together" [344]) and, as we have seen, leads directly to the play-within-a-play: "Let me hear the story of the twin. So we begin. / Photograph. / The sub title. Twin" (344). Bay-Cheng is right to remark on the queer connotations of twins, uncannily similar (their likeness a source of "prejudice") yet distinct, troubling the logic of original/copy prevalent in the discourse of photography. Twins are not duplicates of their source or origin but of one another and in Stein's play raise a basic arithmetical question: Are they one or two, separate or together? Given her medical training at Johns Hopkins and her experiences delivering babies in Baltimore, Stein would have known that so-called identical twins result from the splitting of the zygote or inseminated ovum. Stein's meditation on photography proposes a curious analogy between photographic reproduction and the biological phenomenon of twinning as a kind of self-splitting, and pursues this analogy in the split form of the play itself.

The contribution Stein makes here is to think about photographic and theatrical representation not primarily in terms of mechanical, mimetic copying but organismic splitting, a form of separation that leads not to identity but self-difference. In Stein's play photographs connote familial danger, a brotherhood that results from sexual reproduction via "Madame" and arrives at "Guess McAdam," the sons of Adam, originary violence and murder. Photography raises threats of proximity, competition, and erasure, and the need to defend against these threats. Here is how the play begins:

> For a photograph we need a wall.
> Star gazing.

> Photographs are small. They reproduce well.
> I enlarge better.
> Don't say that practically.
> And so we resist.
> We miss stones. (344)

In what sense do "we need a wall" for a photograph? Not for display, since we most often look down at small photographic reproductions rather than up at them as singular art objects (such as the paintings that Stein exhibited on her salon walls). But a wall may also be used for defense (as a barrier), and the start of this play proposes that we need to "resist" photographs, to defend against what they gain precisely by virtue of their size and reproducibility: their ubiquity or what Benjamin calls their exhibition value. Stein understood the need for some kind of defense against the uncanny visual encounters that commonly arise with photography. In *A Circular Play*, also written in 1920, Stein recommends to her readers this strategy: "It is a good idea to stare. We had our photographs taken, not intentionally but we happened to have seats in the front row near the arena and so when a photograph was taken we were in it."[54] When Stein and Toklas, attending a bullfight, find themselves captured by the camera's gaze, the decision to stare back becomes a wall or defense against those dissociations that accompany the disturbance of photography, the danger that photographs pose to feeling from the inside as they split self-perspective.

We have seen how these duplications and separations would worry Stein in her encounters with the publicity machines of the 1930s and the amplified forms of photographic and filmic dissociation that made possible her celebrity. Notably, she returns to the theme of twins and twinning in her late novel *Ida* on celebrity's self-splitting effects (Logan Esdale has unfolded these issues most lucidly). But in these earlier works such as *Photograph* and *A Circular Play* Stein is already noticing and worrying about dissociation, a consequence of photography's indexical qualities evoked by Stein's phrase "star gazing." Just as starlight strikes our eyes from a distant past, so does a photograph let us look at light materially registered on a sensitive surface at some past moment (Barthes, Benjamin, and Susan Sontag all dwell on photographic indexicality). We encounter starlight again in Act IV of *Photograph* where, once again, it poses some danger ("I am very sleepy and burned. / Burned by the sun to-day" [346]). Photography is a species of dangerous writing that Stein's play identifies and competes with. While photographs "reproduce well. / I enlarge better" (344): acknowledging photography's ubiquity or exhibition value, the play punningly insists on its own superior capacity to contain multitudes, to represent groups back to themselves.

The thematic of twinning in *Photograph*, then, is not only about the capacity for visual duplication (copying) but the self-splitting that accompanies photography and the need to resist or defend against its emotional consequences. Thinking about such defenses I have found it helpful to bring Stein's play into conjunction with the idea of splitting in Kleinian theory, one of a set of primitive defenses anterior to repression (as Freud understood it). Notably, the twin becomes a figure for the splitting defense in Wilfred Bion's remarkable essay "The Imaginary Twin" (1950), a case study of a patient (possibly Beckett) who, in infancy, suffered from the same disease his slightly older sister died from, and whose material brings forward many instances of doubling. In this essay Bion recounts how (after two years of analysis) he is able to observe "a quality which derived from what I can best describe as the rhythm of his associations" as it involves a series of imaginary interlocutors.[55] Bion reports: "I drew his attention to peculiarities of his behaviour, notably the rhythms of 'association—interpretation—association' that indicated that I was a twin of himself who supported him in a jocular evasion" (59). From this case and related clinical experiences Bion concludes that the analyst is often the recipient of projective identifications, those unwanted or split-off aspects that a patient cannot tolerate within the boundaries of the self, ego, or imaged interior and therefore projects into the analyst: "The imaginary twin goes back to his very earliest relationship and is an expression of his inability to tolerate an object that was not entirely under his control. The function of the imaginary twin was thus to deny a reality different from himself" (69).

A similar tone of "jocular evasion" characterizes the first act of *Photograph* and especially its play-within-a-play which begins with a charming and rhythmic floral dance ("Two a twin.—Step in. / Margot.—Not a twin. / Lilacs.—For a twin. / Forget me nots.—By a twin" [*Stein Reader*, 344]) before offering a brief excursus on twin houses:

> Twin houses.
>> We are considering twin houses. I say.
>> Have I read all about twins.
>> And now to walk as twins walk.
>> Two twins have two doors.
>> One twin is a bore.
>> I exercise more. I walk before the twins door. (344–45)

According to *The Autobiography of Alice B. Toklas*, "She [Stein] was born in Allegheny, Pennsylvania, in a house, in a twin house. Her family lived in one and her father's brother lived in the other one."[56] In the 1870s Stein's father, Daniel, and her uncle Solomon were business partners who lived with their families in twin houses, that is, separate mirror-image dwellings that share a wall on a single plot of land ("Two twins have two doors"). The brothers' wives, Amelia and Pauline, did not get along and eventually stopped speaking to one another, which prompted the brothers to dissolve their business partnership and living arrangement. Shortly after Gertrude was born (in 1874) Daniel moved his family to Vienna. The twin houses that appear in *Photograph*, I suggest, recollect this dispute ("One twin is a bore") and the emotional demands that accompany sharing finances and property. They are duplications of domestic space that failed to contain or manage the hostile relations within and between the families.

Just as Gertrude's father and his brother separated or split, so did Gertrude and her own brother Leo's relationship rupture many years later. Brenda Wineapple, in her double biography of the Stein siblings, describes how Leo and Gertrude grew up in crucial psychic relation to one another. The youngest of four siblings, their closeness was in part due to a shared sense of the contingency of their births. Two babies born before them had died in infancy, and insofar as Gertrude and Leo understood their parents to have wanted four children in total, they believed that neither of them would have been born had the babies survived. They were, in a sense, imaginary twins of their deceased siblings (as well as of one another), strongly bonded until they stopped speaking to one another around the time Alice Toklas moved in with Gertrude (more on this in Essay 2). Above I proposed that Stein's plays draw on murky psychic materials of exactly this kind. It is likely that Stein had Leo's voice in her head for many years, both before their separation and after, and that Alice's voice would come to compete with Leo's. Stein puts it this way near the end of *A Circular Play*: "Do I sound like Alice. / Any voice is resembling. / By this I mean when I am accustomed to them their voices sound in my ears" (*Stein Reader*, 341). Stein avows the confusion of familiar voices inside her, sonic afterimages that motivate her playwriting.

This biographical context helps to justify bringing together Stein's and Bion's texts as this conjunction provides insight into the thematic of twinning and photographic separation in this play. It also grounds a speculation about the play's setting. With Dydo's observation about the centrality of looking at a snapshot in mind, and returning to Act III of the play ("A photograph of a number of people if each one of them is reproduced if two have a baby if both the babies are boys"), I speculate that the speakers in *Photograph* are looking at a group family photo, perhaps taken just outside the house that Stein was born in and which includes babies that belong to one or both of the Stein families, possibly one of the babies that did not survive infancy or Gertude and Leo themselves. If such a photo existed it would probably be difficult to date and determine the identity of the baby or babies. This imagined photo would amplify, in several directions at once, the sense of historical belatedness and separation that accompanies all family photographs at the same time that it models and competes with Stein's understanding of plays as depictions of group dynamics.

The question of setting will return shortly in relation to a discussion of Radio Free Stein's interpretation-in-performance of this play. While I find close reading indispensible for thinking with and about Stein's plays, it is never clear in advance how this kind of textual attention helps move us toward performance. As I suggested in this book's prologue, it is in order to answer basic theatrical questions about a Stein play (such as, is any given line a stage direction, setting description, line of dialogue, or something else?) that I bring a number of readers together in workshop to air Stein's words. At the first workshop on *Photograph* one of the participants, Michael Moon, reported that, despite the play's many conversational markers, to him it had more the feel of a monologue than a dialogue.[57] He proposed that we think with the idea of subvocalization, the phenomenon of speaking-to-oneself that takes place at the threshold of consciousness (related, it seems to me, to the idea of a sonic afterimage).[58] Moon's idea prompted the workshop to divide the first lines between a more extroverted voice, which we labeled V, and a quieter subvoice, labeled SV, that elaborates, undermines, or otherwise revises the first voice's lines. Then we heard a third voice, with the lines that follow "Now we sing" appearing to several of us at the workshop as three short songs: "St. Cloud and you. / Saint Cloud and loud," "I sing you sing birthday songs," and "Oh come and believe me" (*Stein Reader*, 344). The composer Dan Davis immediately began thinking of ways to interweave three individual songs or melodies sung by three distinct voices (see figure 2, previously).

This workshop experience led us to decide on three main voices as primary speakers and singers in our performance of the play. The initial libretto that I drafted after the workshop named these voices V, SV, and No. 3. This decision initially thematized a separation or split between voice and subvoice in one individual, but it evolved in later drafts into three members of a household with characters renamed V, ME, and THREE. As we moved toward casting and (eventually) costuming, V became Gertrude-like, ME became Alice-like (as one of the primary voices in V's head), and THREE, originally conceived as an imagined reader or audience, became a cousin who keeps house for the couple, a triangulated figure for a desired outsider internal to the household but external to the couple, at once necessary and apart. In other words, psychic roles that seemed interior became theatricalized, projected outward as characters in an expressionist rather than naturalist mode. We based our theatrical setting on the speculation about a family photograph I describe above: this group of three players are looking at a photograph of a family on the verge of separation. This choice was partly inspired by Claire Laville's observation in workshop that the line "We miss stones" near the start of the play is a cross-linguistic pun (in both German and Yiddish), we miss Steins.

Onstage and in the play's diegesis, then, we begin with the players looking at a photograph of a family on the verge of separation. In staging the opera we decided to interpret this not in biographical terms but in relation to the larger historical moment of turn-of-the-century immigration to the United States from Europe and accompanying separation of families. We explicitly chose not to anchor the play in literal biography, and V is not intended to be a re-creation of the historical figure of Gertrude Stein—V is, rather, a likeness, a twin. In fact, our somewhat perverse interpretation reverses the facts of Stein's own German Jewish family who returned to Europe for a year in the 1870s. But this allowed us to offer an implicit comparison to and contrast with a contemporary United States (in 2018) much more fearful about immigration, one aspect of the opera's connection with twenty-first-century American politics. In Doug Fitch's design the photograph is represented onstage by a frame holding cardboard cutouts of iconically drawn turn-of-the-century immigrants (see figure 6). In the third act's passacaglia these cutouts are placed on the floor and illuminated by glowing eggs that call to mind Stein's analogy beween biological and mechanical reproduction. Before this moment, still in the first act, a miniature boat pulled across the front of the stage helps to illustrate the lines "Miss Nuttall was born in America. / Mrs. Roberts was also born there. / Mr. Andrew Reading went to America. / Mrs. Reading was born in America. / Mrs. Lord was born on the boat" (*Stein Reader*, 345).

In addition to this historical setting, we introduced the distinctive sonic quality of prerecordings to thematize questions of audience and temporal lag that Stein's play explores. Davis's musical setting makes substantive use of prerecordings that the players interact with during performance, for example, in a moving song (in the first act) with the lines: "A language tires. / A language tries to be. / A language tries to be free" (345). To provide a diegetic visual cue for these prerecorded songs and to foreground a phonograph's likeness to the play's title (differing by only a single letter), the stage designer constructed an outsized phonograph or gramophone (see figure 13 in the appendix). Prerecordings and filters are key sonic elements that repeat through the various parts of the opera as a whole. In deciding to use these elements as part of the musical setting, the composer and I discussed how we would both accommodate and create distance from the nostalgia that accompanies the crackling sound of old recordings, closely related to the nineteenth-century sentimentalism by which the technology of photography was often understood, especially in the United States. The discourses of preservation and revelation that enveloped photography from its introduction in the 1840s, powerfully elaborated in the American context of the Civil War, seem to return in yet another postwar moment. In the second act of *Photograph* we evoked these sentimentalizing national and proto-imperial contexts, and the pressures these exert on verbal representation, by creating a farcical shadow play (within the play-within-a-play) of word-silhouettes that eventually concludes with voices humming an utterly deranged, destabilizing version of "The Star-Spangled Banner" mentioned in Stein's text (the composer was acutely aware of the risk involved in using this musical citation).

In our rendering, Stein's play offers modernist perspective on the nostalgia associated with these nineteenth-century graphic technologies. In its fourth and fifth acts the players decide to abandon their performance of the play-within-a-play titled "Photograph" to play, instead, a different, more modern parlor game, What's on the Phonograph? THREE plays records (again, the composer's prerecorded songs are heard) while the musician-guests try and fail to identify the songs, an allegory for a reader's and audience's attempt to guess Stein's seemingly hermetic meanings. The musician-guests soon grow tired of this game, impatient with their frustrating encounter with Stein's sentences, and everyone but the cellist (whose name is George) leaves: the party's over, the play ends. Our abrupt ending segues to the opera's second act, based on Stein's play *Captain Walter Arnold*, set a week later in the same parlor as an erotic encounter between V and ME who has just returned home from a shopping expedition. In the stage design for this act, a gender-indeterminate dressmaker's dummy replaces the phonograph and becomes involved in the stage action. The final act of the opera, based on Stein's *The Psychology of Nations*, stages an election-night party gone horribly wrong. This act features a fourth voice, WE or the voice of the radio (the stage design features an outsized radio console), and contrasts radio's live presentation with recordings from the first act. (Consult the appendix for links to audio and video recordings of the chamber opera as well as additional photographs.)

It is to this last play that I briefly turn my attention. Written in 1920 (like *Photograph*) and published as the final work in *Geography and Plays* (1922), *The Psychology of Nations, or What Are You Looking At* is one of several works in which, as Richard Bridgman points out, "Politics, particularly the kind generated by the peace conferences, briefly entered [Stein's] writing as it had never done before."[59] The dances of its opening lines ("Soultz Alsace dance on the Boulevard Raspail / Spanish French dance on the rue de la Boetie / Russian Flemish dance on the docks") evoke postwar Parisian celebrations and European relief, but the three parts that follow (titled "And now we come to a picture," "PART II.," and "LAST PART"), which center on a U.S. presidential election, are more frightening and ambiguous.[60]

Figure 6. A photograph of a family on the verge of separation, from *SIX. TWENTY. OUTRAGEOUS. Three Gertrude Stein Plays in the Shape of an Opera* (2018), set design by Doug Fitch. Steven Pisano Photography.

The play's main figure is a little boy introduced as "playing marbles with soldiers, he was rolling the balls and knocking down the soldiers" (*Geography*, 416), a form of aggressive play that, Stein implies, threatens social order: "In the middle of the presidential election they had a bonfire. / A policeman stopped them. / What can a policeman do, they said" (416). The bonfire continues in PART II in which short sentences conjure an American political scene of anxiety, surprise, and anti-Indigenous violence: "Suppose a presidential election comes every fourth year. / Startling, start, startles jump again. / Jump for a feather. / A feather burns. / Indians burn have burned burns" (417). The play's sudden changes in register and shifting associations are difficult to follow and understand, but there is an undeniable sense of violence and regret underlying American national celebration ("Do you remember the Fourth of July" [417]). The boy becomes literate, capable, and commanding ("Jump to the word of command. / Jump where / In there" [417]), which the play casts as related qualities: "Read readily and so tell them what I say" (417). In the LAST PART the boy "grows up and has a presidential election" (418), a democratic rags-to-riches story that the play ironizes: "Why do the words presidential election remind you of anything. / They remind us that the boy who was in the street is not necessarily a poor boy. / Nor was he a poor boy then" (418). The EPILOGUE offers a concluding lamentation ("Veils and veils and lying down" [418]) that twines together the political events of the play with personal, familial dynamics ("Who can expect an election. / A boy who is the son of another has a memory of permission" [418]). These familial and political relations ("Kisses do not make a king. / Nor noises a mother" [419]) are both subordinated to a devotion to writing itself ("Benedictions come before presidents. / Words mean more" [419]). The play ends with an ambivalent acknowledgment and a wishful imperative: "I speak now of a man who is not a bother. / How can he not bother. / He is elected by me. / When this you see remember me" (419).

Dan Davis and I completed the libretto and score prior to the 2016 U.S. election but it was impossible not to register that contemporary reality in our interpretation. Our rendering sets the play in the same parlor as the previous two acts of the opera. Here V, ME, and THREE host an election-night party while listening to voting results announced via the radio (the partygoers include several musicans-cum-guests who comprise a Parlor Chorus). On a bifurcated stage separated by the large radio console stage prop, audience members also see and hear the Radio Chorus led by WE, the Voice of the Radio. The libretto distributes Stein's lines among the four main voices, moving back and forth between WE's election announcements and the dancing and conversation in the parlor. In this way, the opera reflexively theatricalizes audience, the experience of listening and responding to the radio, with the music realizing increasingly dissonant relations between Parlor and Radio Choruses, competing realities that clash by the end.

As WE's news becomes more disturbing, V, ME, and THREE express distinct affective responses to what they hear. V, enraged, narrates the violence endemic to American history, ME descends into guilt and panic, while THREE, in utter denial, tries to enliven the party by turning the radio dial back to dance music. There is considerable tension between them until, in our interpretation of the LAST PART, WE and the Radio Chorus emerge from the radio and crash into the parlor. The final election results roll in, the music becomes terrorizing, and WE inflicts a mortal wound on ME. In the lamentation that follows, ME is all but sanctified while the score and libretto's play on the words *bother/brother* unfolds the intractable and intolerable historical reality, the ongoing reorganization of mass democracy (envisaged as fraternity) by contemporary media. The play ends quietly and calmly with a repeated musical motif, followed by an excerpt from Stein's word portrait "Play," which has served to structure the opera as a whole.

"Radio music always seems to be an echo of music coming from a distant place," Adorno observes in his analysis of the similarities and differences between radio and phonograph.[61] In this essay I have suggested that radio's distant place is the introjected microphone-and-studio which becomes available at the point of reception—the parlor. Public and private spaces of studio and parlor (both theatrical stages) contain the listener and are contained by her to ground a phantasmatic phenomenology of listening that suits Stein's theater, especially her early plays and their acousmatics. By reading Stein's plays and theater poetics beside Adorno's writing, I hope to have made explicit her role as yet another media theorist, perhaps the Echo that precedes McLuhan's Narcissus.[62] Radio Free Stein's renderings have led me to unfold phantasies that accompany acousmatic technologies, those that accompany radio and phonograph as well as the literary techne of plays.

Sometimes Stein's thinking resembles Adorno's, as in this passage from *Everybody's Autobiography* on the topic of machines and standardization:

nobody means the same thing by what they say as the other one means and only the one who is talking thinks he means what he is saying even though he knows very well that that is not what he is saying. That is the reason that everybody thinks machines are so wonderful they are only wonderful because they are the only thing that says the same thing to any and every one and therefore one can do without them, why not, after all you cannot exist without living and living is something that nobody is able to understand while you can exist without machines it has been done but machines cannot exist without you that makes machines seem to do what they do. (*EA,* 290)

Perhaps we need Stein to remind us, at this moment of the public emergence of ever more powerful computational technologies and so-called artificial intelligences, of how seductive machines can be, ideal instruments for disseminating the confusions and clarities of propaganda. If Stein hedges her bet on whether humans can live without machines ("it has been done," she claims), her more confident point that "machines cannot exist without you" implies that human projection (of need, of life) is what "makes machines seem to do what they do." Stein acknowledges our willing but unwitting transference with machinic reproduction, and embraces the fact that insistence and repetition, confusion and clarity, hearing and sight are entwined in the techne of language: "A language tires. / A language tries. / A language tries to be free. / This can be called Twinny" (*Stein Reader*, 345). But language cannot easily be standardized, as Stein's writing knows well, or to put this another way, even identical twins are not exact reproductions of the same but consequences of an uneven split. Stein's plays remain fascinated by likenesses, resemblances, and kinships even while they refuse to collapse difference into identity. Like Andy Warhol (as Jonathan Flatley has shown), Stein portrays and accommodates in her writing the inevitable reciprocities and internalizations of humans with machines, the psychic phantasies and confusions that accompany these dependencies.

WHAT HAPPENED

A FIVE ACT PLAY

ACT ONE

One.

Loud and no cataract. Not any nuisance is depressing.

Five.

A single sum four and five together and one, not any sun a clear signal and an exchange.

Silence is in blessing and chasing and coincidences being ripe. A simple melancholy clearly precious and on the surface and surrounded and mixed strangely. A vegetable window and clearly most clearly an exchange in parts and complete.

A tiger a rapt and surrounded overcoat securely arranged with spots old enough to be thought useful and witty quite witty in a secret and in a blinding flurry.

Length what is length when silence is so windowful. What is the use of a sore if there is no joint and no toady and no tag and not even an eraser. What is the commonest exchange between more laughing and most. Carelessness is carelessness and a cake well a cake is a powder, it is very likely to be powder, it is very likely to be much worse.

A shutter and only shutter and Christmas, quite Christmas, an only shutter and a target a whole color in every center and shooting real shooting and what can hear, that can hear that which makes such an establishment provided with what is provisionary.

Two.

Urgent action is not in graciousness it is not in clocks it is not in water wheels. It is the same so essentially, it is a worry a real worry.

A silence a whole waste of a desert spoon, a whole waste of any little shaving, a whole waste altogether open.

Two.

Paralysis why is paralysis a syllable why is it not more lively. A special sense a very special sense is ludicrous.

Three.

Suggesting a sage brush with a turkey and also something abominable is not the only pain there is in so much provoking. There is even more. To begin a lecture is a strange way of taking dirty apple blossoms and is there more use in water, certainly there is if there is going to be fishing, enough water would make desert and even prunes, it would make nothing throw any shade because after all is there not more practical humor in a series of photographs and also in a treacherous sculpture.

Any hurry any little hurry has so much subsistence, it has and choosing, it has.

ACT TWO

Three.

Four and nobody wounded, five and nobody flourishing, six and nobody talkative, eight and nobody sensible.

One and a left hand lift that is so heavy that there is no way of pronouncing perfectly.

A point of accuracy, a point of a strange stove, a point that is so sober that the reason left is all the chance of swelling.

The same three.

A wide oak a wide enough oak, a very wide cake, a lightning cooky, a single wide open and exchanged box filled with the same little sac that shines.

The best the only better and more left footed stranger.

The very kindness there is in all lemons oranges apples pears and potatoes.

Figure 7. Gertrude Stein, *What Happened: A Five Act Play* (1913). In *A Stein Reader*, edited by Ulla Dydo (Northwestern University Press, 1993). Estate of Gertrude Stein.

The same three.

A same frame a sadder portal, a singular gate and a bracketed mischance.

A rich market where there is no memory of more moon than there is everywhere and yet where strangely there is apparel and a whole set.

A connection, a clam cup connection, a survey, a ticket and a return to laying over.

ACT THREE

Two.

A cut, a cut is not a slice, what is the occasion for representing a cut and a slice. What is the occasion for all that.

A cut is a slice, a cut is the same slice. The reason that a cut is a slice is that if there is no hurry any time is just as useful.

Four.

A cut and a slice is there any question when a cut and a slice are just the same.

A cut and a slice has no particular exchange it has such a strange exception to all that which is different.

A cut and only slice, only a cut and only a slice, the remains of a taste may remain and tasting is accurate.

A cut and an occasion, a slice and a substitute a single hurry and a circumstance that shows that, all this is so reasonable when everything is clear.

One.

All alone with the best reception, all alone with more than the best reception, all alone with a paragraph and something that is worth something, worth almost anything, worth the best example there is of a little occasional archbishop. This which is so clean is precious little when there is no bath water. A long time a very long time there is no use in an obstacle that is original and has a source.

ACT FOUR

Four and four more.

A birthday, what is a birthday, a birthday is a speech, it is a second time when there is tobacco, it is only one time when there is poison. It is more than one time when the occasion which shows an occasional sharp separation is unanimous.

A blanket, what is a blanket, a blanket is so speedy that heat much heat is hotter and cooler, very much cooler almost more nearly cooler than at any other time often.

A blame what is a blame, a blame is what arises and cautions each one to be calm and an ocean and a masterpiece.

A clever saucer, what is a clever saucer, a clever saucer is very likely practiced and even has toes, it has tiny things to shake and really if it were not for a delicate blue color would there be any reason for every one to differ.

The objection and the perfect central table, the sorrow in borrowing and the hurry in a nervous feeling, the question is it really a plague, is it really an oleander, is it really saffron in color, the surmountable appetite which shows inclination to be warmer, the safety in a match and the safety in a little piece of splinter, the real reason why cocoa is cheaper, the same use for bread as for any breathing that is softer, the lecture and the surrounding large white soft unequal and spread out sale of more and still less is no better, all this makes one regard in a season, one hat in a curtain that is rising higher, one landing and many many more, and many more many more many many more.

ACT FIVE

Two.

A regret a single regret makes a door way. What is a door way, a door way is a photograph.

What is a photograph a photograph is a sight and a sight is always a sight of something. Very likely there is a photograph that gives color if there is then there is that color that does not change any more than it did when there was much more use for photography.

INTERLUDE 1

WHAT
HAPPENED | PLAYS
A RADIO SCRIPT

The Radio Free Stein project moved through successive stages to render Gertrude Stein's parlor plays as radio and music theater: from brainstorming workshop to script preparation, music composition, performance rehearsals, and finally to the recording studio or theater stage. To convey a sense of the early stages of this process, here is the radio script I prepared based on Stein's *What Happened: A Five Act Play*. The initial workshop, organized by Laura Schultz, was held at the University of Copenhagen on May 17, 2016. The participants included Solveig Daugaard, Lene Asp Frederiksen, Steven Meyer, Martin Glaz Serup, and Samuel Vriezen. Stein's play text is included for purposes of comparison (see figure 7). See Interlude 2 for excerpts from Vriezen's musical setting, and the appendix for links to the audio recording and information on performance and production.

WHAT HAPPENED | PLAYS

A Radio Script
by
Adam Frank
(March 2019)

PREAMBLE.

"Their expectations of what happened in groups of which I was a member were very different from mine . . . I will describe what happens."
—W. R. Bion, *Experiences in Groups*

———————

This radio melodrama or music theater piece is based on Gertrude Stein's first play, *What Happened* (1913), and includes excerpts from her lecture "Plays" (1934). It stages the composition of a play out of parts of speech, a set of movements back and forth between individuated and group (or aggregate) experience.

W, the Writer, is the lead voice (female). The **CHORUS** is an instrumental ensemble whose members also vocalize. Other musical elements may include electronics or prerecorded sound. Over the course of the first act the CHORUS members differentiate into grammatical and logical parts. One of them eventually (by act 3) emerges as A, the voice of an imagined Audience, then fades back into the CHORUS.

The situation: W recalls a recent birthday party, not her own, and writes a play called *What Happened*. In interludes between acts she explains her ideas about playwriting to the audience.

PROLOGUE.

A QUIET, FAINT, OR DISTANT SOUND OF RUSHING WATER. IT APPROACHES, BECOMES MORE COMPLEX AND TEXTURED. GRADUALLY SEVERAL FLOWS EMERGE AND INTERACT WHILE REMAINING SEPARATE. COMPLEXITY AND VOLUME INCREASE, CREATING BOTH CLARITY AND CONFUSION. SOUND ENDS ABRUPTLY, IN ITS WAKE WE HEAR THE FIRST WORDS OF THE PLAY.

THIS SEQUENCE CAN BE A LITERAL RECORDING OF WATER FLOWS, OR AN ELECTRONIC OR INSTRUMENTAL COMPOSITION, OR BOTH.

CHORUS: (OVERLAPPING, DISTINCT INTONATIONS)
What happened? / What happened! / What happened.

W: A Five Act Play. (PAUSE)

QUIET DRONE. W STEPS UP TO LECTERN, TAPS MICROPHONE, BEGINS LECTURE.

W: In a book I wrote
called How To Write
I made a discovery:
that sentences are not emotional
    and that paragraphs are.

This difference is not a contradiction but a combination.

And now I have found out a fundamental thing about plays
also a combination
          and not a contradiction.

That something is this:
The scene as depicted on the stage is
more often than not
          one might say it is almost always

in syncopated time in relation to the emotion of anybody in the audience.

What this says is this:
Your emotion as a member of the audience is never going on at the same time
as the action of the play.

This makes one endlessly troubled about a play,
because not only is there a thing to know
          as to why this is so
but also there is a thing to know
          why perhaps it does not need to be so.

And knowledge
          as anybody can know
is a thing to get by getting.

ACT ONE.

[THE ACTION: INVOCATION. *In her filthy workshop of creation* W *teases out multiple voices, those of the* CHORUS, *from the line of her writing.*]

SCENE 1.

<u>W SITS AT DESK, FLIPS OPEN LAPTOP.</u>

W: Act One: One.

<u>WRITES WHILE SPEAKING.</u>

Loud and no cataract.
Not any nuisance is—depressing.

<u>PLAYS BACK SENTENCES USING LAPTOP SPEECH FUNCTION. COUNTS WORDS IN EACH SENTENCE (FOUR-COUNT, FIVE-COUNT).</u>

(LOW) Nuisance. Nuisance. (LEAVES DESK)

SCENE 2.

<u>W RUMMAGES AROUND AND BRINGS OUT A RECORDING/PLAYBACK DEVICE. PRESSES PLAY AND TRANSCRIBES FROM A RECORDING OF HER VOICE.</u>

DEVICE:	Five.
W:	(WRITES) Five.
DEVICE:	A single sum four and five together
W:	A single sum four and five together
DEVICE:	and one,
W:	and one
DEVICE:	not any sun
W:	not any sun
DEVICE:	a clear signal and an exchange.

W FINISHES TYPING, THEN PLAYS BACK SENTENCE FROM DEVICE AND LAPTOP SIMULTANEOUSLY.

DEVICE: A single sum . . . not any sun
four and five . . . a clear signal
together . . . an exchange
and one . . . and one . . . and one . . . and one . . . and one . . .

FRUSTRATED, W CLOSES LAPTOP. NEW IDEA: W SUMMONS A MEMBER OF THE CHORUS, THE QUALIFIER (CH1). W STANDS AND DECLAIMS.

W: Silence is in blessing and chasing   (W/CONT'D OVER)

INTERLUDE 1 · 61

W (CONT'D):   and coincidences being ripe.
                   A simple melancholy clearly precious
                              and on the surface
                   and surrounded and mixed strangely.
                   A vegetable window
                              and clearly most clearly
                   an exchange in parts and complete.

CH1:   (MUSICAL UNDERLINES)
                   Ripe . . .
                   simple . . . clearly precious . . .
                   strangely . . .
                   vegetable . . .
                   clearly . . . clearly . . .
                   complete

<u>   W SUMMONS A SECOND CHORUS
                   MEMBER, THE SPLITTER OF HAIRS (CH2),
                   WHO ALSO UNDERLINES WORDS.</u>

W: A tiger a rapt and surrounded overcoat
                   securely arranged with spots old enough to be thought useful
                   and witty quite witty in a secret
                   and in a blinding flurry.

CH1:   Rapt . . . surrounded . . .
                   securely . . . old enough . . . useful . . .
                   witty . . . witty . . . secret . . .
                   blinding . . .

CH2:   Old enough . . .
                   quite witty . . .

<u>W BRINGS MORE CHORUS MEMBERS IN, THE SEEKER
OF DEFINITIONS (CH3) AND THE NEGATOR (CH4).</u>

W: Length what is length
                      when silence is so windowful.

CH3:   What is . . .
                      silence is . . .

CH1:   so windowful . . .

CH2:   so . . .

W: What is the use of a sore if there is no joint
                      and no toady
                      and no tag
                      and not even an eraser.

CH3:   What is . . . if there is . . .

CH4:   No . . .
                      no . . .
                      no . . .
                      not even . . .

W: What is the commonest exchange
                      between more laughing and most.

CH3:   What is . . .

CH1:   Commonest . . .

CH2: More laughing . . . most . . .

W: Carelessness is carelessness
and a cake well a cake is a powder,
it is very likely to be powder,
it is very likely to be much worse.

CH3: carelessness is . . .
cake is . . .
it is . . .
it is . . .

CH1: Well . . .
likely . . .
likely . . .
worse.

CH2: Very . . .
very . . .
much worse.

CH4: Worse.

W: A shutter and only shutter
and Christmas, quite Christmas,
an only shutter and a target
a whole color in every center
and shooting real shooting
and what can hear, that can hear
that which makes such an establishment
provided with what is provisionary.

CH2:   Only shutter . . .
        quite Christmas . . .
        only shutter . . .
        whole color . . . every center . . .
        real shooting . . .

CH1:   only . . .
        only . . .
        whole . . .
        real . . .

CH3:   what can hear . . .
        that which makes . . .
        what is provisionary.

CH4:   is provisionary.

SCENE 3.

<u>W, PLEASED, APPROACHES THE CHORUS. EMBOLDENED, THE CHORUS BECOMES MORE EXPANSIVE.</u>

W: Two.

        Urgent action is not in graciousness
        it is not in clocks
        it is not in water wheels.

CH1:   urgent . . .
        water . . .

CH3:	urgent action is . . .
	it is . . .
	it is . . .
CH4:	not in . . .
	not in . . .
	not in . . .
W:	It is the same so essentially,
	it is a worry a real worry.
CH1:	so essentially . . .
	real . . .
CH2:	the same . . .
	a real worry
CH3:	It is . . .
	it is. . . .

<u>W PLAYS WITH INTONATION.</u>

W:	A silence a whole waste of a desert spoon,
	a whole waste of any little shaving,
	a whole waste altogether open.
CH1:	whole . . . desert . . .
	whole . . . little . . .
	whole . . . altogether open . . .
CH2:	any little shaving . . .
	altogether . . .

SCENE 4.

<u>THE CHORUS IS CARRIED AWAY AND LEAVES W BEHIND.</u>

CHORUS: (SUNG) Two!
Paralysis why is paralysis a syllable
why is it not more lively.

Why is paralysis a syllable (LITTLE SONG)

CH3: why is . . . why is . . .

CH1: more lively . . .

CH2: more lively . . .

CH4: not more . . .

<u>AT SOME POINT W BEGINS WHISPERING POINTEDLY.
HER REPEATED LINE ENDS THE SCENE.</u>

W: A special sense a very special sense is ludicrous. (EMPHASIS ON SIBILANTS)

SCENE 5.

<u>THE CHORUS HAS BEEN CHASTENED. W
BACK AT HER DESK. RETURN TO MUSICAL
UNDERLINING, MORE SUPPLE NOW.</u>

W:	Three.
	Suggesting a sage brush with a turkey
	and also something abominable
	is not the only pain there is
	in so much provoking.
		There is even more.

CH1:	Sage . . .
	abominable . . .
	only . . .
	so much . . .
	even . . .

CH2:	With a turkey . . .
	the only pain . . .
	so much provoking . . .
	even more.

CH3:	There is . . .
	there is . . .

CH4:	Is not . . .

W:	To begin a lecture is a strange way
	of taking dirty apple blossoms
	and is there more use in water,
	certainly there is
		if there is going to be fishing,
	enough water would make desert and even prunes,
	it would make nothing throw any shade
	because after all
		is there not more practical humor (W/CONT'D OVER)

W (CONT'D):   in a series of photographs
                              and also in a treacherous sculpture.

CH1:   Strange . . .
            dirty . . .
            more . . .
            certainly . . .
            enough . . . even . . .
            more practical . . .
            treacherous . . .

CH2:   A strange way . . .
            More use . . .
            enough . . . even . . .
            after all . . .
            more . . .
            also . . .

CH3:   Is there more use . . .
            certainly there is . . .
            if there is . . .
            is there not . . .

CH4:   Make nothing . . .
            not more . . .
            treacherous . . .

<u>W'S LAST LINES OF THE ACT SPOKEN WITH NO MUSICAL ACCOMPANIMENT.</u>

W: Any hurry
            any little hurry   (W/CONT'D OVER)

INTERLUDE 1 · 69

W (CONT'D):   has so much subsistence,
it has and
choosing, it has.

INTERLUDE.

<u>W RESUMES HER LECTURE WITH
DRONE ACCOMPANIMENT.</u>

W: Plays are either read
      or heard
          or seen.

That the thing seen
and the thing felt about the thing seen
are not going on at the same tempo,
      that is what makes anybody nervous.

Nervousness consists in needing to go faster or slower so as to
get together.

At the theater there is the curtain
and the curtain already makes one feel nervous.
Then beside the curtain there is the audience
and the fact that they are or will be
      or will not be
           in the way when the curtain goes up
that too makes for nervousness.

(W/CONT'D OVER)

W (CONT'D):   And is it a mistake that
        that is what the theater is
        or is it not.
There are things that are exciting
as the theater is exciting
        but do they make you nervous
            or do they not.

Let us think of three different kinds of things that are exciting and that make
        or do not make
            one nervous.
First any scene which is a real scene
        something real that is happening
            in which one takes part.
Second any book that is exciting,
third the theater at which one sees
        an exciting action.

In each case the excitement and the nervousness
and the being behind or ahead in one's feeling
        is different.

First anything exciting in which one takes part.
There one progresses forward and back
emotionally
and at the supreme crisis of the scene
        the scene in which one takes part,
in which one's hopes and loves and fears
        take part
at the extreme crisis of this thing
one is almost one with one's emotions,
        the action and the emotion go together,

(W/CONT'D OVER)

W (CONT'D): there is but just a moment of this
coordination,
> but it does exist
>> otherwise there is no completion.

When any people are living an exciting moment
they go on and on and on
> until the thing has come together.

Now when you read a book how is it.
> Well it is not exactly like that
no not even when a book is even more exciting
than any excitement one has ever had.
In the first place one can always look at the end of the book and so
> quiet down one's excitement.
The excitement having been quieted down
one can enjoy the excitement
> just as any one can by remembering
and so tasting it over and over again
> but each time
>> less intensely
and each time
> until it is all over.
Those who like to read books over and over
get continuously this sensation of the excitement
as if it were a pleasant distant thunder
> that rolls and rolls
>> and the more it rolls
>>> well the further it rolls
>> the pleasanter
> until it does not roll any more.

Now the theater has still another way of being
> all this to you.

ACT TWO.

[THE ACTION: CIRCULATION. *Voices sift through memories and associations, primarily in song.*]

SCENE 1.

<u>THREE DISTINCT SHORT SONGS, SUNG OR VOCALIZED PRIMARILY BY W WITH CHORAL SUPPORT. (ONE CHORUS MEMBER, A, BEGINS TO EMERGE IN THIS ACT.)</u>

W: Act Two: Three.

W/CHORUS: (SUNG) Four and nobody wounded,
five and nobody flourishing,
six and nobody talkative,
eight and nobody sensible.

W/CHORUS: (SUNG)
One and a left hand lift that is so heavy
        that there is no way
                of pronouncing perfectly.

W/CHORUS: (SUNG) A point of accuracy,
a point of a strange stove,
a point that is so sober that the reason
left is all the chance of swelling.

SCENE 2.

THREE SONGS, VARIATIONS ON THE PREVIOUS SCENE'S.

W: The same three.

W/CHORUS: (SUNG) A wide oak a wide enough oak,
a very wide cake, a lightning cooky,
a single wide open and exchanged box
filled with the same little sac
         that shines.

W/CHORUS: (SUNG) The best the only better
and more left footed stranger.

W/CHORUS: (SUNG) The very kindness there is
in all lemons oranges apples pears
         and potatoes.

SCENE 3.

THREE MORE SONGS, THIS TIME WITH HINTS OF A DUET BETWEEN W AND A.

W: The same three.

W/CHORUS: (SUNG) A same frame a sadder portal,
a singular gate
         and a bracketed mischance.

(W/CHORUS/CONT'D OVER)

W/CHORUS (CONT'D):   (SUNG) A rich market where
there is no memory of more moon
than there is everywhere
and yet where strangely
    there is apparel
        and a whole set.

W/A: (SUNG/SPOKEN)
A connection, a clam cup connection,
a survey, a ticket and a return to laying over.

INTERLUDE.

<u>W RETURNS TO LECTERN. THE CHORUS MEMBER, A, LISTENS MOST ATTENTIVELY.</u>

W: What happens on the stage
and how
and how does one feel about it.

Is the thing seen or the thing heard
the thing that makes most of its impression upon you at the theater.
How much has the hearing to do with it
   and how little.
Does the thing heard replace the thing seen.
Does it help or does it interfere with it.

And when you are taking part
   in something really happening,
does the thing seen or does the thing heard affect you.
Can you wait to hear or can you wait to see   (W/CONT'D OVER)

W (CONT'D): and which excites you the most.
And what has either one to do with the completion of the excitement.

In reading an exciting book one sees
    but one also hears
and when the story is at its most exciting
does one hear more than one sees.

I am posing all these questions because
    of course
in writing, all these things are really
    most entirely really exciting.
And in asking a question one is not answering
    but one is
        as one may say
            deciding about knowing.
In asking these questions

A: although there is no one who answers them
W: there is in them that there is knowledge.
    Knowledge is what you know.

ACT THREE.

[THE ACTION: RUMINATION. *A takes a more active part, which brings a change in balance to W's composition.*]

SCENE 1.

<u>COUNTERPOINT, APPROACHING FUGUE.</u>

A: Act Three. Two.

W/A: (CHANTED/INTONED)
           A cut, a cut is not a slice,
           what is the occasion for representing a cut
                   and a slice.
           What is the occasion for all that.

           A cut is a slice,
           a cut is the same slice.
           The reason that a cut is a slice
                   is that if there is no hurry
           any time is just as useful.

SCENE 2.

<u>FUGUE PLUS ECHO. CHORUS UNDERLINES
WITH DISTINCT EMPHASES, SIBILANTS,
CAMERA SHUTTER CLICKS.</u>

A: Four.

W/A: (CHANTED/INTONED)
           A cut and a slice is there any question when a
                   cut and a slice are just the same.

CH1:   ssslicce . . . sssslicccceee

CH2:   any question . . . just the same . . .

CH3:   is there . . .

CH4:   *click . . . click*

W/A: (CHANTED/INTONED)
A cut and a slice has no particular exchange
    it has such a strange exception
        to all that which is different.

CH1:   sssliccee . . . strange . . . different

CH2:   such a . . . all that which . . .

CH3:   that which is different . . .

CH4:   *click* . . . no particular . . . exception

W/A: (CHANTED/INTONED/ALTERNATING?)
A cut and only slice,
    only a cut and only a slice,
the remains of a taste may remain
    and tasting is accurate.

CH1:   ssliccee . . . ssliccee . . . accurate

CH2:   only . . . only a . . . only a . . .

CH3:   tasting is accurate . . .

CH4:   *click . . . click . . .*

78 · RADIO FREE STEIN

W/A:	(CHANTED/INTONED/ALTERNATING?)
	A cut and an occasion,
	a slice and a substitute
	a single hurry and a circumstance
	that shows that, all this is so reasonable
		when everything is clear.

CH1:	sssliccee . . . single . . . reasonable . . . clear . . .

CH2:	all this . . . everything . . .

CH3:	this is so . . . everything is clear . . .

CH4:	*click* . . . clear . . .

SCENE 3.

<u>W DISMISSES THE CHORUS. SHE BELIEVES HERSELF TO BE ALONE, BUT A REMAINS NEAR, LISTENING AND TAKING PART.</u>

A:	(LOW) One.

W:	(CHANTED/INTONED)
	All alone with the best reception,
	all alone with more than the best reception,
	all alone with a paragraph
	and something that is worth something,
		worth almost anything,
	worth the best example there is

(W/CONT'D OVER)

INTERLUDE 1 · 79

W (CONT'D):   of a little occasional archbishop.

                           This which is so clean is precious little
                                   when there is no bath water.
                           A long time a very long time
                           there is no use in an obstacle that is original
                                   and has a source.

A: best reception . . .
                           the best reception . . .
                           something . . . something . . .
                           anything . . .
                           example . . . occasional . . .
                           time . . . long time . . . original . . .

<u>WHISPERING, A REPEATS HER WORDS.</u>

INTERLUDE.

<u>RETURN TO LECTURE FORMAT. MUSICAL DRONE WITH MORE VARIATION AND CHORAL PARTICIPATION.</u>

W: I remember very well the first play I wrote.
                           I called it What Happened, a Play.
                           I think and always have thought
                                 that if you write a play
                                    you ought to announce that it is a play.

                           I had just come home from a pleasant dinner party and I realized then
                                 as anybody can know

                                                                   (W/CONT'D OVER)

W (CONT'D):	that something is always happening.
	Anybody knows a quantity of stories,
	there are always plenty for the newspapers
	and there are always plenty in private life.
	Everybody knows so many stories
ALL:	(LOUD) What is the use of telling another story!
W:	Everybody knows so many and tells so many.
	So naturally what I wanted to do in my play
	was what everybody did not always know
	nor always tell.
	By everybody I do of course include myself.
	And so I wrote What Happened, a Play.
	Then I wrote a lot of plays.
	I concluded that anything that was not a story
	could be a play.
	I had before I began writing plays
	written many portraits.
	I had been enormously interested
	all my life
	in finding out what made each one that one
	and so I had written a great many portraits.
	I came to think that
	since each one is that one
	and that there are a number of them
ALL:	(LOUD) each one being that one,

W: the only way to express this thing

ALL: each one being that one

W: and there being a number of them
                                     knowing each other
                was in a play.
                          And so I began writing plays.

                 And the idea in What Happened, a Play
                            was to express this
                without telling what happened.

                 I have of course
                        always been struggling with this thing
          to say what you nor I nor nobody knows,
                      but what is really
                          what you and I and everybody knows,
          and as I say everybody hears stories
          but the thing that makes each one what he is
                      is not that.

          I slowly came to feel that
          if a play was exactly like a landscape
          then there would be no difficulty
                    about the emotion of the person looking on
          being behind or ahead of the play
                  because the landscape
                              does not have to make acquaintance.
          You may have to make acquaintance with it,
                  but it does not with you.

                                                                                          (W/CONT'D OVER)

W (CONT'D): The landscape has its formation and
 after all a play has to have formation
 and as the story is not the thing
 then the landscape
 not moving but being always in relation,

W/CHORUS: the trees to the hills
 the hills to the fields
 the trees to each other
 any piece of it to any sky
 and then any detail to any other detail,

W: the story is only of importance
 if you like to tell
 or like to hear a story
 but the relation is there anyway.

 And of that relation I wanted to make a play
 and I did, a great number of plays.

 So you do see what I have after all meant.

ACT FOUR.

[NO ACTION, JUST LANDSCAPE. W, *recalling a recent birthday party, creates an expanded sense of space for the play she is writing, a blossoming, another order of polyphony.*]

W: Act Four. Four

CHORUS: and four more

> THESE FIRST LINES SERVE AS REFRAIN, REPEATED
> AS OFTEN AS NEEDED. MUSICAL UNDERLINING
> RECALLS ACT ONE, BUT ACCOMPANIMENT
> IS MORE SUPPLE, PLAYFUL, JOYOUS.

W: A birthday, what is a birthday,
a birthday is a speech,
it is a second time when there is tobacco,
it is only one time when there is poison.
It is more than one time
when the occasion which shows
an occasional sharp separation
is unanimous.

CH3:   What is a birthday . . .
it is . . .
it is . . .
it is . . .
unanimous.

CH1:   What . . .
a second . . .
only one . . .
more than one . . .
occasional sharp . . .
unanimous.

CH2:   is a . . .
is a . . .
is a . . . when there is . . .

(CH2/CONT'D OVER)

CH2 (CONT'D): is only . . . when there is . . .
is more than . . .
is unanimous.

CH4: unanimous.

CHORUS: (REFRAIN) and four more

W: A blanket,
what is a blanket,
a blanket is so speedy that heat
    much heat
is hotter and cooler,
very much cooler
almost more nearly cooler
than at any other time

CH3: What is a blanket . . .
a blanket is . . .
much heat is . . .

CH1: So speedy . . .
much heat . . .
hotter and cooler . . .
very much cooler . . .
almost more nearly cooler . . .
any other . . .

CH2: Is a . . .
is so . . .
very much . . .
almost more nearly . . .

CH4:   Any other time often.

CHORUS: (REFRAIN) and four more.

W: A blame
             what is a blame,
             a blame is what arises
             and cautions each one to be calm
             and an ocean
             and a masterpiece.

CH3:   What is a blame . . .
             a blame is . . .
             an ocean . . .
             a masterpiece.

CH1:   Each one to be calm . . .

CH2:   Is a . . .
             is what . . .
             each one . . .

CH4:   A masterpiece.

CHORUS: (REFRAIN) and four more.

W: A clever saucer,
             what is a clever saucer,
             a clever saucer is very likely practiced
             and even has toes,
             it has tiny things to shake   (W/CONT'D OVER)

W (CONT'D): and really
    if it were not for a delicate blue color
would there be any reason
    for every one to differ.

CH3: What is a saucer . . .
a saucer is . . .
it has . . .

CH1: Clever . . .
clever . . .
clever . . . very likely
tiny things to shake . . .
really . . . delicate blue . . .
every one . . .

CH2: Is a . . .
even has toes . . .
tiny things . . .
every one to differ.

CH4: If it were not . . .
any reason . . .
every one to differ.

CHORUS: (REFRAIN) and four more.

<u>BEGINS AS DUET BUT A FADES OUT.</u>

W/A: The objection and the perfect central table,
the sorrow in borrowing

(W/A/CONT'D OVER)

W/A (CONT'D): and the hurry in a nervous feeling,
the question is it really a plague,
is it really an oleander,
is it really saffron in color,
the surmountable appetite which shows
　　inclination to be warmer,
the safety in a match and the safety in
　　a little piece of splinter,
the real reason why cocoa is cheaper,
the same use for bread
　　as for any breathing that is softer,

W: the lecture
and the surrounding large white soft unequal
　　and spread out sale
　　of more and still less
is no better,
all this makes one regard in a season,
one hat in a curtain that is rising higher,
one landing
　　and many many more,

CHORUS: and many more many more many many more.

<u>INTERLUDE.</u>

<u>SILENCE, OR VERY QUIET, AMBIENT SOUNDS.</u>

<u>ACT FIVE.</u>

[THE ACTION: EPILOGUE, CODA. W *completes her play.*]

<u>W RETURNS TO DESK, OPENS LAPTOP. SOME USE OF SPEECH FUNCTION AGAIN. QUIET OR AMBIENT MUSIC CONTINUES, WITH UNDERLINING.</u>

W: Act Five. Two.

A regret
a single regret
makes a door way.
What is a door way,
a door way is a photograph.

CH1: Single . . .

CH2: Is a . . .
is a . . .

CH3: What is a door way . . .
a door way is . . .

CH4:   A regret . . .
             regret . . .

LAPTOP: (PLAYBACK)
             What is a door way,
             a door way is a photograph.

W: What is a photograph
             a photograph is a sight
             and a sight is always
                         a sight of something.
             Very likely there is a photograph
                     that gives color
                             if there is then
             there is that color
                     that does not change
                             any more than it did
             when there was much more use for photography.

CH1:   Always . . .
             very likely . . .
             that color . . .
                     that does not change . . .
                             any more than . . .
             much more use . . .

CH2:   Is a . . .
             is a . . .
             is always . . .
             there is that color . . .   (CH2/CONT'D OVER)

90 · RADIO FREE STEIN

CH2 (CONT'D): any more than . . .
when there was much more use . . .

CH3: What is a photograph
a photograph is a . . .
a sight is . . .
there is a . . .
there is that . . .

CH4: A sight . . .
a sight of something . . .
that does not change . . .

LAPTOP: A sight of something . . .
that does not change . . .

END.

ESSAY 2

SPEECH, ACTS, PARLOR PLAYS: STEIN WITH AUSTIN

These pages begin with an intuition: that reading, listening to, and thinking with Gertrude Stein's early plays will help us to untangle, if only to retie differently, some of the intricate knots that bind linguistic performativity to performativity in its theatrical sense. This intuition has accompanied the Radio Free Stein project from the start, but, I admit, it has not been easy to make good on its promise. What is called *performativity* is well-trodden if still thorny theoretical ground, its entwined meanings emerging in distinct contexts of use and polemic across a variety of disciplinary locations (philosophy of language, literary theory, theater and performance studies, the wider humanities).[1] No doubt, the term is well past its paradigmatic prime, the heyday of 1990s queer theory, a party I was at and to which this feels like a very (*very*) belated contribution. But the term continues to play a significant role in contemporary discourse, usually in a manner that either assimilates its linguistic and theatrical meanings reductively (sometimes egregiously so, as in the popular use that means *(merely) acted* or *going through the motions* as in "He apologized but it was only performative") or brackets them off from one another completely (in analytic philosophy's distinction between serious and nonserious language). I have the strong sense that it is worth returning to the muddle of resemblances and differences between and among this term's related meanings by way of Stein's plays which break down theatrical experience in specifically linguistic terms.

By linguistic performativity I refer, in the first instance, to the concept of *performative utterances* famously introduced and provisionally theorized by J. L. Austin in the William James Lectures given at Harvard in 1955 which were collected, edited, and published under the title *How to Do Things with Words*. Austin's lectures ran strongly athwart then prevailing winds in analytic philosophy of language with its near-total emphasis on the truth-value of statements inherited from logical positivist and empiricist projects of the 1920s and '30s, themselves based in the work of Frege (who Austin translated), Russell and Whitehead, and the early Wittgenstein. Austin's initial gesture, perhaps his most sustained and radical one, is to point out that we do (and ought to do) many other things with and in language than only describe, assert, or constate facts. Putting into practice the methods and techniques of ordinary language philosophy for which the intricacies of everyday speech may indicate evolved structures of meaning and being, Austin identifies a kind of utterance, *performatives*, which he defines this way: "A. they do not 'describe' or 'report' or constate anything at all, are not 'true or false'; and B. the uttering of the sentence is, or is part of, the doing of an action."[2] In performatives, most explicitly exemplified by sentences in the first-person singular present indicative mood, such as those that begin "I bet," "I promise," or the "I do" of a marriage ceremony, "the issuing of the utterance is the performing of an action" (*How*, 6), whether a bet, a promise, or a marriage, "(in, of course, the appropriate circumstances)" (6).

Austin's parenthetical qualification turns out to be one main reason the performative utterance has been so generative for thinkers across disciplines. The baggy category of "appropriate circumstances" invites analysis of those pragmatic, contextual, and nonverbal aspects of language that mid-century analytic philosophy tended to ignore. In particular, Austin's emphasis on the key role for norms or conventions in what he calls the felicity conditions for performatives appealed strongly to thinkers interested in the institutional authority of language, such as Judith Butler and Eve Sedgwick, who saw a promising connection between performative force and the imbrications of language with power in Michel Foucault's work.[3] Austin himself is not keen to take his concept beyond what he considers ordinary circumstances even while his imaginative, at times perverse examples incite readers to expand these horizons. But his attraction to inappropriate circumstances, to all the ways that performative utterances can go wrong or be unhappy (what he named the "doctrine of the *Infelicities*" [*How*, 14]), resonated with queer theory's politicizing tendencies toward trouble and the non-normative, toward gaps between otherwise rigidly aligned and ideologically enforced meanings of gender, family, sexuality, and identity. Reading Austin's wry, witty, and enormously understated lectures, it is evident that much of his own enjoyment lies in the infelicities, the challenges these pose to his own analytical project and the dangers of philosophical reduction more generally ("we must at all costs avoid over-simplification, which one might be tempted to call the occupational disease of philosophers if it were not their occupation" [38]).

For literary theorists and their fellow travelers, then, Austin's theory of performatives has offered a promising conceptualization of linguistic force even while it appears to exclude from its account literary and theatrical circumstances as peculiarly inappropriate. Austin consistently brackets such "nonserious" uses of language, most infamously in the second lecture: "A performative utterance will, for example, be *in a peculiar way* hollow or void if said by an actor on the stage, or if introduced in a poem, or spoken in soliloquy. This applies in a similar manner to any and every utterance—a sea-change in special circumstances" (22). Austin's point, made rich and strange by way of *The Tempest*, is that on the literary page or theatrical stage all promisings, marryings, and other explicit performatives are hollow or void (these terms refer to specific kinds of infelicity that Austin has adumbrated and to which I will return) insofar as they are spoken in quotation marks: "Language in such circumstances is in special ways—intelligibly—used not seriously, but in ways *parasitic* upon its normal use—ways which fall under the doctrine of the *etiolations* of language. All this we are excluding from consideration" (22). He repeats a similar exclusion in a footnote toward the end of lecture 7 at a key moment in the overall arc of the lectures: "We shall not always mention but must bear in mind the possibility of 'etiolation' as it occurs when we use speech in acting, fiction and poetry, quotation and recitation" (92).

More on etiolation in a moment. But first, I would observe the consistent use of scare quotes in Austin, citations to other uses, often unspecified, of a word or phrase (including to his own previous use of *etiolation*). Clearly, as his unmarked use of a Shakespearean phrase indicates, Austin understands that the citational is not restricted to literary or theatrical language and must be present in everyday speech as well as in works of philosophy. Second, intimately related to this, I accept many aspects of Jacques Derrida's critique of Austin in "Signature Event Context" including his theorization of the citational structure of all utterances, the fundamental iterability of the mark that permits writing to break with its context by way of the force of rupture, and his deconstruction of the distinction between serious and nonserious language. Yes. At the same time, I would point out that Austin's consistent use of playful, ironized, literarily allusive, self-distancing, not-always-quite-seriously-doctrinal language in the stand-up comedy routine delivered as the William James Lectures effectively deconstructs itself. Indeed, as many readers have noticed, Austin's initial, careful, and persuasive exploration of the performative/constative distinction leads to an engaging breakdown as a result of his failed attempts to identify a grammatical criterion that would distinguish between them (something that Derrida notes appreciatively). By lecture 8 we encounter a major shift: unable to repress his taxonomic urges, Austin decides to supplement (but not exactly replace) his binary scheme with a tripartite one (locutionary, illocutionary, and perlocutionary acts) whose relation to performative and constative utterances remains unresolved. These aspects of Austin's lectures, their bracing mix of grounded observational clarity, self-deprecating humor, far-ranging speculation, and a willingness to face and fail to accommodate ever-increasing linguistic complexity, have left literary theorists, philosophers, and linguists with an enormously rich, promising, and promise-breaking collection of concepts and terms, examples and problems, methods, techniques, and affective dispositions.

So it should be evident that I am not returning to Austin here in a primarily deconstructive mood.[4] As my repeated references to promising indicate, I am informed at least as much by Shoshana Felman's performative reading of Austin as by Derrida's constative one, her analysis of the pleasures of Austin's seductive Don Juanism and the logic of the broken promise (my psychoanalytic reference points, however, are not Lacanian). But of all these important commentators, I have been most drawn to Sedgwick's uptake of the performative which veers closest to Austin's nondualist commitments to a phenomenology of ordinary language.[5] As she puts it in the context of one of several discussions of Austin's concept:

> I assume that the line between words and things or between linguistic and nonlinguistic phenomena is endlessly changing, permeable, and entirely unsusceptible to any definitive articulation. With Wittgenstein, however, I have an inclination to deprecate the assignment of a very special value, mystique, or thingness to meaning and language. Many kinds of objects and events mean, in many heterogeneous ways and contexts, and I see some value in not reifying or mystifying the linguistic kinds of meaning unnecessarily.[6]

I don't think that Sedgwick means this to be a controversial or esoteric point. The sound of rustling or crunching dry leaves or the feel of cold hands, the sight of a flashing neon sign or a broken ceramic plate, an orgasm: these are just a few of the many kinds of objects and events that mean in many ways and contexts, and whose meanings are not primarily linguistic. Language inevitably comes to be intimately involved in their meanings when we wish to think and communicate about them (as I am doing here, if only as examples of the nonlinguistic). But the physiological (sensory, affective) aspects of these experiences have or evoke meaning independently of our abilities to describe them in language, even or especially when our linguistic descriptions seem retrospectively to offer a good account of them.

My approach to Stein's writing takes up the endlessly permeable line between words and things as a methodological, even a meta-methodological premise. Rather than enlist Austin's concept in the service of an antiessentialist epistemological project to arrive (again and again) at a generalized performativity understood in terms of the production or construction of reality by language, these pages seek to unfold in more detail what Sedgwick calls (after Paul de Man) "this unsettling aberrance between performativity and theatricality" and the key role for the affective in this aberrant relation.[7] A still-current critical promise of Austin's lectures lies in their ways of theorizing a variety of linguistic forces vis-à-vis both norm (or convention) and motive (or affect). This is to return to what Felman calls the scandal of the speaking body but to locate it in Stein's modernist theater, a Faustian laboratory characterized by devil's bargains and improvised conventions, in which language is aberrantly framed and unframed in a manner that lets us perceive locutionary, illocutionary, and perlocutionary forces in tension with one another. When we pay close attention to Stein's early plays we will see that these tensions emerge from her proposed conventions that reflexively forge theatrical elements (dialogue, scenes) out of grammatical, prosaic, and poetic ones (sentences, paragraphs, meters). Whether or not readers or audiences give their consent to such unusual theatrical conventions (or even recognize them), Stein's plays invite us to engage with them via what Austin calls the "total speech situation."

I read Austin with Stein precisely because they are both ordinary language philosophers who share a conception of language associated with American pragmatism and are committed to analyzing the conventions of ordinary language.[8] On offer, for both, are: (1) a fine-grained attention to minimal linguistic differences and their surprising, meaningful, not-only-linguistic consequences (realized, for example, in their obsession with prepositions); (2) a Nietzschean perspective on the contingency and provisionality of the subject's relation to utterance; (3) a supple understanding of labile, contextual frames for verbal communication; and (4) a willingness to wade pleasurably (often comedically) into the muddle of scenes of utterance in their verbal and nonverbal aspects and labile frames. Given especially these latter two shared dispositions, it is no accident that both thinkers are powerfully, ambivalently drawn to theater. Austin evokes theatrical scenes and figures to exemplify the varieties of linguistic force that he wishes to analyze even while he subordinates these examples. In this context, his description of theatrical and poetic language as etiolated—that is, parasitic, feeble, bleached, a plant deprived of sunlight, a pale imitation of green vigor—strikes me as counterintuitive at best, or, really, just plain wrong. In the theatrical works that Austin has in mind (Euripides as well as Shakespeare show up in the lectures), utterances, far from etiolated, are more like hothouse flowers or plants. Placed under special lights, framed, artifactualized, theatrical language on the page or stage (or screen) has, if anything, more power or force for its readers and hearers, if not always the same kind as offstage. A promise or vow made in a play, a trial verdict on television or in film, is, often enough, brought into sharp relief, we audience-witnesses put on our toes, alert to possible narrative or other consequences. Like a gun in a Chekhov or Ibsen play, the theatrically framed placement of an explicit performative utterance, certain to fire or misfire, is consequential no matter its diegetic felicity. The consequences of such theatrical utterances may resonate off the stage and into everyday language as well as philosophy.[9]

Here is a road map for this three-part essay. The first part centers on Austin's main theatrical example in *How to Do Things with Words*, his citation of a brief excerpt from Euripides's play *Hippolytus* to support an analysis of promising. Austin describes Hippolytus's promise as hollow, an infelicity that is also, as Samuel Weber has observed, a structural condition for theater. The peculiar way that theater and theatricality open up hollow, interior spaces leads some of Austin's most astute interpreters (Stanley Cavell, Eve Sedgwick) to seek a role for the affective in what Austin calls "the total speech situation," a role that I redescribe by way of Melanie Klein's notion of the total situation of the transference. This essay then brings Klein's notion with its expanded role for witnessing, or performativity's scenic aspect, back to a reading of Euripides's play while paying particular attention to spaces of indeterminate diegesis (the *skene*, the audience) as these become important structural conditions for the in/felicity of Hippolytus's promise. I conclude with a brief performative analysis of Austin's use of scare quotes, a grammatical technique for navigating indeterminate diegesis, to argue that he puts thinking on the line between commitment and provisionality.

The essay's next two parts wend their way through readings of several of Stein's early parlor plays, including *He Said It: Monologue* (1915), *What Happened: A Five Act Play* (1913), and *White Wines: Three Acts* (1913), to pursue the question: What does the hollowness of theatrical and poetic language sound like? While it may strike a reader as perverse to locate in Stein's theater (of all things!) any possible answer to a question about spatial emptiness, given the sheer linguistic density of these early plays, rendering them as radio theater has required that my collaborators and I seek their hollowness, and we have profited from the way, in radio, the Athenian *skene* has become the studio with all its interiorizing dynamics (as discussed in Essay 1). We have found that *He Said It* sets multiple voices in extroversive and introversive relations to one another, that *What Happened* creates play form itself (scenes and acts) from prosaic building blocks (sentences and paragraphs), and that *White Wines* traces the reciprocal dynamics of containment between domestic and theatrical space. That is, the spaces of these plays emerge from utterances and parts of speech, elements of dramatic form, and the situation of the parlor. These all exemplify the forms of hollowness that define theater.

THE FIRST AND MOST EXPLICIT evocation of theater in Austin's lectures is a citation to Euripides's *Hippolytus* in lecture 1. There he anticipates an objection to his definition of performatives, and with specific reference to promising, poses a question half in the voice of his objector (and with his characteristic scare quotes): "Surely the words must be spoken 'seriously' and so as to be taken 'seriously'?" (*How*, 9). His reply is complex and worth quoting at length.

> But we are apt to have a feeling that their being serious consists in their being uttered as (merely) the outward and visible sign, for convenience or other record or for information, of an inward and spiritual act: from which it is but a short step to go on to believe or to assume without realizing that for many purposes the outward utterance is a description, *true or false*, of the occurrence of the inward performance. The classic expression of this idea is to be found in the *Hippolytus* (l. 612), where Hippolytus says
>
> ἡ γλῶσσ' ὀμώμοχ', ἡ δὲ φρὴν ἀνωμοτός,
>
> i.e. 'my tongue swore to, but my heart (or mind or other backstage artiste) did not.' (9–10)

There are many things worth unfolding here, and I will have to proceed slowly and selectively. In the most immediate context, Austin is using the citation to Euripides in order to argue against a constative theory of promising, one that asserts the truth value of the utterance insofar as it is a report or description of some other, inward act. In the play Hippolytus breaks a promise he has just made to Phaedra's nurse not to betray the secret that his stepmother (Phaedra) is passionately in love with him. Hippolytus justifies his choice to betray the secret, which will lead to Phaedra's suicide, this way (in an early Harvard Classics translation): "'Twas but my tongue, 'twas not my soul that swore."[10] As Austin puts it, such a constative theory of promising "provides Hippolytus with a let-out, the bigamist with an excuse for his 'I do' and the welsher with a defence for his 'I bet.' Accuracy and morality alike are on the side of the plain saying that *our word is our bond*" (10).

Second, and in a slightly larger argumentative context, Austin is clearly rejecting any dualism that requires a mind or soul or other idealized agent to ground the act, and in this he resembles his antimetaphysical logical positivist predecessors. He is oriented (scientifically, as it were) toward exteriority, toward what he will later call the illocutionary force of the utterance with its supporting norms.[11] But, and significantly, Austin does not reject interiority as such, as a footnote just after the reference to "backstage artiste" makes clear: "But I do not mean to rule out all the offstage performers—the lights men, the stage manager, even the prompter; I am objecting only to certain officious understudies, who would duplicate the play" (10). Readers acquainted with Sedgwick's writing on queer performativity in Henry James's prefaces may hear associations between Austin's backstage artiste and anal erotics, the theatricalizing of a bodily, resourceful interiority that founds James's poetics. In his characteristically compressed, hyper-arch manner Austin uses these theatrical figures to label multiple interior systems such as perception (lights men), volitional and motor impulses (stage manager), language competence (the prompter)—psycho-physiological systems that interact off the stage of consciousness. Austin expresses considerable interest in such dynamics elsewhere in his writing, as Felman points out, and theater offers him precisely a queer, somewhat disavowed figure for such psychic complexity and multiplicity ungrounded in unitary intention. I will be returning to an entirely avowed version of this figure in Stein's conception of the multiple sensory aspects of plays.

But (and this is a third point in a yet larger argumentative context) there appears to be a tension between Austin's example and what follows in lecture 2, his characterization of the doctrine of the infelicities. There Austin distinguishes between misfires and abuses, that is, between acts "purported but void" and acts "professed but hollow" (18). If you and I marry but we are already married to others and the law of our land prohibits polygamy, then our marriage ceremony and its attendant performatives are void. On the other hand, my promise to drive you to the airport when I have no such intention (like Hippolytus's promise to Phaedra's nurse) is hollow. The hollowness of unhappy performatives invokes a gap between intention and expression, precisely the same psychical gap whose relevance for assessing performative force Austin has been at some pains to dismiss. Significantly, hollowness does not obviate (or void) the force of the utterance (*our word is our bond*).[12] What I noted above as a contemporary popular use of the term *performative* ("He apologized but it was only performative") assimilates the general term to a specific infelicity, the abuse of hollowness.

We may wonder why such a reduction of meaning has taken place in popular discourse. Perhaps this has something to do with an impoverished uptake of Butlerian performativity combined with an influential critique of the inadequacy of performative utterances in specific institutional contexts.[13] For my purposes here, I would simply observe that the contemporary, reduced meaning of performative does point to something that Austin clearly implies but nowhere explicitly states: that the gap or discontinuity between intention and expression (or act), a felicity condition for the promise (and other performative utterances, such as the apology), is a defining condition for theatrical experience. In the long history of antitheatrical discourse this gap is almost always construed as evidence for theater's fundamental insincerity, its falseness, nonseriousness, and manipulativeness.[14] But I find Samuel Weber's deconstructive approach to theatricality much more generative. Weber takes up Austin on precisely this point to interpret the hollowness of performativity as a structural condition for theater: "Such hollowness marks separation as a kind of inner space rather than an interval in-between. Theater takes place in the hollow of this separation, which it deploys and to which it responds."[15] Weber's argument, in its Nietzschean implications, evokes a potential genealogy of reciprocal relations between interiority and theater, with its broken promises and exhilarating betrayals. Austin's use of theater to figure multiple interior agencies, as both metaphor and more than metaphor, gestures toward such a genealogy. In a footnote Weber characterizes hollowness specifically in terms of "the abrupt modulations of the voice" in a Peking Opera performance, an "'expressionist' dynamics . . . without expressive 'pathos.'"[16] Such an emphasis on vocal intonation, as well as the scare quotes around "expressionist" and "pathos," points to some defining or constitutive role for affect in the hollowness of both theatricality and the performative utterance. As a good Derridean, however, Weber is concerned that any explicit reference to affect flirts dangerously with intentionality or self-presence.

I would like to extend this line of thinking about theatrical separation in relation to an interiorizing hollowness here. There are robust conceptualizations of affect that do not subscribe to notions of idealized self-presence in which affect may serve as a hinge category that links linguistic performativity and theatricality. Other theorists of a late Wittgensteinian bent have pursued similar intuitions about the role or place of affect in conceptualizing this link. Sedgwick has offered the notion of periperformatives, those utterances that cluster around or negatively refer to explicit performatives (such as "I cannot promise" or "I don't ask anything whatever of you") in order to bring into focus situations where there are no existing norms or agreed-upon conventions. Her goal, as she puts it, is not to "hiv[e] off a depersonalized understanding of performative force from a psychologized and spatial understanding of affective force."[17] A similar psychologizing and spatializing impulse can be found in Stanley Cavell's notion of the passionate utterance, which takes up and expands Austin's idea of perlocutionary force.[18] These theorists all practice the kind of attention that Austin, at some moments in his lectures, invites: "what we have to study is *not* the sentence but the issuing of an utterance in a speech situation" (*How*, 139); or, again, "The total speech act in the total speech situation is the *only actual* phenomenon which, in the last resort, we are engaged in elucidating" (148).

Rather than see in Austin's total speech situation a familiar fantasy of taxonomic mastery or exhaustive description of context (precisely what Derrida has shown to be impossible), we may hear rather what Kleinian object relations calls the total situation, that is, the transferential circumstances of interpretation in which nothing is, in principle, off-limits or excluded from analysis.[19] In Melanie Klein's revised and expanded notion of transference based on her experience using play technique with children, the total situation includes not only the patient's speech but also their bodily gestures and postures, facial expressions, vocal tones, and inflections, as well as the analyst's feelings (the countertransference). To return to theoretical formulations I have discussed elsewhere, by supplementing Derrida's early critique of structuralism with a theory of motivation that makes use of Kleinian affect theories, we may begin from the idea that any instance of language uses both frames and is framed by affective experience, that affect serves a specifically metacommunicative function: affective expressions put in place a labile frame for verbal (and other) communication.[20] When we call someone's behavior or a given performance style *theatricalizing*, we mean that it is highly reflexive about the reciprocal framing relation between language and affect, that it casts doubts on seriousness, and that it raises the specter of hollowness.

Theatrical space, with its dynamic relations between onstage and off, offers a laboratory for approaching the total speech situation. Austin's consistent return to questions of audience uptake, Cavell's emphasis on the passionate relations of exchange rather than only the utterance itself, and Sedgwick's spatialized approach to the neighborhoods of the periperformative all invoke performativity's scenic aspect and the crucial role for witnessing, including the witnessing of metacommunicative affective frames. No accident that these theorists consistently invoke highly theatricalized operatic moments in their treatments of Austin and performativity: Weber, as I mentioned, briefly describes a Peking Opera performance, Sedgwick interprets what she calls an "extraordinary periperformative aria" (*Touching*, 73) in Henry James's *The Golden Bowl*, and several key examples in Cavell are from the canon of European opera. Word-music configurations, opera in particular, appear at just that moment when affectivity is summoned to make sense of linguistic performativity with respect to the reciprocal containment of scene and utterance. The Radio Free Stein project has consistently approached Stein's plays with affective metacommunication in mind to experiment with and conceptualize the relations between scene and utterance as fundamental to linguistic peformativity and to theatricality as such.

I would like to return briefly to Austin's citation of Euripides both to bring my current discussion of Austin to a provisional conclusion and to demonstrate what an approach to performativity's scenic aspect might offer. The performative question, What exactly is Austin doing in and by citing *Hippolytus*?, has certainly been asked, most assiduously by Stanley Cavell, who suggests that Austin's choice is, in relation to the play itself, an odd one. In Euripides's play, Cavell asserts, Hippolytus "is incapable of breaking his promise. . . . It is exactly a consequence of this fact (is it a character flaw?) that the ensuing tragedy triples, or say generalizes, drawing Hippolytus and his father, Theseus, to their deaths after Phaedra."[21] But *Hippolytus* offers so many examples of oaths taken and either adhered to or not that Austin's recollection of it as a possible case study of the infelicities of the promise, and of speech acts more generally, is, if anything, overdetermined. As Aphrodite puts it in the prologue which explains her role in the play's action (the punishment of chaste Hippolytus through Phaedra's desire), "So runs my word; and soon the very deed / Shall follow" (l. 9–10). I cannot pursue a full reading of this play here but would begin by pointing out, contra Cavell, that Hippolytus does initially break his promise (even if he keeps it thereafter), that Theseus does not die, and that the question of seriousness at stake in Austin's citation should be analyzed not primarily in terms of sincerity but commitment.[22]

Perhaps the most significant fact about Hippolytus's promise, and one reason Austin may have been drawn to this scene, is that it is made offstage. The audience never hears Hippolytus utter his promise to Phaedra's nurse; readers of the play never read such an utterance. Rather, we are only informed of it retrospectively in the moment that he breaks it. The scene proceeds as follows: Hippolytus and the Nurse have just entered the stage from Theseus's palace, represented by the *skene*, the shed or structure that serves in ancient Athenian theater both as change room and prop or set. Phaedra has been listening at the palace door to a heated exchange in which (we are about to learn) Hippolytus has rejected the Nurse's invitation to assuage Phaedra's sexual desires. Once onstage the Nurse tries to prevent Hippolytus through an act of supplication from speaking in front of Phaedra and the Chorus of Troezenian women. Here is the exchange (in rapid lines of *stychomythia*):

> **NURSE:** Oh, by thy knees, be silent or I die!
>
> **HIPPOLYTUS:** Why, when thy speech was so guileless? Why?
>
> **NURSE:** It is not meet, fair Son, for every ear!
>
> **HIPPOLYTUS:** Good words can bravely forth, and have no fear.
>
> **NURSE:** Thine oath thine oath! I took thine oath before!
>
> **HIPPOLYTUS:** 'Twas but my tongue, 'twas not my soul that swore. (lines 641–49)

In the context of Austin's intervention, it is difficult not to interpret this exchange as professing two distinct approaches to language. The more pragmatic Nurse, seeking to help her mistress who is dying of sexual shame and inhibited desire, emphasizes precisely language's force, its potential destructiveness, and appropriate circumstances for speech and silence. Hippolytus, on the other hand, insists that speech, when good or true ("guileless"), stands alone, independent of context. Clearly Austin sides with the Nurse here and seeks to describe Hippolytus as a hypocrite: "It is gratifying to observe in this very example how excess of profundity, or rather solemnity, at once paves the way for immorality" (*How*, 10).

There is little for a contemporary reader to approve in Hippolytus (at least, at this point in the play), whose proud, cruel, and harsh rejection of Phaedra (he offers an extended misogynist fantasy of a world without women and biological reproduction) leads rapidly to her suicide (and there would be much more to say about his commitment to Artemis, to chastity and sexual purity, and the play's relation to homosexuality).[23] As in so much Greek theater, the mother's sexuality introduces disorder into patriarchal social bonds and she is punished. At the end of this play Theseus is reconciled with his dying son, their homosocial bonds first broken and then remade almost literally over Phaedra's dead body. But something else may have drawn Austin to this scene. I noted that Hippolytus's promise is not witnessed by the audience but, in the play's diegesis, takes place just prior in the palace, that is, the *skene*, that peculiar space, at once onstage and off, whose interior is invisible to us. I suggest here that the *skene* realizes precisely the hollowness or interior separation that Austin requires as a felicity condition for the promise, and may serve as a figure for the variety of agencies (thoughts, feelings, volitions) that he wishes to include in the total speech situation. Perhaps this is why Hippolytus's unwitnessed promise, broken in the act of reporting on it, is nevertheless kept for the rest of the play: the audience is forced to become witness to the effects of its betrayal and are made to hold Hippolytus to it, despite what they might otherwise wish. Theatrically hyper-felicitous, this line from Euripides became an ancient commonplace (Plato quotes it in the *Symposium*, Aristophanes in *The Frogs*) precisely because it raises the specter of hollowness, at once theatrical and linguistic. This is performativity's scenic (*skenic*) aspect at an early moment in theater's interiorizing history.

Austin never settles the question of seriousness that Euripides's play is meant to resolve. By no means does it disappear, but neither does it remain a question of the constative. *Serious* cannot simply be opposed to *insincere*, for as Cavell points out, it is not reasonable to suppose that Hippolytus is insincere when he utters his promise to the Nurse. If he does not take his oath seriously, this is less a function of his insincerity (Hippolytus is nothing if not sincere to a fault) than of his attitude toward his diegetic audience: the Nurse, the Chorus of Troezenian Women, and Phaedra herself are all women, in front of whom it is doubtful that Hippolytus considers himself held to an oath (only when it is restated in front of the theater audience that includes Athenian men will he count himself beholden to it). I suggest that the question of seriousness, analyzed in performative terms, is about commitment and being held to commitment. To engage briefly in some Austin-style analysis of ordinary language, consider how we use the word in sentences like "She's a serious tennis player" or "He's serious about practical jokes." The opposite of serious, in this sense, is flippant or dilettantish, uncommitted to the practice of tennis or joking, just trying it out. Flippant is precisely how Austin is worried that his theory of performatives will be received ("Such a doctrine sounds odd or flippant at first" [7]), and so he uses scare quotes to navigate the question of serious versus nonserious language use. Scare quotes let Austin try out a word or phrase without committing to it, and usually there is good reason not to, some use to which it can be put that he is not yet clear about or does not agree with ("Surely the words must be spoken 'seriously'" [9]). This is why we rarely say, about a promise, that it is serious, for this qualification is redundant insofar as to utter a promise is already to make a commitment. To speak of promising or marrying "seriously" would shed dubious light on the committed aspect of these acts. What is serious about the serious use of language, then, whether in philosophy, literary criticism, theater, or everyday speech, is a commitment to the choice of specific words and their entailments. It is not primarily to assert the continuity of intention over time but to acknowledge that this very assertion may be hollow but nevertheless forceful, that is, it may be undermined by the contingency of and conflicts between norms and motives, including our motive to abide by or to alter the norm of making sense or meaning what we say.

THIS ESSAY HAS, SO FAR, engaged primarily with some of the literature on performativity. These next sections will engage with scholarship on Stein's theater, although Austin will continue to appear along the way. The expanded field of attention that Austin's lectures foster, an orientation to performativity's scenic aspect, is what Stein's writing invites as well. But I should declare at the very start that I am a visitor to the field of theater studies, and as such, have been dismayed to encounter a somewhat recalcitrant opposition between the literary and the theatrical, an opposition that takes place, it seems, within a largely Hegelian framework. The affect theoretical approach that I take here and elsewhere, a kind of nonreductive materialism, begins from the idea that writing itself can be more or less theatricalizing, more or less reflexive about how writing as event happens in space and time on the ground of the page that is a stage for the minimal performance of reading. There are differences between reading a text silently, reading it aloud to oneself, reading it aloud to one person (a lover, say), reading it in front of an audience of strangers, and creating a fully staged theater piece or sound recording. The formal and aesthetic differences between these will depend on any number of conventions—of reading, courting, recording—as well as varying means of production.

The Radio Free Stein project has explored Stein's plays as they foreground the continuities between writing and performance, and having grant funding has expanded the range of conventions that we can use. In the prologue and in Essay 1, I suggested that the most salient conventions of radio performance (the close-mic and intimate enclosure of the studio, the presence of the script, the acoustic bridge between music and words) open up practical, technical possibilities for realizing Stein's early plays in performance. That is, radio lets us entertain and explore the fantasies (and phantasies) of audience that accompany Stein's theater. By shifting attention away from the theater stage and toward the studio-as-stage I have tried to sidestep the critical commonplace that insists on Stein's modernist antitheatricality, that sees the linguistic density of her plays and their rejection of legible dramatic conventions as distinctively untheatrical qualities.[24]

In doing so, however, I may be accused of avoiding (or voiding) the tension between language and bodily performance that one of the most important critics of Stein's theater argues is exactly what her plays require us to encounter. According to Jane Palatini Bowers, Stein's "metadramas" are "self-reflexive plays that question the way language functions in the theater and that are concerned with the interaction between textuality and performance."[25] As will become clear in my readings of Stein's plays, I have found many aspects of Bowers's writing incisive and helpful, such as, for example, her careful tracking of the emergence of Stein's playwriting out of group portraiture (*"They Watch Me,"* 9), and her location of Stein's theater poetics, not in a European avant-garde tradition (exemplified by Artaud) that aims to shock or antagonize audiences and that minimizes the importance of text and language, but in an American tradition committed to the categories of experience, poiesis, and an aesthetics of the contemporary.[26] At the same time, her argument that Stein's plays "oppose the physicality of performance" (2) and address a fundamental condition of theater, the many ways that language in performance is "overwhelmed, transformed, subordinated, menaced, and dissolved" (7), strikes me as overstated. In part this is because Bowers positions her argument against Betsy Alayne Ryan's work, at that time the only previous book-length treatment of Stein's plays, which emphasizes Stein's poetics of perceptual immediacy, "a relational, physical, present-tense theatre."[27] While Bowers offers a much-needed corrective to Ryan's undeconstructed commitment to theatrical presence, something has gone missing in the opposition between text and performance: reading as utterance, the vocal and bodily performance of speech acts, the scandal of the speaking body.

Consider Bowers's assertion, with regard to what she influentially termed Stein's conversation plays (those written between 1915 and 1919), that they "appear to be written records of speech acts, and nothing more. They are not windows onto a nonlinguistic world. They are themselves the world—a world of conversations without stories" (*"They Watch Me,"* 11). Bowers evokes speech act theory but does so in line with the linguistic interpretation offered by Émile Benveniste, who emphasizes the self-referential quality of performatives: "The act is thus identical with the utterance of the act. The signified is identical with the referent."[28] This claim normalizes Austin's concept and presents a formalist approach in which the linguistic and extralinguistic become "two entirely different categories," an approach that departs from the spirit of Austin's lectures with their emphasis on the total speech situation and inclusion of gestural, vocal, and other circumstantial aspects.[29] (See also Shoshana Felman's critique of Benveniste: "The performative has the property of subverting the alternative, the opposition, between referentiality and self-referentiality.")[30] Bowers's readings, echoing Benveniste's emphasis on linguistic reflexivity and with a disciplinary investment in theater semiotics, do not accommodate the many ways that Stein's plays invite both linguistic and nonlinguistic consideration, her writing's thoroughgoing commitment to exploring the intricate relations among verbal and nonverbal aspects of language itself.

For Bowers, a typical Stein conversation play "functions as an autonomous world of discourse without apparent connection to the world beyond words" (*"They Watch Me,"* 14). For example, she suggests that the title of Stein's short play *Can You See the Name* does not "evoke a central object, action, or condition that underlies all the talk of the play" (14) as play titles normally do (say, Beckett's *Endgame*). Instead, it is the first line of the dialogue which follows: "The name that I see is Howard. / Yes. / And the water that I see is the sea. / Yes. / And the land is the island" (12, in *"They Watch Me"*). No question that its title initiates the play's dialogue (and, perhaps, invites us to treat it as a poetic dialogue), but it also, at the same time, points to its topic, one of the main topics of Stein's theater, how we sense words and the relation between seeing words and hearing them, evident from the homonyms in these first lines: Howard/how word, see/sea, island/eye-land. Far from being a "closed system of discourse" (14), this play explores words' fundamental embeddedness in and openness to varieties of sensory and perceptual experience, those material aspects of utterance and reception that conjure with the enigmatic but undeniable impurities of the sign that are a condition for the theatricalization of writing in uttered speech. I would reformulate Bowers's remark that Stein's plays "are not windows onto a nonlinguistic world" this way: Stein's plays compose, spatialize, and re-create a linguistic and nonlinguistic world that they are already complexly interwoven with. This interweaving of the verbal with the nonverbal is less an opposition than an unpredictable, generative muddle of reference and self-reference, norm and motive, a variety of forces. Orienting toward Austin's total speech situation becomes a prerequisite when reading Stein's plays, insofar as they open up analysis of language to such muddles.

Consider *He Said It: Monologue* (1915), one of the conversation plays that Stein wrote during the year she and Toklas spent in Mallorca to escape the zeppelin air raids and coal shortages of wartime Paris (see figure 8). The play immediately poses a problem for readers. Its subtitle implies that we should read the text as if recited by a single masculine voice (a monologue), but its first lines appear to contradict this idea: "Spoken. / In English. / Always spoken. / Between them."[31] These lines describe aspects of the play's situation, its linguistic situation (the play is in English) and its performance situation: the lines are to be spoken as a dialogue between at least two persons. The conversational give-and-take between first- and second-persons that follows supports such a dialogic performance interpretation. In the Radio Free Stein workshop on this play we debated how best to resolve the tension between subtitle and dialogue form.[32] Peter Quartermain suggested that the play could be interpreted as a monologue insofar as there is one hearer, the reader of the play. (Amusingly, I misheard Peter's English accent and thought he was insisting on there being one *hero* of the play.) Others proposed that a monologue in performance inevitably becomes a kind of dialogue spoken between performer and audience, while still others heard three distinct voices in the play text, somehow realized by only two players. The libretto that I developed after the workshop (in collaboration with Ada Smailbegović) cast the play for piano and the voices of two women, whom we named Speaker and Hearer. The action of the play (as it were) consists of the recollection and re-creation of a man's monologue, described musically by the piano. (Formally, the piece is melodrama in the late eighteenth-century sense in which instrumental music introduces and is interspersed between spoken dialogue.) In our rendering each woman speaks in two distinct registers, a more extroversive voice addressed to the other and a lower, quieter subvoice addressed to the self that qualifies, contradicts, or otherwise reinflects what has just been said. For example, in these lines from the beginning—"This is what we give. We give it with a hat. Dear me. A great many people are precious. Are they. I do not ask the question" (267)—"Dear me" and "Are they" are uttered in the quieter, self-questioning subvoice. The pianist serves as Narrator and, as the play progresses, occasionally comments on the recollections and re-creations of his speech. The genre, we decided, is distressed comedy.

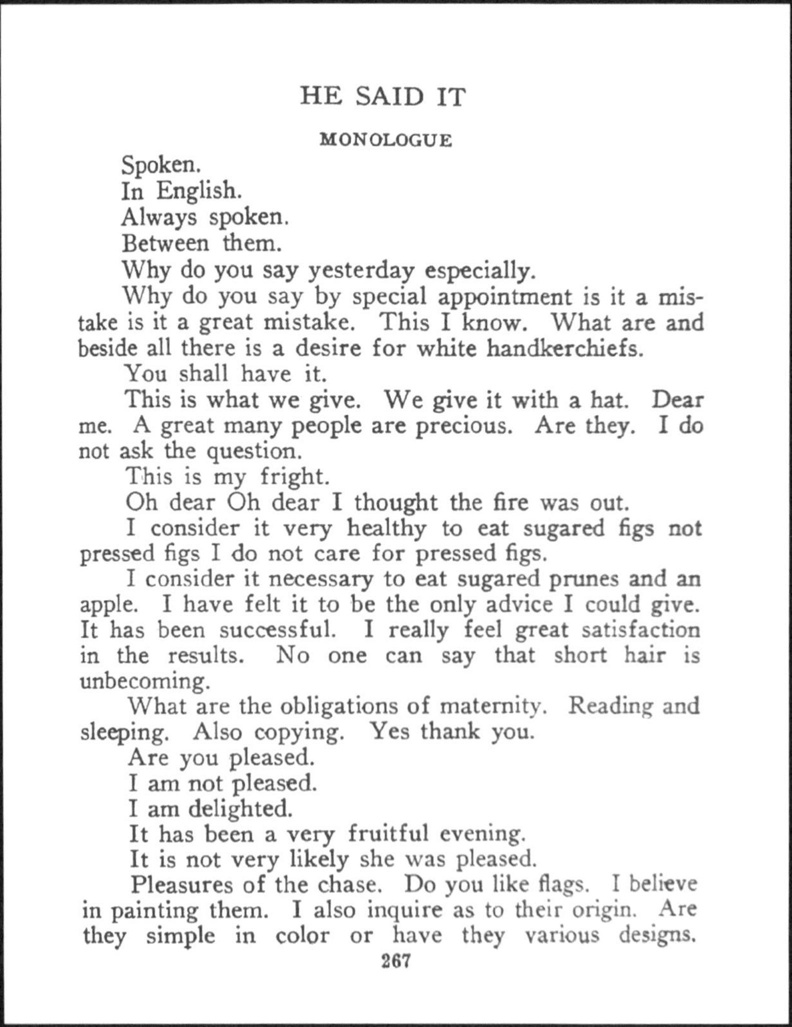

HE SAID IT
MONOLOGUE

Spoken.
In English.
Always spoken.
Between them.
Why do you say yesterday especially.

Why do you say by special appointment is it a mistake is it a great mistake. This I know. What are and beside all there is a desire for white handkerchiefs.

You shall have it.

This is what we give. We give it with a hat. Dear me. A great many people are precious. Are they. I do not ask the question.

This is my fright.

Oh dear Oh dear I thought the fire was out.

I consider it very healthy to eat sugared figs not pressed figs I do not care for pressed figs.

I consider it necessary to eat sugared prunes and an apple. I have felt it to be the only advice I could give. It has been successful. I really feel great satisfaction in the results. No one can say that short hair is unbecoming.

What are the obligations of maternity. Reading and sleeping. Also copying. Yes thank you.

Are you pleased.

I am not pleased.

I am delighted.

It has been a very fruitful evening.

It is not very likely she was pleased.

Pleasures of the chase. Do you like flags. I believe in painting them. I also inquire as to their origin. Are they simple in color or have they various designs.

Figure 8. Gertrude Stein, *He Said It: Monologue* (1915). From *Geography and Plays*, by Gertrude Stein with an introduction by Cyrena N. Pondrom. Reprinted by permission of the University of Wisconsin Press. Copyright © 1993 by the Board of Regents of the University of Wisconsin System. All rights reserved.

Listeners to the Radio Free Stein recording may hear the illocutionary force of almost every line of Stein's play, even while there are few explicit performative utterances. This force can be assessed by way of the various classes of utterance that Austin lists in his last lecture, examples of which include verdictives such as the appraisal "I consider it very healthy to eat sugared prunes" (267); expositives such as "This is what I said" (268) or "This is the way I say it" (269); and behabitives such as "I am not pleased. / I am delighted" (267). You will be delighted, or at least relieved, that I have no wish to classify all the utterances in Stein's play. I prefer to bring your attention to the exchanges that take place in our radio rendering, both between Speaker and Hearer and within each of the voices as well. Speaker's and Hearer's subvoices create the kind of hollow spaces between intention and expression that Austin has identified and bring into relief the distinct perlocutionary effects that reframe communication in affective terms. To listen to Stein, to give voice to her words, is to become aware of the reciprocal interplay between doing and feeling in words, an awareness that multiplies sensory modalities in a manner that does not exclude reference. Rather, and this is Stein's particular contribution, reference comes to have no greater significance, but also no lesser significance, than illocutionary acts and perlocutionary effects. For example, we can read "a desire for white handkerchiefs" (267) as a wish to witness a gesture of surrender, in the play's historical context, an end to the war that had displaced Stein and Toklas from their home. "You shall have it" (267), then, becomes an omnipotent gratification of such a wish for peace that is immediately, hopelessly ironized: "Dear me" (267).

One way to conceive of Stein's landscape theater poetics is in terms of a re-creation of a more even linguistic field on which locution, illocution, and perlocution play out in constant relation to one another. Reference and locution may be relatively deprivileged, but they need not be discarded or disregarded, a point I would insist on against readings of Stein that consider her language to be anti-referential (or only self-referential).[33] At the same time, I see no need to track down contextualizing sources for every line of Stein's play. Rather, we can simply notice that—like other Mallorcan plays such as *For the Country Entirely* and *Please Do Not Suffer*—*He Said It* explores the everyday space of two American women who watch the war from the sidelines of neutral Spain.[34] This context is scattered throughout in sentences referring to flags ("Do you like flags. I believe in painting them" [267], "Here are my stars and stripes" [273]), navies ("Who can be willing to leave an American boat" [268]), and politics ("Governed. Do be governed" [268], "I am not certain I like liberty" [270]), but, as always in Stein's writing, historical context is intertwined with the process of writing in its intimate and domestic settings. In the first few exchanges the lines invoke defecation (the advice to eat dried fruit and its satisfying results) and reproduction (copying as one of the "obligations of maternity" [267]), physiological analogues for making or producing. In the act/scene structure we developed the play expands out from this bodily space via gossip to include wider social relations, then returns to focus on aesthetic re-creation and authority. After what seems to be a digressive memory of travel ("This afternoon we went to New York and we spent the day together" [271]), the play winds down with a picnic that features "False smuggled contraband tobacco.

You mean by that that it isn't tobacco. No it's only leaves. I laugh" (274). The phrase "False smuggled contraband tobacco" is almost a triple negative that can be parsed in a number of ways depending on which words modify which (is it false tobacco or false contraband?), and the expositive ("You mean by that that it isn't tobacco") brings our attention to these layered meanings that don't quite cancel each other out. We are left with "only leaves," that is, the paper on which the play has been written, and the statement "I laugh," a pararhyme with "leaves," another ironized response to wartime conditions that abandons readers to their own devices.

I want to unfold more carefully the constitutive role or place of the affective in Stein's theater by turning to *What Happened: A Five Act Play* (1913), her first complete play, published in *Geography and Plays* (1922) and subsequently in Ulla Dydo's *A Stein Reader* (1993) (see figure 7, in Interlude 1). According to the reading that emerged from our Radio Free Stein workshop, *What Happened* is a metatheatrical piece that depicts the experience of writing a play in the wake of a party. As she reports in her lecture "Plays," "I remember very well the first one I wrote. I called it What Happened, a Play. . . . I had just come home from a pleasant dinner party and I realized then as anybody can know that something is always happening" (*Lectures*, 118). Dydo, in her headnote, provides the context of "a dinner party for the birthday of the painter Harry Phelan Gibb (1870–1948) on 8 April 1913" which conversation and "atmosphere Stein's play reproduces."[35] The workshop participants were not entirely persuaded by the idea that Stein's play "reproduces" the party's conversation or atmosphere, however, for it did not substantively help our reading experience. While biographical and historical context is useful for reading Stein, her plays consistently and reflexively work with the processes and materials of composition itself, regardless of their sources, to make us aware of the experience of writing and re-creation. By the end of the workshop we had concluded that what happens in the play is not the party itself but resonances or memories of the party and a meditation on the role that these memories play in the act of composition. *What Happened*, then, does not directly depict the emotional dynamics of a group of friends and acquaintances at Gibb's birthday party. Rather, the party's emotional dynamics become, after the fact and by way of writing, an occasion for thinking.

The workshop's sudden orientation toward understanding this play as metatheatrical or metacompositional emerged only after pondering what is probably the most pressing of this play's many interpretive problems: What do the numbers mean? And what should a theatrical interpreter do with this paratext? In the version published in *Geography and Plays*, small numbers, written out and in parentheses, are interspersed with the lines of the play. Are these highly compressed stage directions that refer to the number of voices or characters? In the version Dydo published (based on the manuscript), these numbers are centered, an unusual placement for stage directions but a more common one for character names or scene titles.[36] At the workshop I observed that these numbers (with two exceptions) count paragraphs, and we arrived at the sense that they serve to structure the play by separating the five clearly delineated acts into scenes, with each scene comprising one or more paragraphs. It appeared to us, then, that in this play Stein proposes a new dramatic convention: the paragraph as a fundamentally scenic unit.

Why would Stein choose to count paragraphs, to innovate the unusual convention of building scenes from paragraphs, in her first play? Counting, addition, measurement, and other number operations do occur frequently in this play. Its second paragraph, which became act 1, scene 2, in the radio script that I developed, begins this way: "A single sum four and five together and one, not any sun a clear signal and an exchange" (*Stein Reader*, 205). At the workshop Steven Meyer pointed out that the numbers in this sentence count the words in the sentences that precede it: "Loud and no cataract" has four words, "Not any nuisance is depressing" has five. Stein's play is observing something fundamental, that individual words add up to sentences ("A single sum four and five together"), and that sentences add up to paragraphs ("and one"). These aggregates of words do more than add up; they combine to form another unit, a paragraph. This is a kind of transmutation: the wordplay of *sum/sun* and *single/signal* foregrounds the transformation of number words into images of a distinctly expressive kind. We may begin to glimpse an analogy here between the way an aggregate of words can form a sentence, an aggregate of sentences a paragraph, and an aggregate of persons (one and one and one, in Stein's idiom) a group with its own emotional dynamics. These first words, sentences, and paragraphs enact and observe meaningful phenomena: that quantity turns into quality, that individual units combine rather than only sum, that a number of words in sequence can somehow evoke images, sensations, or emotions.

As Laura Schultz has observed, combination is a key concept for Stein, who begins her lecture "Plays" by recalling "a discovery which I considered fundamental, that sentences are not emotional and that paragraphs are . . . this difference was not a contradiction but a combination" (*Lectures*, 93).[37] That emotional paragraphs are made up of a succession of unemotional sentences fascinated Stein, who experimented with this idea in her writing of the late 1920s in a series of meditations published under the title *How to Write* (1931). Meyer has offered a lucid explication of Stein's discovery in relation to William James's theory of emotion (as second-order auto-sensation) and Wittgenstein's (mis)characterizations of James's theory. As he puts it, for Stein "sentences and paragraphs were related in exactly the same way that sensations and emotions were," that is, Stein's thesis is "a variation on James's theory of emotion, only extended to writing."[38] It is not uncommon to find in Stein's work concerns that stretch over decades. Fifteen years earlier, in *What Happened*, she explored a related phenomenon, that emotional paragraphs can combine to become theatrical scenes.[39]

Stein's choice of the paragraph as a hinge unit to help compose her first play is not arbitrary. In most classical and naturalist theater the scene is a basic building block that consists of one or more characters engaging in action (including speech) in a fixed setting at a continuous time. This scenic action is motivated, that is, it implies or includes an emotional or affective underpinning, hence the quintessential twentieth-century actor's question, What's my motivation in this scene? A spectator's attention at a staged play is often absorbed as she tries to understand a given scene's action and underlying motivations as these relate to the larger plot (recall that this makes Stein "nervous," as she puts it in "Plays"). In the metatheatrical piece *What Happened*, Stein tries for the first time to build a play's scenic action, the action of writing, from the sentences and paragraphs that she knows how to write already. How do we get from prose to plays, from sentences and paragraphs to scenes and acts, she wonders? By way of combination, by building sequences of emotional paragraphs into scenes to re-create what happened, the writing of the play itself. Stein must have appreciated the role of counting in developing play form: it is by counting that the writer gets from scenes (scene 1, scene 2, scene 3 . . .) to acts, and from acts (act 1, act 2, act 3 . . .) to the play as a whole. In our reading, then, *What Happened: A Five Act Play* bootstraps itself into existence by counting various linguistic elements in order to move from prose to play. Stein theatricalizes the combining of words into sentences, sentences into paragraphs, paragraphs into scenes, and scenes into the acts out of which the play is formed.

The radio scenario I prepared after the workshop took up some of these ideas in an attempt to render Stein's conventions in performance (see Interlude 1). In its final form, the script integrated excerpts from the lecture "Plays" between the acts to make explicit the play's metatheatricality as well as the lecture's theatricality. We cast the play for a lead voice, the Writer (W), and a Chorus consisting of a musical ensemble whose members also vocalize (sometimes by way of their wind instruments), and who take on roles of distinct grammatical forms. In workshop we observed a handful of patterns in the play: a repetition of the phrase "What is"; looping adjectival and adverbial forms ("clearly most clearly," "a worry a real worry"); a fastidious use of quantifiers and other modifiers of logical domains ("only," "enough," "every"); and a healthy dose of negation. To capture these gramatical patterns, the chorus members took up individual roles as the SEEKER OF DEFINITIONS, the QUALIFIER, the SPLITTER OF HAIRS, and the NEGATOR. The lead voice W gradually invokes these choral voices in the first act, teasing them out from the lines of her writing, and they eventually move toward chanting or singing as if to compensate for their grammatical limitations.

Act 2 explores various impulses toward counting, rhythm, and song as a way to sift through memories and associations, something W has a knack for but is ambivalent about. She knows that song and memory will please a projected or imagined audience, a figure that begins to emerge from the chorus as a distinct voice, A. However, W is ambivalent about giving A what it wants. Act 3, the crux of the play, offers a rumination, in fugue form, on a kind of writing that cuts through habitual associations and received conventions. In this act A makes trouble for W's triumphant assertion that she is "All alone with the best reception, all alone with more than the best reception, all alone with a paragraph and something that is worth something" (*Stein Reader*, 207). In act 4, the recollection of a recent birthday party creates an expansion, a new order of polyphony ("four and four more") and group experience. Finally, act 5 serves as an epilogue, coda, or exit out of the play's framework: "What is a door way, a door way is a photograph" (209). The complex temporality and regretful mood of the final scene or paragraph, its treatment of photography as a frame, at once analogy for and antithesis to playwriting (paragraph/photograph), lets writing go or releases it. The play, as we understand it, re-creates an experience of being alone to write while in the midst of various multiplicities: of words, sentences, and paragraphs, of memories, sensations, and emotions connected to the social event of the party and its aftermath, shaped into dramatic structures, scenes and acts. (Essay 3 offers

Samuel Vriezen's account of his compositional choices in preparing a musical setting for this play.)

With this interpretation of the centrality of affect and convention in Stein's first play, and her early plays more generally, we have entered the murky critical and speculative realm of experience that Raymond Williams called *structures of feeling*. Williams may be an unlikely critic to turn to for help understanding Stein, absent as she is from the all-male list of prominent playwrights (more than thirty) he discusses in *Drama from Ibsen to Brecht* (1973). Nevertheless, his book, which includes chapters not only on writers of drama (Ibsen, Strindberg, Chekhov, Pirandello, Shaw, Ionesco, etc.) but on writers of poetry who wrote plays (Yeats, Eliot, Auden, etc.), offers a critical framework that does not oppose text to performance.[40] For Williams, conventions are precisely what permit one to navigate between text and performance insofar as they offer "the terms upon which author, performers and audience agree to meet. . . . [This is] by no means always a formal or definite process; much more usually, in any art, the consent is largely customary, and often indeed it is virtually unconscious."[41] Dramatic and theatrical conventions, "customary" and "unconscious," may also be (at least in their initial discovery or invention) technical solutions to problems of writing and performance. Because anything might serve as a convention if it offers an expressive solution that operates within the constraints of theatrical production and is agreeable to writer, director, performers, or audience members, the question of consent becomes central. This is precisely the issue in Stein's plays, which require readers to observe the absence of received theater conventions and therefore to entertain new ones in order to find ways to read or stage them.

Williams's lucid discussion of convention leads to his famous, somewhat vague, but nevertheless methodologically useful concept *structure of feeling*, for this lets him locate the difficult-to-specify realm of audience agreement: "What I am seeking to describe is the continuity of experience from a particular work, through its particular form, to its recognition as a general form, and then the relation of this general form to a period" (*Drama*, 17). The key word here is *experience* which, as Sean Matthews points out, Williams emphasizes as "a tool to open up an analytic perspective otherwise unavailable . . . it brings together elements in an analysis that are otherwise kept separate."[42] In its focus on the experience of an individual work (I would include experiences of the writer, producer, director, actors, as well as readers and audiences) and lived relations to a more general historical condition, the structure of feeling concept offers a materialist revision of Zeitgeist (reminiscent of Stein's own concept of composition as explanation). For Williams, structure of feeling is "a critical term" (*Drama*, 19) and, at the same time, "an experience, to which we can directly respond . . . communicated in a particular form, through particular conventions" (19). If drama and performance conventions index structures of feeling, then a reader's emotional or affective experiences offer resources for understanding and articulating the relations between an individual work, its formal features, and the larger historical moments it participates in (although this is not easy: "The most persistent difficulty, in the analysis of structures of feeling, is the complexity of historical change and . . . the coexistence, even within a period and a society, of alternative structures" [20]).

Practically, Williams's writing on drama invites us to ask two critical questions: What conventions does a given Stein play propose? And what structures of feeling are indicated by its conventions? My reading of her first play's use of paragraphs and counting is one answer to the first question. While our attempt to render Stein's paragraph-to-scene convention in the Radio Free Stein performance remains less legible than I woud have liked (at least in the current iteration of the piece), I believe that we have captured Stein's radical commitment to new theatrical forms and her attempt to develop these forms as conventions. Radical though it is, Stein's commitment is also ambiguous, motivated at once by an uncompromising sense of writing's independence or autonomy and by the writer's wish for audience consent and agreement (an ambiguity that our rendering seeks to capture). Many readers, encountering Stein's writing and its commitments, either do not consent to her conventions or read her in terms of an utter rejection of all convention (and meaning as such). What I have tried to show is how Stein's commitments involve her in a fundamental rethinking of theater's verbal building blocks, with all the risks for legibility and consent that this entails.

And what is the structure of feeling of Stein's first play? It seems to emerge out of W's (the Writer's) movement back and forth between solitary and group experience, a disorientation and dispersion that is, at the same time, a startlingly precise reorientation to linguistic experience as a site of group impingement. With Williams's help I would locate Stein's drama between Chekhov and Brecht. On the one hand, we have Chekhov's attempt "to develop a new kind of dialogue. . . . An unfamiliar rhythm is developed, in which what is being said, essentially, is not said by any one of the characters, but, as it were inadvertently, by the group" (109). No question, the mood of *What Happened* is very different from that of *The Cherry Orchard*, but Stein's dialogue also conveys the feeling of a disintegrated (internal) group, difficult to express by any one voice. And on the other hand, Stein's early plays resemble Brecht's reflexive, critical theater which, as Williams suggests, tried "to show the action in the process of being made" (279), a "complex seeing" (285) that "*is* the action, in a profound way" (285). For Williams, the conventions of Brecht's epic theater point to the contradictions of capitalism in a way that those of naturalism and expressionism could not. Rather differently, Stein's early plays index tensions between motives and conventions for speech and writing. In *What Happened* the specific conventions of dramatic writing (act-scene structure), the place of memory and association in mimetic narrative, and the need for audience consent all become subject to vigorous linguistic recombination.

IN GIVING THIS ACCOUNT of Stein's first play and its proposed paragraph-to-scene convention, it may appear that I have strayed from Austin and the concerns with performativity that I began with. But this is not the case. I have been arguing that Stein's early plays are laboratories for thinking about performativity's scenic aspect or what Austin calls the total speech situation, which includes the conventions that serve as felicity conditions for both performative utterances and theatrical performance as well as the multiple and contradictory motives that accompany spoken language and exchange. These latter are notoriously difficult to assess, and Stein's early plays involve us in an estranging process: first, they betray our desire to disappear into the agreed-upon conventions of written drama by discarding them (or warping them beyond recognition); and second, they invite us to become aware of the tensions that arise between conventions and our motives, such as, for example, what might motivate consent to a given convention in the first place. Established theatrical conventions and norms for speech are not arbitrary but they are often calcified, indexes to historical institutions that do not necessarily meet a given reader's or audience's contemporary needs. Sounding out Stein's plays and trying out new conventions for performance requires readers and audiences to attend to these misfits or historical archaisms, to think with Stein's efforts to re-create the confusing muddle of aesthetic experience and its transformations in and by language.

Austin too shows a lot of interest both in utterances and their actual issuing, their tones, cadences, and other aspects that are difficult to capture in writing or put into words other than through mimicry (and paratext). This interest appears throughout *How to Do Things with Words* but most powerfully in the middle lectures when the initial distinction between performative and constative utterances begins to break down. On the way to offering what is sometimes called the mature speech act theory (the distinction between locutionary, illocutionary, and perlocutionary acts) Austin proposes, at the end of lecture 7, a different tripartite distinction between phonetic, phatic, and rhetic acts. He does not remain with this distinction long, but it lets him differentiate between "the utterance of certain noises, the utterance of certain words in a certain construction, and the utterance of them with a certain 'meaning' in the favorite philosophical sense of that word, i.e., with a certain sense and with a certain reference" (*How*, 94). It is in the midst of a dense investigation into the difference between "performance of an act *in* saying something as opposed to performance of an act *of* saying something" (99–100) that Austin introduces the idea of illocutionary force and insists on the difference between force and meaning. And this, in turn, leads to the distinction between locution, illocution, and perlocution (the latter as performance of an act *by* saying something), that is, between a variety of acts that it is possible to perform when issuing an utterance: a locutionary act that means something (via sense and reference), an illocutionary act that may take forceful effect (via norm or convention), and a perlocutionary act that has consequences (especially emotional consequences). For example, "Beware of the dog" may be uttered as a locutionary act, an imperative that means that its addressee should be aware of some dog; it may be uttered as an illocutionary act, a warning (when spoken by a friend who I am on a walk with) or a threat (when printed on a sign); and may be uttered with perlocutionary effects such that I become alert, afraid, or intimidated.

No accident that these illustrations are fundamentally scenic (they require some minimal description of situation, props, motive). No accident either that Kenneth Burke, in a far-reaching essay that locates and interprets Austin's lectures in relation to his own dramatistic model of linguistic action, takes up the phonetic/phatic/rhetic distinction to suggest that "the mere noise of words (phones) is related to their role as speech acts (phatic acts, rhetic acts) as the realm of non-symbolic motion is to the realm of symbolic action."[43] I am quoting Burke here as a gesture toward the kind of interpretation I would like to be able to offer, and as a way to clear a space for a speculative revision of my own. For while there is no doubt that the differences between force and meaning and consequence are significant, from another angle it is possible to recast these as follows: locutionary, illocutionary, and perlocutionary acts are each associated with a distinct kind of force. Locutionary acts are associated with logical force, in accordance (or not) with truth conditions. Illocutionary acts are associated with the force of norm or convention, in accordance (or not) with felicity conditions. And perlocutionary acts are associated with the force of motive, in accordance (or not) with the conditions of exchange or affective relations between speaker and hearer(s). Note, none of these kinds of force is identical with what Derrida calls the force of rupture, what comprises the mark in its iterable being, although each may be implicated in that force, and none is uncontaminated by any other.

My purpose has been to work at a different scale, a middling scale at which we may notice that illocutionary force is often suffused with both logical and motive force, and how the latter may (at rare moments) play a role in originating those norms or conventions that are felicity conditions for illocution. This is the realm that Derrida explores under the category of primary or originary performatives, the analysis of which he initiates in a reading of the impossible signatories of the American Declaration of Independence. James Loxley helpfully summarizes Derrida's various writings on such foundational illocutionary acts:

So in this situation [the founding of an institution], the illocutionary force that characterizes an act performed rightfully, according to prior conditions of authorization, is intertwined with a more violent force that serves to validate the act by splitting it from itself. The first kind of force is a function of an institutional framework of conventions that accords validity to acts performed through this framework: it is this that allows us to distinguish rightful or effective marriage ceremonies, for example, from their parodic, non-binding or invalid opposites. If the second kind of force can be described as violent it is not because weaponry, physical force or assaults on the citadels of power are necessarily involved. It is violent only because this force is not simply derived from conformity to prior felicity conditions. Derrida's analysis shows that such different kinds of force do not finally, or even originally, exclude each other, and that there can be no pure legitimacy.[44]

I have been glossing this "more violent force" as the force of motive or affect, identical neither to the force of norm or convention, nor to logical force, nor even to physical force, as important as these may be to the effectiveness of illocutionary acts, foundational or otherwise. Motive forces, always present in exchanges between speakers and hearers (or writers and readers), set the conditions for those basic relational realities that permit groups to form commitments to one another or to break those commitments. While it is not clear why one couple survives the pandemic with renewed commitment and appreciation while another dissolves its compact, why one university humanities department rises to the challenge of decolonizing its curriculum while another devolves into toxic guilt and paranoia, or why one government incites an insurrectionary coup attempt while another may not (for some salient examples), it is clear that an analysis of norms or conventions will not suffice to explain these differences. Rather, understanding the various and contradictory motives, the imagery, ideologies, and phantasies that guide affective exchange among these couples or groups, would be integral to such an analysis. And while actual motives or affective conditions are largely unconscious and therefore notoriously difficult to know, emerging both from individual histories and group dynamics, and even more difficult to describe (for many reasons, including the role that calcified conventions play in their description), they are nevertheless real and can undermine norms or motivate their establishment.

Stein understands something about how the force of motive and the conditions of affective exchange contribute to the dis/establishment of norms. Her theater, in aiming to arrive at what she calls "completion" or new emotional proportions (*Lectures*, 108), seeks the emergence of new knowledge and norms. In the final pages of this essay I turn to another of Stein's early plays, *White Wines*, and to one emergence of this kind. The play registers a sigificant shift in Stein's living arrangements: the physical and psychical separation from her brother Leo Stein and establishment of a new household with Alice Toklas. In my reading of this play, I am less interested in the new norm itself (the Stein-Toklas marriage) than in the process of its establishment, what Wilfred Bion calls "catastrophic change" or a transformation in relations of container-contained that necessarily accompany "real change," as Stein's play puts it. The resources that are called upon to survive such change are significant. Stein's play realizes the precarious relations of container-contained and those disruptive qualities that accompany thinking as it evolves. I read Stein's theater along the lines that Bion proposes to evoke an awareness of these motivational realities.

White Wines: Three Acts (published in *Geography and Plays*) was written not long after *What Happened*, probably in spring of 1913 (see figure 9, or read the entire play on the project website). While it uses the earlier play's paragraphs-to-scenes technique, it also offers a more legible theatrical structure by beginning with a list of the play's three acts ("1. All together / 2. Witnesses / 3. House to house" [*Geography*, 210]) followed by the parenthetical direction "(5 women)" (210). In Stein's manuscript notebook we can read names of four of these women (one is crossed out): Harriet, Jane, Sylvia, and Therese.[45] These names seem to refer to several women in her circle of friends and acquaintances (Sylvia Beach, Harriet Levy, Jane Peterson, Theresa Ehrman). Once again, Stein is exploring group dynamics in play form. After our reading and discussion of the play in the Radio Free Stein workshop, the composer Dorothy Chang and I decided to cast the play for four women's voices and a percussionist who occasionally vocalizes.[46] The scenario I developed interpreted *White Wines* as taking an audience through the process of finding or making a new space of sexual, emotional, and

WHITE WINES

THREE ACTS

1. All together.
2. Witnesses.
3. House to house.
   (5 women)

All together.
    Cunning very cunning and cheap, at that rate a sale is a place to use type writing. Shall we go home.
    Cunning, cunning, quite cunning, a block a strange block is filled with choking.
    Not too cunning, not cunning enough for wit and a stroke and careless laughter, not cunning enough.
    A pet, a winter pet and a summer pet and any kind of a pet, a whole waste of pets and no more hardly more than ever.
    A touching spoon a real touching spoon is golden and show in that color. A really touching spoon is splendid, is splendid, and dark and is so nearly just right that there is no excuse.
    The best way is to wave an arm, the best way is to show more used to it than could be expected.
    Comfort a sudden way to go home, comfort that and the best way is known.
All together.
    Hold hard in a decision about eyes. Hold the tongue in a sober value as to bunches. See the indication in all kinds of rigorous landscapes. Spell out what is to be expected.
    Show much blame in order and all in there, show much blame when there is a breath in a flannel. Show the tongue strongly in eating. Puzzle anybody.
    Violet and the ink and the old ulster, shut in trem-

Figure 9. Gertrude Stein, *White Wines* (1913). From *Geography and Plays*, by Gertrude Stein with an introduction by Cyrena N. Pondrom. Reprinted by permission of the University of Wisconsin Press. Copyright © 1993 by the Board of Regents of the University of Wisconsin System. All rights reserved.

architectural containment for the work of composition or writing. In our rendering, the play explores the definitional relations between theater and domestic space, in particular, the speech situation of the parlor.

I choose the word *parlor* with some care and with the goal of redescribing what Bowers calls Stein's conversation plays as parlor plays.[47] This term retains the connotations of speech (*parole, parler*) but locates speech within a shared, psychically charged domestic situation. We have seen how, in Stein's plays, larger social and political contexts are relocated in affective, physiological daily life. Stein's parlor, a space of writing as well as talking, eating, and living, foregrounds the compositional continuities between writing and her life with Alice Toklas and their salon associates. We have taken advantage of this in the Radio Free Stein production of *He Said It*, for example, where the piano, so often found in parlor spaces of bourgeois performance, serves as more than background: it offers reciprocal relations of containment for Stein's re-creation. And the parlor that contains speech, music, writing, and domestic life will come to contain the radio as well.

To be clear, Stein's plays are not parlor plays in the professional theater sense, that is, closet dramas intended for so-called private performance. In the prologue I pointed out that Stein did not think of her plays this way. When Carl Van Vechten, the drama critic for the *New York Press* during the 1910s, expressed immediate interest in publishing her first plays in a Sunday supplement of that newspaper, Stein refused because she did not want them published before they were staged. She also refused the poet Donald Evans's request to publish a volume of her plays through his Claire Marie press, sending him instead the manuscript that would be published in 1914 as *Tender Buttons*.[48] None of the three of the plays I discuss in this essay (all published in *Geography and Plays*) were staged during her lifetime. In fact, *White Wines* was not staged (as far as I can tell) until the 1990s, and there are few references to this play in the critical literature.[49] This is precisely because Stein developed new conventions for playwriting out of her own epistemic needs, conventions that create the dispersion characteristic of her theater. In these early plays Stein re-creates the tension between convention (or norm) and affect (or motive) in speech and exchange as these take place in the everyday situaton of the parlor.

The notion of parlor play that I am proposing here attends to continuities between the stage and domestic space, and in the case of *White Wines* (as with the play *Photograph*, discussed in Essay 1) we can associate this continuity with biographical context. Stein wrote this play around the time her brother Leo moved out of their shared accommodations in Paris, the well-known salon at 27, rue de Fleurus. Brenda Wineapple's dual biography of the Stein siblings is helpful (once again) for understanding the intricacies of the Gertrude–Leo relationship, which came under increasing strain when Leo dismissed his sister's writing and became more stridently negative as she achieved greater recognition. Toklas had moved into their apartment three years earlier, displacing Leo from his role as Gertrude's primary partner and support. In 1913 he initiated a move to Florence and began to leave the Paris apartment. Later that year the siblings split up the household they had shared for so long, their art collection, finances, and furniture. Stein and Toklas actively looked for another apartment but ended up staying and renovating. The break with Leo would be final.

White Wines takes up this substantial reconfiguration of Stein's domestic and emotional life, which had begun several years earlier but was now intensifying and arriving at a point of no return. The play's three acts move though different aspects of this rearrangement. Act 1 evokes bodies in sexual and domestic relation, emphasizing erotic acts or gestures ("not cunning enough for wit and a stroke and careless laughter" [*Geography*, 210], "a pet, a winter pet and a summer pet" [210]), household objects ("a touching spoon" [210]), food and various bodily imperatives (such as "Change the sucking with a little sucking" [211]), all of which we rendered by way of playful fugal sequences of chase, escape, capture, in which you can hear a strong concern for "home" (210) or going home. If in act 1 the voices seek a new female space for sexualized domesticity, act 2 ("Witnesses") calls upon others to bear witness, stabilize, and develop this new arrangement, especially in the absence of conventions for lesbian marriage. In our interpretation, the scenes in this section evoke preparations for a party. In one scene the women's voices renovate their domestic space ("Pile in the windows, freeze with the doors, paint with the ceiling, shut in the floors" [212]), and in other scenes we hear snippets of campy dinner conversation ("an army of invincible and ever ready moustaches and all the same mind" [212]), comments on the dishes and silverware ("a splendid spout of little cups and colds, a splendid big stir, a splendid glass" [212]), a late-night/early-morning drunken declamation ("in the condition of pretty nearly saying that yesterday is today, and tomorrow, tomorrow is yesterday" [213]), and dessert ("The whole swindle is in short cake and choice cake is white cake and white cake is sponge cake and sponge cake is butter" [213]). This is domesticity theatricalized, performed and displayed, a rearrangement that requires a set of witnesses and sexual-political allies. (The Radio Free Stein sound recording can be heard at https://radiofreestein.com/plays/white-wines/.)

Until this point the play is mainly about the domestic space of a queer marriage, but, as is always the case with Stein's theater, it re-creates this vis-à-vis the space and time of composition. Stein often wrote at night during the salon years. In the wake of the highly social evenings she would stay up to work, then sleep in the next morning. In act 3 of *White Wines*, titled "House to house" (we directed the vocalists to pronounce this phrase as noun followed by verb), the guests have left and we are in a quieter space of composition. The scenes, as we interpret them, comprise a series of meditations on habit, change, and composition as it makes nature strange. Its first scene addresses a variety of habits through dense, qualitative, largely positive descriptions ("a habit which brightened the returning butter fly and the yellow weed and even tumbling, the habit which made a well choose the bottom and refuses all chances to change" [213]). Here habit is associated with the norms of domestic living ("the habit which credited a long touch with raising the table and the hour glass and even eye glasses and plenty of milk" [213]), norms that are at once comforting and difficult ("a habit that is cautious and serious and strange and violent and even a little disturbed, a habit which is better than almost anything, a habit that is so little irritating, so wondering and so unlikely is not more difficult than every other" [213]). By contrast the second scene defines change largely through negation: "a change is no touch and buzzing and cruelty" (214), "no darkness and swinging and highness" (214), "not place," "not church," "not more clad" (214). For Stein, "real change" cannot be located in space or observed by the bodily senses, but is a second-order function of composition: "a real change is made by a piece, by any piece by a whole mixture of words and likenesses" (214). Change rules composition, as far as Stein is concerned ("and the change is the kind and the king is the king and the king is the king and the king is the king" [214]).

I read this string of *kings* as the generation of self-difference in which the accretion of minimal differences (from *kind* to *king*) sets identity at odds with itself, an ironic contrast with an unbroken patriarchal or genealogical line of the selfsame. This scene of composition as differentiation belongs to what she will later call "the human mind," a phrase from Stein's work *The Geographical History of America* (1936), subtitled "The Relation of Human Nature to the Human Mind." In this work she associates habit with nature ("Human nature is what any human being will do") and mind with composition: "The human mind is the mind that writes what any human mind years after or years before can read, thousands of years or no years it makes no difference."[50] Writing breaks with its temporal context, and in this way stands outside the ordinary events of human nature. But what the human mind thinks or writes about, what it takes as subject or topic, is human nature. I bring up this later work of Stein's, if only very briefly, because *White Wines* offers a way to think about the necessary and fraught relations between writing or mind and domesticity or nature. If one idealizing view of the poet's vocation involves a heroic, masculinist isolation that requires feminine support but disavows such dependence, Stein's play avows and takes seriously as a topic the complex domesticity that lets her engage in writing in the first place. In this reading of the play (similar, in part, to my reading of *What Happened*), Stein seeks to accommodate the necessary, inevitable place of others for the writer: sexual partners, friends, family members, partygoers, intellectual compadres, anyone who may come into one's home and salon life. While Stein famously asserted in *The Making of Americans* that "I write for myself and strangers," her plays are murky acknowledgments of how much she depended on the people she knew, initially her brother Leo, then her partner Alice, as well as allies and enemies, acquaintances, portrait subjects.

White Wines explores these relations of dependence and independence during a moment of significant change for her, and offers a container for their difficult dynamics. Richard Bridgman has noted about Stein's writing at this time that it is "marked by a vocabulary of containers, colors, food, and light."[51] The word "container" shows up in this play at the end of act 1 ("make a best container with no speed" [*Geography*, 211]), and another container appears at the end of the play ("all the old clothes are in the best bag" [214]), both qualified as "best" as if Stein is seeking to make the best parlor play she can. Indeed, the title of this play names something fluid that must be contained in order for it to be used or enjoyed, while the penultimate scene begins with the question "Could there be the best almost" and plaintively concludes "Can there be water, can there be water and water. Can there be water. Can there be" (214). Here the writer wonders what kind of container can accommodate the play of fluid dynamics she is most concerned with.

The idea of container-contained that has guided my thinking on Stein's plays comes from Bion's work. As Thomas Ogden explains in a helpful essay, "In Bion's hands, the central concern of psychoanalysis is the dynamic interaction between, on the one hand, thoughts and feelings derived from lived emotional experience (the contained) and, on the other, the capacity for dreaming and thinking those thoughts (the container)."[52] Briefly, for Bion, part of the analyst's role is to serve as a container for the patients' projective identifications, to modify them so that they can be reintrojected by the patient in a more acceptable form. His model of container-contained begins from the constant to-and-fro of projection and introjection in the infant-mother and sexual dyads but expands these reciprocal or reversible relations to describe those between analyst and analysand, word and meaning, group and individual, and thinker and thought.[53] Bion considers the reversibility of container-contained to be crucial for the possibility of growth insofar as substantial change involves an unsettling of relations, "a destructuring of the theories and a re-establishing of new conjunctions," as Robert Hinshelwood puts it.[54] Hinshelwood goes on to explain that this destructuring or fragmentation involves "severe emotional demands" since "change involves a potential catastrophe" when the structure of the thinking apparatus falls apart to be reconfigured anew, and thus requires "the capacity to withstand and contain the elements of the process which represent annihilation and death."[55]

It is this reversibility of relation between container and contained that strikes me as most useful for thinking not only about Stein's play in its treatment of domesticity and writing but more generally about the relation between theater and domesticity. On the one hand, it is remarkable how often plays take marriage, family, and the household as setting, situation, or obsession. This remains as true of modernist theater (from Ibsen and Chekhov to Pirandello, Brecht, and Beckett) as of ancient Greek royal family dramas. At the same time, domesticity is utterly theatrical (compare Sedgwick "Around the Performative" on the mobile proscenium of marriage): not only must a marriage and household be witnessed by others outside the couple, but members of this group are alternately actors of and spectators to the actions and events taking place within it. That the stage can be a household, and a household a stage, is an index to the possibility of what Bion would call catastrophic change, the disruptions that take place in both theater and domesticity alike, precisely as a function of their reversibilty. Stein's *White Wines* addresses such change and the role this plays in destruction as well as growth, as its last line puts it: "This is not a claim it is a reorganization and a balance and a return" (*Geography*, 214). Stein's theater proposes plays themselves as reversible containers for exploring domesticity and its everyday catastrophes, those changing ratios of affective relation that lead to new knowledge and new norms in and around the parlor.

Not a claim but a reorganization: here is the performativity of Stein's theater as it explores the limits of theatrical legibility. Part of my purpose in this essay has been to render some of the provisional conventions proposed by Stein's theater somewhat more legible, to unfold the variety of forces (especially the tensions between norm and motive) that make up this theater, both verbal and nonverbal, and to unfold the implications of her plays for thinking about the concept of linguistic performativity. To return to Burke's essay on Austin for a moment:

> The very nature of the relationship between a speech act and the circumstances ("context of situation") in which any such act takes place forces us (in *ultimately* dramatistic terms) to ask how such "conventions" (such verbal or "symbolic" action) must relate to nonconventional, nonverbal, nonsymbolic ground or context that, by the very "dialectical" nature of the case, must be there somehow. For don't the dialectical conventions of speech itself force us to recognize that our aptitude with *words* emerges from a realm of *wordlessness*?[56]

The most remarkable aspect of Stein's plays is their realization of this meta-dialectic, their evocation of a "realm of *wordlessness*" in the very midst of so many ordinary words and forces. (Perhaps this description makes Stein sound more like Beckett than has been previously acknowledged.) Returning to Stein and Austin by way of the total speech situation and performativity's scenic aspect has let me track a variety of linguistic and theatrical forces and the variable landscapes of their interaction.

INTERLUDE 2

WHAT HAPPENED | PLAYS

A SCORE

Samuel Vriezen composed a musical setting for *What Happened | Plays* during the winter and spring of 2019 based on the radio script that I prepared (see Interlude 1). Here you may read a synopsis of his musical setting, general performance notes, and excerpts from parts written for W (the Writer) and the Chorus. A performance of this piece took place at the Hôtel de Lauzun in Paris on June 26, 2019. See the appendix for more information and links to recordings.

WHAT HAPPENED

with

PLAYS

Music theater

by

ADAM FRANK

and

SAMUEL VRIEZEN

on texts by

GERTRUDE STEIN

DRAMATIS PERSONAE

W — *The Writer.* Mezzo-soprano

A — *The Imagined Audience.* Cello, also singing (mezzo voice) (also Vc)

Ch — *The Choir*, consisting of four parts, all using voice as well as intruments:

Ch1 — *The Qualifier.* Alto flute and flute

Ch2 — *The Splitter of Hairs.* Alto saxophone

Ch3 — *The Seeker of Definitions.* Bass clarinet

Ch4 — *The Negator.* Trombone

Gtr, Va, Vc — *Guitar, Viola, Cello.* Various roles and functions

---

On stage:

A writing desk, with a laptop on it, connected to the PA system, with text editor program running and speech function readied

A lectern

Chairs

SYNOPSIS AND GENERAL PERFORMANCE INDICATIONS

PROLOGUE

P 1   OPENING GESTURE: CASCADE

Vc, Va, and Gtr playing cascading harmonics on open strings, ending suddenly

Ch, Vc, Va, and Gtr all say: "What happened?" simultaneously but not together, each with individual expression.

W answers speech/singing: "A five act play."

P 2   FIRST LECTURE FRAGMENT

W moves to lectern. Ch seated as audience.

Vc, Va, and Gtr in the background play a drone/ostinato. W clears throat and reads.

ACT 1

W moves to writing desk.

SCENE 1

W types two lines while speaking them out loud, words non legato. Ch echoes the text instrumentally after each line. This becomes their ostinato motif (the four parts gradually drifting apart) from here into scene 2.

SCENE 2   IN FIVE SECTIONS, A–E

a) W keeps typing, listening to the results through automated speech function.

b–e) Dissatisfied, W stops the auto-speech and erases the text from the document.

She then starts speaking in a way that becomes ever more songlike. On certain syllables, the members of Ch are evoked one by one from their ostinato, to join in with a text-echoing counterpoint.

SCENE 3

W's spoken "Two" shuts down the counterpoint, which immediately begins anew as W resumes singing, this time louder and higher, and increasingly like classical song.

Halfway through, Vc and Va enter with a slow glissando downward.

SCENE 4

Vc and Va cut off the polyphony by loudly saying "Two!"

Ch, Vc, and Va start playing and repeating a little song (in parallel chords). W, taken aback, listens, then joins for two repeats. Then the ensemble song starts falling apart as all members increasingly get excited about their own favorite sections.

W interrupts the chaos, first singing then whispering a line that shuts Ch, Vc, and Va up one by one.

SCENE 5

W again sings, more calmly; Ch again echo and Vc, Va follow W heterophonically.

Ch, Vc, and Va gradually become fainter and drop out, leaving W to speak the final lines alone.

INTERLUDE 1

W moves to lectern and delivers the second part of the lecture, addressing the ensemble, in a speech style around reference pitches. This time, Ch, Vc, Va, and Gtr all accompany with a relay game, passing the note B to one another as W speaks to them.

ACT 2

Gtr repeats a faster version of the cascade figure from the opening, ending it by saying "Three!"

This triggers a set of short "birthday songs" sung by everyone except W. One performer starts, the others join in. In the second or third repeat, one member starts the second song, and the others follow and join in; then the third song. This is followed by a brief improvisation where people start any of the songs and others can join in, together or not quite, and multiple lines may happen at the same time.

Gtr then again performs the gesture, leading up to "The same three!" The same song process is repeated with three different versions of the same songs. This time, during the improvisation, Ch, Vc, Va, and Gtr can also use their instruments.

Gtr then once again performs the gesture leading up to

"The same three." Again, the songs in different versions; this time, during the improvisation, all instruments go into different transpositions of the song material. After an all-too-brief glorious chaos, the polyphony quickly fragments and collapses into snippets, then quickly fading away into nothingness.

INTERLUDE 2

Lectern now placed to address the real audience, W resumes her Lecture, which becomes much more chantlike. She is accompanied by a drone by Ch, Vc, and Va, but the ensemble members gradually fade away one by one, until only Vc (A) is left. Lecture ends in a short dialogue between W and A, who now uses her voice.

ACT 3

SCENE 1   INTRODUCTION, 1A AND 1B

Introduction: a short cello solo and viola duet using high harmonics that all approach a C sharp, ending in a glissando down to C sharp above middle C.

1a   W and A singing and playing together in octaves
1b   The two parts start drifting apart a bit as the cello embarks on a very slow glissando down

SCENE 2   FOUR MEDITATIONS ON A CUT AND A SLICE

Throughout these four, the cello very gradually keeps glissandoing down, while W and A sing their lines quite independently on slow glissandi themselves. Members of Ch also enter occasionally with a slow glissando, echoing one of the text's words.

In this scene, Gtr and Va act as the Photographer. Making a camera shutter sound, once during every meditation they "freeze" the scene, along with the sounds and the glissando at whatever harmony happens to be sounding at that point, setting it in motion again with a second such sound.

Vc's glissando ends on the open C string.

SCENE 3

W now glissandoes down very slowly on an extensive text, while Vc now makes a combined gliss / harmonic gliss on the C string upward to the 15th partial (which is a

B), again heterophonically shadowing W's diction in her bowing articulation.

W's final word, "Source," is sung on a B which is taken up by the entire ensemble to become the drone for the following interlude section.

INTERLUDE 3

W resumes her lecture, but no longer at the lectern. This time, she addresses the ensemble as if it is a circle of friends. They surround her and sing a drone on B.

Eventually, during this longer lecturing section, they participate in the delivery in a responsorial singing mode. End in silence.

ACT 4
FOUR (A–D) AND FOUR MORE (E) A–D:

a–d:
Four times: Vc starts the section by saying "Four" and playing the next open string (C, G, D, A) sforzando, then Vc and Va start a very slow harmonics glissando across the entire string. Ch responds to this by loudly responding "And four more." On top of this, a very varied, highly improvised polyphony is created by Ch and Gtr. These polyphonies start out in a kaleidoscope of very different modes of playing, largely improvised, and containing pre-echoes of the morphology of W's text.

The variety of playing styles gradually diminishes and the dynamics go down, until Vc reaches the exact half point of the string. At this point, the textures become more homogeneous, and W enters with a short aria.

e:
Now Vc and Va go through the four strings again, but a little faster, while W sings/recites her lines improvisationally using the overtone series of the open string that Vc and Va use, and Ch plays notes from the same series (sometimes freely inflecting them a bit off the harmonic norm).

The final lines (after Vc and Va have exhausted their open strings) are sung on an E, to Gtr's open string harmonics ostinato, ending with the entire ensemble chiming in (individually, not together): "and many more, many more, many many more."

INTERMISSION/INTERLUDE 4 and ACT 5

W again goes to the lectern, but there is nothing more to say, so she puts the lectern to the side. She sits down at her writing desk again and opens the laptop (which is still on) and thinks.

Meanwhile, Gtr, Va, and Vc detune the open strings so that the high harmonic B is the same for all strings (becoming the 5th on the A strings, the 7th on the D strings, 11th on G, 16th on C, and the guitar retunes its strings in similar fashion). Tuning is done only through this harmonic, so we hear different intonations of the same high B. Ch plays very sparse, soft, short B sounds as well.

Retuning done, Vc, Va, and Gtr then proceed to a very slow, soft, final version of the opening cascade gesture, with a harmonics gliss down across all open strings. W delivers the final lines of the play, echoed by Ch, as she types them into her laptop. Gradually, W's delivery becomes more and more like ordinary speech, and Ch's echoes disappear into whispers. Laptop speech function gets the final word.

PERFORMANCE NOTES—WINDS

GENERAL

<u>Textual articulation keys:</u>

Underlined text in the score are textual articulation keys.
These are related to the text that is recited or sung by W.

In instrumental playing, try to follow this text by means of articulation and timbral changes, but not literally speaking through the instrument. It's not necessary that the text is literally comprehensible, but it should merely echo (or prefigure) the delivery from W.

If multiple keys are written for a section, you can choose them freely in any order. Mostly (especially in act 1 and act 5) it's best to wait until W has used a word before using it.

Sometimes the key is in parentheses. This indicates that the use of a text key is optional here; the material can also be played regularly.

<u>Special indications for applying the keys:</u>

1/2 A: This means using the articulation key less clearly, only half.

A—> 1/2 A: Use articulation key most clearly first time, in repeats use 1/2 A.

0 A: only follow the text in terms of rhythm, do not follow its timbral character.

W: whispered—mostly air, no tone.

1/2 W: half-whispered—lots of air, thin tone.

Notation

Microtonal accidentals

    ↑   quarter tone sharp
          (related to 11th harmonic)
    L   sixth tone flat
          (related to 7th harmonic)
    ♯   third tone flat
          (related to 13th harmonic)

<u>text that is underlined</u>   is to be used as articulation key

    ½ A   less than full articulation
    ∅ A   only use text key for rhythm
    W   "whispered", (almost?) no tone, mostly air
    ½ W   lots of air, thin tone

[MODE OF PLAYING] → Begin section playing this way
          and end section playing → [THIS WAY]

[0 : x-y]   make phrases of between x and y notes from the line written

↺   the line notated loops (the last note can be followed by the first)

//   choice

[o]   in Act IV : a harmonically central pitch that may be given more emphasis as the section progresses

o—o   use glissandi   o(—)o   glissando is optional

ō ō   non legato   ♩, ō   portamento towards note

≡   flatterzunge

W   PROLOGUE

Cataract of sounds from strings ends in sudden cut-off guitar chord. Ensemble – except W – all say 'What happened'. Short pause and W responds:

A five act play

Then W moves to LECTERN as DRONE of strings starts. The following text is spoken, against the 3/4 pulse in Guitar (more or less one fragment or white line per bar), using as reference pitch the same B that the previous phrase ended on.

In a book I wrote // called How to Write // I made a discovery:
     that sentences are not emotional // and that paragraphs are.

And now I have found out // a fundamental thing // about plays.

That something is this: // The scene as depicted on the stage is
     more often than not // one might say // it is almost always in syncopated time
          in relation to the emotion // of anybody in the audience.

Your emotion as a member of the audience is // never going on at the same time
     as the action // of the play.

This makes one nervous // and endlessly troubled // about a play.
     Not only is there a thing to know // as to why this is so
          but also there is a thing to know // why perhaps it does not need to be so.

And knowledge // as anybody can know // is a thing to get by getting.

(Wait for drone end, then move to writing desk)

Act One

SCENE ONE [SPOKEN]

PENSIVELY, while writing on laptop [NON LEGATO]   [ensemble responds]

Act one: one.   loud   and   no   cataract

[Ensemble responds]

not   any   nuisance   is   depressing

SCENE TWO

(2A) [Sung] [still pensively, writing]

Five.   [P]   A single sum four and five together   and one,   not any sun,

[Playback from laptop speech function]   (2B) [no longer writing but singing to ensemble?]

a clear signal and an exchange.   Silence is in blessing and chasing

→ CUE Flute

and coincidences being ripe.   A simple melancholy clearly precious and on the surface and surrounded

and mixed strangely.   A vegetable window and clearly most clearly an exchange in parts and complete.

(2C)   → CUE SAX

A tiger a rapt and surrounded overcoat securely arranged with spots old enough to be thought useful

W Interlude One

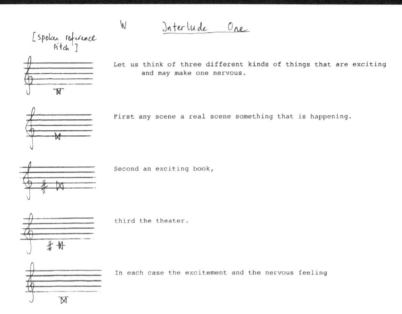

[spoken reference pitch]

Let us think of three different kinds of things that are exciting and may make one nervous.

First any scene a real scene something that is happening.

Second an exciting book,

third the theater.

In each case the excitement and the nervous feeling

[sung]

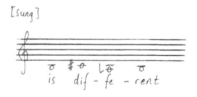

is dif - fe - rent

ACT TWO

Act 2 consists of three times three songs which are "the same three."

All songs are birthday songs or party songs. The act portrays people at a party, the mood is festive, somebody starts singing and others join in. Then the song gets interrupted by another song. The (non-vocally trained) members of the ensemble are the singers, and at any given moment you will have a spontaneously different combination of voices singing one song or another, with overlap and some chaos. The act ends in a grand improvised "fugue" with three subjects.

Structure:
W announces "Act two."

Gtr plays a fast "cascade" figure, a quick continuous irregular strumming across the six strings while lightly touching these with a bar and moving it across the full length to produce a sextuple overtone glissando effect, ending in open strings, then says "Three."

Then one of the members of the orchestra stands up and starts singing the first song (the drinking song, "Four and nobody wounded . . ."). One by one, others join in, repeating the song until everybody is singing.

At some point, one of the singers gets bored and changes the tune to the next song ("One and a left hand . . ."). Some chaos with two overlapping songs, but one by one all orchestra members change to the second song.

Then again one singer gets bored, and starts singing the third song: "A point of accuracy . . ." The same thing happens, and when everybody is singing the third song together, the song speeds up.

This ends when Gtr plays its cascade figure again, now announcing "The same three!" The next three songs ("A wide oak," "The best," "The very kindness") are sung in the same way, again ending in an accelerando romp and a guitar cascade figure.

Then again "the same three" songs: "A same frame," "A rich market," "A connection." This time however, people bring in their instruments and the singing becomes a sort of jam session. After everybody has come together on the third song ("A connection"), players start playing fragments from all three songs at will, at various speeds, and also at various transpositions (the notes can be transposed up or down a pure fifth or a major ninth), generating a glorious spontaneous fugal mess. After some two minutes of this it just breaks down and stops.

Then W clears her throat, continuing with the next interlude.

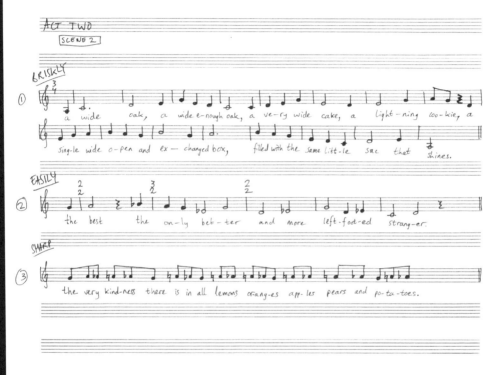

Act III - Scene I

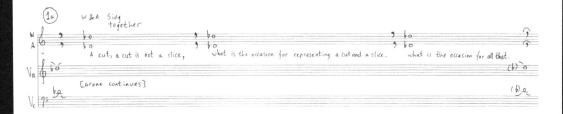

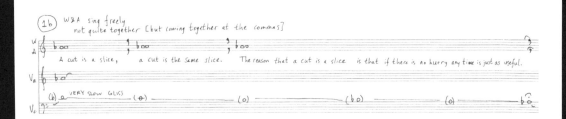

Act III   Scene II   W & A [+ v.]

WHEN CUED BY "camera shutter" click sound from Gtr or Va, <u>freeze</u> on the sound of that moment until next cue, then continue.

(2a) | "Four."   W&A only together at the start of each line

A cut and a slice is there any question when a cut and a slice are just the same.

(2b)

A cut and a slice has no particular exchange it has such a strange exception to all that which is different.

(2c)

A cut and only slice, only a cut and only a slice, the remains of a taste may remain and tasting is accurate.

(2d)

A cut and an occasion, a slice and a substitute. a single hurry and a circumstance that shows that, all this is so reasonable when everything is clear.

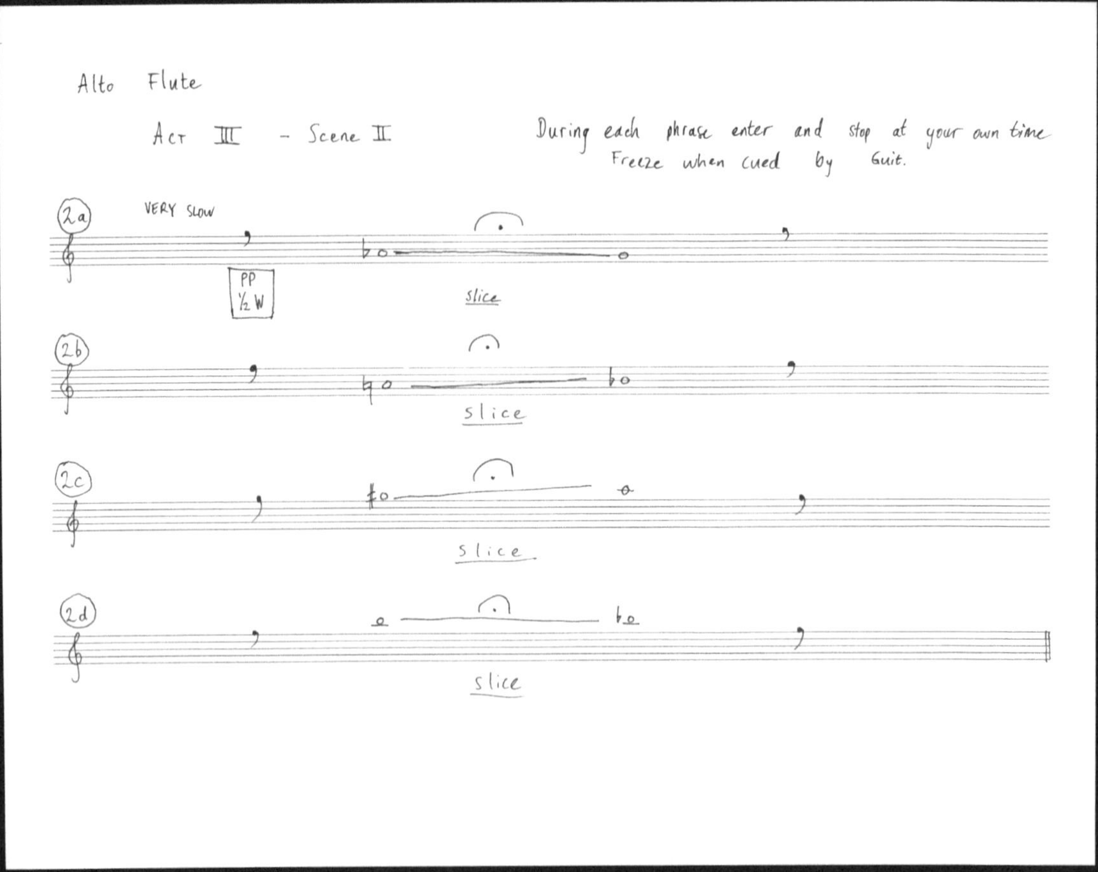
Alto Flute
Act III - Scene II
During each phrase enter and stop at your own time
Freeze when cued by Guit.
2a
VERY SLOW
PP
½ W
slice
2b
slice
2c
slice
2d
slice

Act **III** Scene **III**

W performs very slow gliss from c to b across the full text, below
V_c performs a slow gliss of finger position up to the 15th harmonic on the C string,
using bowing to articulate, very softly, a shadowing of W's text delivery
while very gradually varying finger pressure (freely) between stopped note, harmonic, and open string.
Underlined text to be shadowed slightly more pronouncedly.

③

W: One. → cue choir/ Interlude III
V_c: ...source
IV.15

[SOFT and getting softer]

Text   All alone with the _best reception_, all alone with more than _the best reception_, all alone
with a paragraph and _something_ that is worth _something_,
worth almost _anything_, worth the best _example_ there is
of a little _occasional_ archbishop.
This which is so clean is precious little when there is no bath water.
A long _time_ a very _long time_ there is no use in an obstacle that is _original_
and has a source.
→ cue choir

INTERLUDE 2 · 143

INTERLUDE 2 • 145

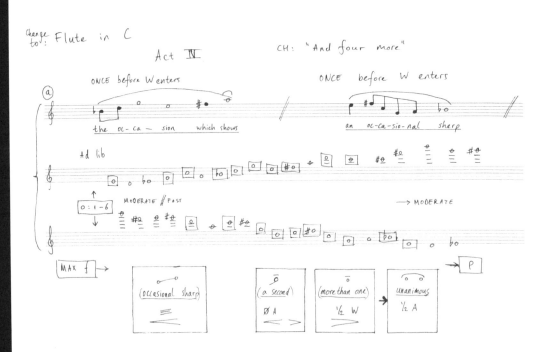

Act Five [Starts after all three strings have commenced their slow bowed harmonics gliss in interlude IV.]

SPOKEN [Pensively, while writing. Take a lot of time for pauses.]

(a)

Act Five. Two. |P| A regret   a single regret   makes   a doorway.

what is a doorway,   a doorway is   a photograph

(b) [Gradually moving from song to speech.]

|pp| ⎯⎯⎯⎯⎯⎯⎯⎯⎯⎯⎯⎯→ SPEECH

what is a photograph
a photograph is a sight
and a sight is always a sight of something.
very likely there is a photograph that gives color
if there is then there is that color that does not change
any more than it did when there was much more use
for photography.

[LW hits laptop speech function to close the piece.]

INTERLUDE 2 • 147

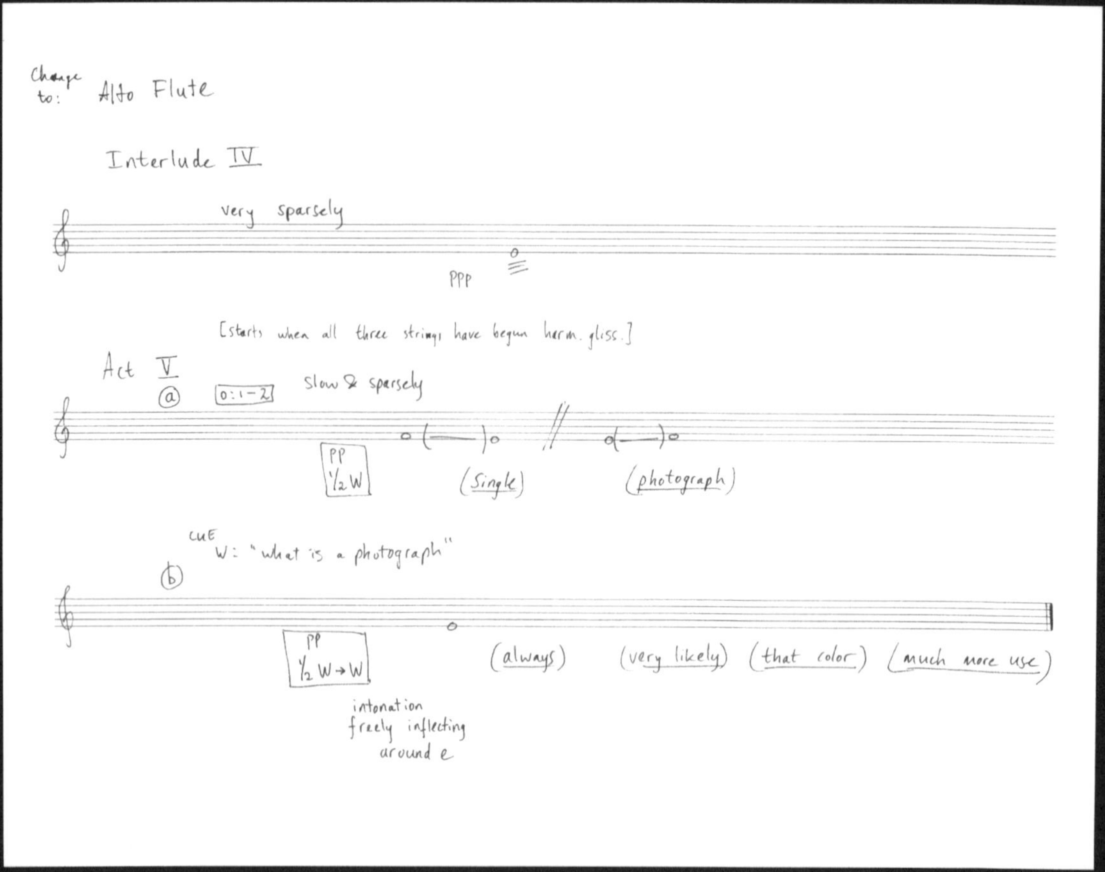
Change to: Alto Flute
Interlude IV
very sparsely
ppp
[starts when all three strings have begun harm. gliss.]
Act V
a
0:1–2
Slow & sparsely
pp
½ W
(Single)
(photograph)
cue
W: "what is a photograph"
b
pp
½ W → W
(always)
(very likely)
(that color)
(much more use)
intonation
freely inflecting
around e

INTERLUDE 4

Instructions for viola, cello, guitar

The music consists of tuning all the strings to the same overtone, given by the high B 12th partial of the low E on the guitar.

To this end:
—Viola tunes down A string to E (3rd partial), D string to B (4th), G string to E (6th), C string to A (9th).
—Cello tunes down A string to G (5th partial), D string to C# +31cts (7th), G string to F +49cts (11th), C string to B (16th).
—Guitar E strings unchanged, B, G and A strings tune their 4th, 5th, 9th partial respectively, D down to C# +31cts (7th).

When playing a note to check the tuning, play musically. Tuning need not be completely perfect before moving on to Act 5.

ACT 5

In the course of this act, Va, Vc, Gtr hand position slides very slowly from bridge to neck ends of the string for a slow harmonics gliss.

Va, Vc, and Gtr all bow the strings.

Va, Vc always bowing one or two strings, gradually shifting across the four strings. Va and Vc start on the I string and end with an open IV string.

[GTR—to be workshopped]

Very soft

Music to end just after the beginning of the final lines read by the laptop.

ESSAY 3

COMPOSING *WHAT HAPPENED*

SAMUEL VRIEZEN

ANY TIME IS JUST AS USEFUL

Being a genius, Gertrude Stein could not go to a dinner party without that dinner party sparkling with insights. Being a composer, I tend to interpret those insights as being all about time. This should not be too controversial: most Stein readers will agree that her work somehow meditates on time, on tense, on rhythm. Certainly, her being a genius itself has everything to do with time, given that a genius is "one who is at the same time talking and listening."

So what is this "same" time, this time of genius? Is it something like a split second in which an infinitesimal talking and an infinitesimal listening are both happening, as if the talking and the listening pass into each other through the narrow point of an hourglass? Two processes, coinciding time point by time point, like two functions both depending on a single variable t? Being a genius then would involve giving those two processes both full living attention, clearly not easy. This is probably the common spontaneous way of picturing this "same time." But rereading the third act of *What Happened: A Five Act Play*, I'm starting to have a different picture.

Here is the text of the first two scenes:

Two.

A cut, a cut is not a slice, what is the occasion for representing a cut and a slice. What is the occasion for all that.

A cut is a slice, a cut is the same slice. The reason that a cut is a slice is that if there is no hurry any time is just as useful.

Four.

A cut and a slice is there any question when a cut and a slice are just the same.

A cut and a slice has no particular exchange it has such a strange exception to all that which is different.

A cut and only slice, only a cut and only a slice, the remains of a taste may remain and tasting is accurate.

A cut and an occasion, a slice and a substitute a single hurry and a circumstance that shows that, all this is so reasonable when everything is clear. (*Stein Reader*, 271)

Here, a cut and a slice are represented. The object, one assumes, could well be a birthday cake, since the play is a written memory of a birthday party that Gertrude Stein had just attended. I picture the cake being cut into slices, the slices being tasted, something remaining of the taste in memory and then being recalled as the writer is later sitting at home, writing the play, "all alone with the best reception" (271) as the text says in the third scene. But something about that memory occasions an investigation into cuts and slices more generally, and that something might well be the act of remembering itself, the ways in which past events are framed and packaged. All over *What Happened* you can find many references to frames, framing devices, photography: "silence is so windowful," "a same frame a sadder portal, a singular gate and a bracketed mischance," and many, many more. Cuts and slices certainly have a lot to do with photography and film. "Cut!" says the director, cutting off a slice of film, a technical operation that organizes time into twenty-four frames per second—practically speaking, for humans, that is already continuity. So a first approach would say something like: a cut cuts into time marking a singular *moment*, an instant of something happening in "real time," whereas the slice is more like a (framed) *period* of time, taken out of a continuity.

However, reading the meditation above, things aren't so clear-cut. There's a lot of ambiguity in the relation between a cut and a slice. For instance, first a cut is not a slice, and then a cut is a slice, specifically "the same slice." So which is it? Can you still make sense of this when thinking with photographic or cinematic technology? You guessed it, dear reader, I am about to step in as a composer and say, wait, let's think sonically instead! Because this confusion about the nature of frames happens naturally when you try to think what an instant of sound could be, the point being that sound always has duration—even when freezing sound into something static. Electronic music composers have learned to use the engineering language of signal processing for such operations when they talk about Fourier transforms. Why not follow this lead? Surely, talking and listening at the same time has got to be a form of signal processing.

Briefly, then, a technical excursion. In Fourier theory, you get, once again, two functions that articulate the same event (or "signal"), but here they do not depend on the same variable *t*. Instead, they are like a dual description, the one describing the signal as an amplitude that varies depending on time—this function takes place in the "time domain"—and the other describing the same signal nontemporally, as a spectrum consisting of pure periodic component signals at different frequencies—the "frequency domain." The Fourier transform is an operation of integral calculus that takes any function describing a signal from one domain to the other. In the time domain, you trace the event "in real time," instant by instant; in the frequency domain, you see the event as composed of regular oscillations (and the more "noisy" the signal is, the more complex this spectral composition will be). You could say that the frequency domain describes the event as a harmony—and the time domain then maybe as a "melody"? as a sequence of impulses or articulations? In any case, this technique is used a lot in electronic sound manipulation in order to slow down or speed up sounds, without changing their pitch—possibly even "freezing" a sound.

In practice it's never the sound at an ideal, zero-duration instant that can be treated like this; sound always needs a little bit of time to be understood in terms of regular frequencies. So what you end up doing is you take a temporal window, let's say one-twentieth of a second. The Fourier transform can then extract the spectrum of the frequencies that comprise the sound during the time of that window—making the sound into a harmony, a chord or a drone if you will, representing the sound at that moment, though indexed not at one single instant but at that entire window of time. This spectrum can subsequently be transformed back into the time domain, possibly being made to fill up shorter or larger spans of time. By repeatedly doing this, always shifting the window a little bit, you can stretch or compress a longer, developing sonic event while preserving its harmonic structure.[1] Contrary to the situation with frames in film, which are fully discrete, these windows of sound will typically overlap—so if you use windows of one-twentieth of a second, you might shift them by, say, one-fortieth of a second, to make the results more smooth.

What this shows is that in sound, there are no single cuts (ideal instants) that define a "sound moment." Moments of sound always have duration and they are always blurry, tending in all sorts of ways to confuse the cut and the slice. This is no problem of course. "If there is no hurry any time is just as useful" (271). Such blurry and extended moments are the time on which the Fourier transforms operate in sound processing—and this is an exchange, not particular to the sound but applying to all sounds in general, between the time and frequency domains. I would now like to suggest seeing the exchange between talking and listening, or maybe between attending a birthday party and writing about it, as similarly taking place not in sequences of instants but in blurry moments of varying duration. I do not want to insist upon a literal equivalence, but I like to associate "talking" with the time domain (real time events) and "listening" with the frequency domain (where the resonances and the overtones live). Or, to stretch these associations even further, time domain / talking / lived experience and frequency domain / listening / memory.

This very general exchange has certainly guided my process in composing *What Happened | Plays* for solo singer, flute, saxophone, bass clarinet, trombone, viola, cello, and guitar, with the instrumentalists all also using their voice as Chorus. In what follows I will try to explain how this played out. I will start with a rough sketch of how my musical thinking developed from the moment of my first encounter with Stein.

FROM MISTAKES TO HARMONIES

I credit the writing of Gertrude Stein with pushing me into my mature musical work. Specifically her ideas in "Poetry and Grammar," which I probably moved over to my work mistakenly, but I do hope, mistaken right. Particularly impressive was her description of syntactic categories in terms of how much life they bring to a text: the verbs and adverbs being more able "to be mistaken" (*Lectures*, 212) than nouns and adjectives, meaning that "they are, so to speak, on the move" (212), and especially the prepositions that "can live one long life being really being nothing but absolutely nothing but mistaken" (212). My interpretation of that had to do with how prepositions always point elsewhere, to what follows them (or precedes them, as the case may be)—to me, what was implied was a relation between this mistakenness, motion, syntactic function, and sense of rhythm. This led me to try to find what a "preposition" in music could be and if I could make a musical syntax that would always be "on the move," not ending in the static literalness of the nouns. Being a pianist, I found an analogue in fast motives that were essentially just broken chords—directional sequences of notes, that would normally lead into some other melodic gesture; what I did was let each such arpeggio lead into another, but without providing closure, spinning entire webs of them, creating a dense sense of voice leadings, without ever making it to a cadence. It was a way of understanding rhythm as something you build up out of these units of characteristic motion, weaving them together, rather than constructing a rhythm in terms of the subdivision of some given regular meter. It was a bottom-up rather than top-down notion of meter. It made me not even bother to write time signatures anymore.

In a further development, I found I could put a kind of further cubist spin on this by having multiple layers of these motivic complexes overlap at different tempos, getting them to develop auditory interference patterns (starting in my pieces *Toccata III* for two glockenspiels [2001] and *20 Worlds* for two pianos [2005]). I say "cubist" for the emergent multiplicity of perspectives, though in time rather than in space, rhythmical layers feeding into one another and blending together as if into some higher order of meter. I thought of this as akin to Stein's writings with extensive landscape-like paragraphs, rhythms always shifting, and the almost-repeating formulas that seemed to lead somewhere else all the time. On the move, one long life, nothing but mistaken.

Similarly in these pieces I was writing, patterns of motives would recur—and this recurrence would generate a sense of harmony. Again, a bottom-up perspective, now on harmony. By contrast, in classical music theory harmony is usually pictured as deriving from hierarchical top-down models: the fundamental pitch at the center with a hierarchy of more and less remote pitches and more and less stable sonorities being organized around it. This view also provides strict control over time. In classical music, we tend to speak of "harmonic rhythm" and the way a rhythm of chord sequences creates a "phrase" then ends in a "full cadence": like a sequence of slices of time, each characterized by its harmonic identity or "chord function," and when you take them together it becomes a complete sentence. What I had was not so much a chord as multiple instances of a motive, each executing one move within time, like a cut—but when you have a number of these cuts recurring, each occurrence mirroring the others and resonating, then perceptually, taken together, they will form a more extended "slice" of time, a harmony of some duration. However, contrary to most classical harmony, defined in terms of chord progressions, my harmonic durations were blurry and sometimes only vaguely determined, since multiple fields of these motives could be superimposed, interact, and move independently between foreground and background. (*20 Worlds* has the clearest expression of this.)

So, in order to focus on the dynamics of the moment itself, I needed to keep the definition of durations somewhat undetermined. This led me increasingly to investigate how I could create dense polyphonic textures while leaving key parts of timing and coordination to the players, who would not be approaching them from a common, all-encompassing count (or the control of a conductor) but from their interactions, for instance, by having them give one another cues, or allowing them to decide when to bring in new material. Bottom-up, once again, but now involving what you could call social relationships between performers, as they were to react to one another in moving from section to section, maybe negotiating time during play. I became interested in modeling such interactions, structuring them more like games than like classical scores. As this strand in my work developed, I began more and more to think of harmony as something that does not just include the pitches sounding at a given moment. Rather I wanted to have a more extended notion of harmony that includes this open temporal management and the coordination between players. A theory of harmony loosened from temporal control, with harmony as a putting-into-relation, not only of sounds in time but also of players making those sounds across time—and therefore organizing time, from the inside out.

More and more, then, I began to understand composition not as the invention of remarkable sonorities and gestures—still very much the dominant notion in modern composition—but as the establishment of systems of resonance in time that would allow performers to bring themselves into relation.

This finally also shifted my understanding of, and interest in, pitch. Throughout much of the last two centuries, pitch and harmony had been the main carriers of musical expression. Open a random book about the recent history of musical composition and you're very likely to find an account of how harmonic language was expanded by various composers into polytonality, atonality, microtonality, and so on. This history has given composers working today enormously rich resources to work with, but nowhere new left to go. Instead I began to understand pitch not as the thing itself, but as a means of resonance. Players playing the same pitches could use them in their games of relation, referring to one another's actions. This made me desire to find ways to reinvent something akin to the modal systems known to so many musical cultures, where pitch is not primarily the material out of which to construct more complex sonorities, but always embedded in musical actions—melodic formulas and methods of playing. Pitch in such musical traditions seems to function more as an intermediary between performers, while also relating the real-time performance to a modal repertoire—and therefore, a resonance of a (cultural) memory.[2]

This idea of pitch as the agent of resonance and deep memory also gave me an insight into what song does. Again, in a lot of modern composition, text setting sounds like adding gestures of expressivity and intensity to words; but I started understanding song rather as giving words resonance, duration, and focus, simply by singing them at some pitch. I became interested in writing songs where singers would move between various manners of delivery, often with one being more speechlike and another more chant-like, where I would simply pick words from the text to be given a slower, pitch-based delivery, that would allow them as it were to detach from the running time of speech and float in the resonant time of song, opening up those words to let their meanings blossom. This, too, I understood as relating to a memory function, as if singing a word simply transfers it to the time of memory.

MANY TRANSFORMS

Let's distinguish "memory" from "remembering." This will be helpful in a Gertrude Stein context. We know from her lecture "Portraits and Repetition" that, for her, the act of remembering is a problem because it confuses time, introducing repetition (of what is remembered) into the living moment of looking and listening. If I invoke memory here, it is not as a faculty of such repetition, but of resonance, and it seems to me this was what happened in *What Happened*. As she explains in her lecture "Plays," while attending a birthday party, Stein realized that "something is always happening" (*Lectures*, 118); getting home, all alone, she worked this insight into a play, in which "the idea was to express this without telling what happened" (118). I understand this as a form of memory that is not a remembering. That is, the temporal distance between partying and writing is there, but not as repetition, with no rule of some formalized past over the present. Memory, as resonance across a temporal interval, is included in the moment of writing, which therefore includes the dimension of duration.

I'm interested in this back-and-forth between the event in time and its resonance in memory. Playing music takes place in the present; composing (in my view) is about finding forms that will allow resonances. Very informally I might think of the one as closer to the time domain, and then of the other—being related to harmony in my very broad sense, including interaction—as closer to the frequency domain. The two domains are not contrasted though, rather they correspond, allowing transformations from one domain to the other (for example, in music, performing a composition—actualizing its forms in real time—would be one such "transform").

Certainly there was a lot of back-and-forth before the opera was finished. Of course it all started with Stein's attending the party (time domain), going home and putting "the essence of what happened" into a form, and a very traditional one at that: the five-act play, with all the resonances that can provide. A century later, Adam Frank had the idea of collaborating with composers and others on making Stein's plays into radio pieces. This happened on the basis of workshops—living social events, where people who enjoy reading Stein get together to enjoy reading Stein together and talking about what they read. Our session on *What Happened: A Five Act Play* in Copenhagen, which included, besides Adam and myself, Solveig Daugaard, Lene Asp Frederiksen, Steven Meyer, Laura Schultz, and Martin Serup, was like a slightly belated hundredth anniversary party for the play, a party once again in real time, like a transform again in the inverse direction, collectively reading the text, teasing out the resonances of Stein's many games, plays, and resonances. It yielded many strands of thought that Adam subsequently worked into the libretto that he adapted from the play. Our next job as librettist and composer was to rebuild a resonant form, a structure that could accommodate all these strands once again, and to stage it. This involved more extensive back-and-forth between Adam and me, and later between Adam, me, and Didier Aschour of Ensemble Dedalus, and ultimately between Adam, me, Didier, seven members of the ensemble, and Aurélie Nyirabikali Lierman, the singer in the solo role.

Over the course of multiple drafts the libretto expanded a set of salient elements to be included in the final composition. In the first group reading, we had discussed the many forms of counting that are going on in Stein's text, and "counting" was included as a theme in the libretto. We had discussed the complex relationships between the monophonic nature of the text ("all alone with the best reception") and the polyphonic nature of the myriad voices that are integrated in, or emerge from, the play and how they could emerge as resonances and echoes from the text. Adam accounted for this in his libretto in the concept of a "chorus" of four emergent voices, each associated with a specific syntactic or affective component of Stein's language. In the composition, these ended up being represented by the four wind players. And so there were many, many more angles coming to us from the text.

It took me a while to realize that my main job as a composer would be to come up with the structures that would allow all of these elements to fall into place again, to be realized for a fourth time (after the party itself, Stein's moment of writing, and our moments of reading and discussing) on the stage, one more resonance extending the original event from 1913. For me, the challenge was not so much to find adequate notes and sounds for each individual event as to find the general space within which the entirety of the musical setup could operate to accommodate the relationship of each element to the others—to resonate together. I will now turn to one of the main problems treated in my composition: the relation of speech to song and how it was incorporated into the whole of the piece.

TWO WAYS OF STYLIZING SPEECH

Adam's libretto contained a rich panoply of compositional allusions, referring to various modes that could go from speaking to singing. Speaking, declaiming, playing with intonation, chant-like, song-like, fugue-like, a blossoming of polyphony. Especially in the first act there was a clear development path which would go from speaking to more song-like speaking to an actual "little song." So the compositional setup would require "speechness/songness" to become a parameter, and it looked like each of the five acts—as well as each of the scenes—would require its own delivery coloration. Because the play features at least thirteen scenes (the exact number is not quite clear-cut), a great variety of setups would be needed.

This in itself is already quite a challenge. At first, I imagined that I would use some version of my technique to employ speaking, speaking around a tone (related to Robert Ashley's idea of a "reference pitch"), choosing pitches for words to be sung, or longer motives, all the way to setting entire lines to pitches, by which time there is full singing. This setup allows for a lot of nuance between speaking and singing and would allow itself to be conceptualized along a single dimension, which is helpful for composing transitions.

However, the challenge became more complicated as another layer was introduced into the libretto: fragments of the lecture "Plays," interspersed between the scenes as intermezzi. These would have to be different in atmosphere—we thought to make them more drone-based, more static declamations, since the lecture, which reflects theoretically on the writing, could be allowed to take place in a more contemplative mood. Or maybe even a kind of sermon-like mood, underscoring the formality of the lecture setting. You could say that these intermezzi introduced a second domain into the setup of the play. The piece as a whole was to feature both the writing itself—as event reconstituting the original party event by resonance—and a more distanced reflection, like a third layer (after the events of partying and writing). Having these intermezzi may seem at first sight like a simple structural idea—adding something constant to the variability of the play—but, given that *What Happened* by itself is already such a wild and rich text, they ended up yielding a rather complicated architecture of self-reflection and memory. This translated into a tricky compositional problem, because the intermezzi also required going from speech to chant, as well as for the involvement of the chorus, just like the acts themselves. But if intermezzi are to be intermezzi, that is, a structural background supporting the articulation of the complex architecture of the play's acts, they should have their own logic and follow their own paths.

This meant that another way of thinking about moving between speech and song would be required. The way I ended up doing this was to think of two kinds of departures from speech that would move it into song— one more related to a "melodic" interpretation of speech, looking at how the speech pitch moves up and down in time, and the other related to a more "harmonic" way of interpreting speech, relating speech to harmonic resonances. In the first perspective, speech could be stylized into song according to the natural intonations of speech melody. In the second perspective, speech would gradually adapt to some kind of drone with its overtones.

The two approaches both led to melodic sung settings, but according to different conceptualizations of the pitches to be sung. I thought of speech melody as essentially a basic tone that modulates up and down, sometimes but not always leading to areas of stability (that is, held pitches). Technically I would develop sung melodies from this by departing from a central tone in the middle register and adding pitches to that at certain intervals up and down from it. A scale could result based around this central tone, constructed out of patterns of intervals, and melodies could be constructed from such scales. By contrast, in the second approach, I would depart from a low drone as a fundamental tone, and I would let the voice find its way to pitches that are in salient harmonic relations to it, such as overtones. This, too, could lead to a scale with which melodies could be made, so ultimately the two approaches could lead to similar results—but the constructions would be a bit different and lend themselves to different contrapuntal treatments.

Additionally, with the scales constructed according to speech melody/interval thinking, I would in many places indicate that pitches could be connected by portamentos, gliding from pitch to pitch, sometimes to be stylized as very slow glissandi. I thought of such portamentos as a speech realism, speech usually not being tethered to held pitches. The second principle, based on drones, also involved a technique specific to it: microtonal inflections that correspond to the overtone series (certain overtones being just a bit off with respect to the tuning of pitches in the regular Western system of twelve tones. For instance a seventh partial is a sixth of a tone flat, and an eleventh is a quarter tone flat).

The acts were based around the speech-melody-to-interval-scale principle, the central pitch from which the scales would spring usually at middle C—though in some acts the scales would move around quite a bit or grow into elaborate constructions that may hide this centrality (in particular, act 3 has a kind of "modulating" progression, and in act 4, the "blossoming of polyphony" in Adam's libretto, scale constructions become extremely rich, leading to a harmonically highly nuanced counterpoint). The intermezzi were based on drones mostly related to a low fundamental pitch B. Taken together, the entire pitch setup for the composition was based on moving between this C and this B, sometimes appearing in the score as a very slow glissando downwards, from the C of the "happening" acts to the B of the "reflective" lecture. (One example: the fourth intermezzo is a musically performed retuning of all the strings in the ensemble, with the lowest cello string C tuned down to B.)

CATARACTS AND STRANGE EXCEPTIONS

The two approaches could sometimes enter into relation with one another, thanks in particular to a basic feature of strings. On a bowed string, you make a glissando by pressing your finger on the string and sliding it up or down—this gives you a sliding tone, not unlike the portamentos of the stylized speech melodies in the first approach above. However, if you don't press the string fully but only very lightly, at the pressure where a string can produce harmonics, and then you slide the finger up or down, overtone melodies will be produced as the finger moves across the harmonic nodes on the string, which is related to the second approach. This very basic idea proved useful not only to relate these two worlds of melodic technique but also for integrating another element indicated in the libretto, the "cataract." At the very opening, Adam's libretto indicates sounds of rushing water that develop and grow, and suddenly stop, having to do with the opening sentence of the play, "Loud and no cataract."

I decided to compose this as emerging from varying bowings (bouncing, col legno, occasionally regular arco), at first getting the higher harmonics of the strings, then by means of harmonic glissandi running to lower harmonics. The gesture indeed produces a waterfall-like sound. You might think of a technique like this as also being a "transform" of sorts between domains. The outside-time domain of the overtones lying at their nodes on a string is transformed into a real-time event by means of the harmonic glissando playing technique, the overtones being sounded one by one as real-time events, sounding out the string's resonance. For that reason, I came to relate such gestures to acts of memorizing—a notion that allowed me to give this cataract a structural rather than a merely anecdotal role in the composition. The cataract of the opening is that which has already disappeared when the play begins ("loud and no cataract"), so it appears as a memory trace. Act 2 was a sequence of three songs; in my reading, these were songs people might sing at a party (and that being decided, I could only read the opening line of the act as a drinking song: "Four and nobody wounded, five and nobody flourishing, six and nobody talkative, eight and nobody sensible"). A quick cataract-like gesture on the guitar would act as a memory trigger, bringing the scene back in time. Later, a slower upward "cataract" glissando on the C string of the cello accompanies the lonely moment of the main character, W, at the end of act 3: "All alone with the best reception . . . ," being understood as a moment of receiving memory while writing ("all alone with a paragraph and something that is worth something"). Finally, act 5 is also interpreted as a memory act in the form of a meditation on photography; this is accompanied by a very much slowed-down version of the cataract gesture—now exclusively bowed and on slightly detuned strings, ending the piece on the open strings, their color changed by the detuning in the fourth intermezzo into an unusual chord of subharmonics of a high B.

The inverse "transform" is present in the piece too. The second scene of act 3 turned out to be the most musically surprising result for me. The libretto here asks for a "fugue plus echo," interspersed with "camera clicks" (among other sounds) from the chorus. I ended up taking a very liberal approach to the fugue form, quite simply deciding that the "fugue subject," to be interpreted by Aurélie as the character W and the cellist, Deborah Walker, doubling as the singer character A, would consist of a very slow glissando down a minor third, with a very slow glissando up a perfect fourth for its "countersubject," both voices drawing out the lines of text across this glissando while being not quite together. This is one of the most stylized forms of the speech melody approach with portamentos appearing in the composition. The four wind players, too, perform such very slow glissandos (articulated to mirror certain key words from the text in rhythm). Taken together, all of these slow glissandos outline very blurry slow chord changes.

The camera shutter sounds were then given to the viola and guitar players, to be played as evocative noises on their instruments. A little game was introduced within the glissandi: every time a shutter sound would be played, the other parts would freeze at the sound and pitch they were holding at that moment, until a second shutter sound would be played. The concept is obvious: it's like taking a "sonic photograph" of a stage of the morphing from one chord into another. Or, you could say, taking one point from the real-time sequence and closely examining its spectrum. In other words, very much like the kind of manipulation in electronic music as sketched above, taking a short window of sound and trying to hold its frequency information for a longer period. Except that in this case, it is not done by computers using the Fourier transform on sound data, but by live musicians using their performing bodies. Given however that a bowing string has to move, or that singers and wind instruments

ESSAY 3 · 159

depend on continuing breath, it is also clear that such a moment cannot be held indefinitely.

The results of this little game were surprising to me in two ways. First, it was strangely impossible for me to predict what the frozen sonority would sound like. Even though the notes between which the performers were transitioning were prescribed, in every performance completely new chords would be produced, because somehow every one of the six transitioning voices would be at just a different stage when halted—and the combination of these variabilities produced a sonic variation far beyond what I had been able to imagine in advance. I think these resultant sounds were just as surprising to the performers themselves as they were to me, listening. Indeed, every chord in every performance always sounded very much like a "strange exception to all that which is different" (*Stein Reader*, 271). Second, there's the game element itself: by playing with the timing of the shutter sound interruptions, the composition was giving some freedom to the viola and the guitar to test the limits of the rest of the ensemble. This introduces a very subtle tension and uncertainty in the sound, which can never be perfectly stable.

Here, in other words, a little party game with a camera shutter cuts into real time, transforming it or maybe extracting from it a resonant moment, like an instant memory. However, the exchange is not only in this direction. Reciprocally, this moment with its unpredictable chord that is extended—which it can be if there is no hurry—is itself invaded by the real time of the performers playing and singing with their bodies in a game of times. The result is a sonority that I did not choose as a composer, one that escapes specification, very much not a particular chord but, you might say, the sound of the exchange between the real time of transitions and the memory time of resonances.

Of course, to be fully alive in the moment, whether talking, listening, partying, writing, or playing, both times are just as useful. And this is the reason that, after all, a cut is a slice.

ACKNOWLEDGMENTS

FIFTEEN YEARS AGO I SCRATCHED some notes into a new blank workbook under the header "melodramatic stein: a project to adapt and record gertrude stein." A list followed of what it would take to get this project started, then this: "I think it would fly. Do I want to do it? Yes." Coming down now, on the other side of this thrilling, at times perilous flight (I'm not a confident flyer), brings some clear feelings (substantial relief, deep appreciation, poignant regrets) along with the murky, overwhelming sense of having had a lot of experience. This project has let me keep vibrant company with so many creative people across practices and disciplines, and brought real opportunities to learn with them. I want to thank these "many, many more" before taking a bow and signing off.

First, and most practically, none of this would have happened without funding from several different organizations and institutions. Initial seed funding from the University of British Columbia's HSS and Hampton Funds (2010, 2012) gave the project some lift and led to a couple of attempts to secure larger funding. Major support came from a Social Sciences and Humanities Research Council of Canada Insight Grant (2013–19) (File 435-2013-1684), which made everything else possible. The Institut d'études avancées de Paris (IEA) supported initial writing on this book manuscript as well as a performance of *What Happened | Plays* at the extraordinary Hôtel de Lauzun in Paris during a sabbatical year fellowship (2018–19). A UBC Public Humanities Fellowship (2019–20) funded a course release for the Radio Free Radio YouTube broadcast and further work on the manuscript. Support from UBC's Scholarly Publication Fund helped with the preparation and publication of this book. I am very grateful to anonymous members of the many adjudication committees for seeing something in this unconventional project.

Workshops are crucial to the Radio Free Stein process. Many thanks to the participants who were game to think with me during nine challenging, lively play workshops held between 2014 and 2017 at the University of British Columbia, the University of Copenhagen, and Emory University: Melanie Adams, Phanuel Antwi, Heather Arvidson, Rizvana Bradley, Guy Conn, Solveig Daugaard, Lene Asp Frederiksen, Kristin Hoff, Lynne Huffer, Aaron Goldsman, Claire Laville, Kevin McNeilly, Steven Meyer, Michael Moon, Tania Ørum, Aaron Peck, Meredith Quartermain, Peter Quartermain, Katie Rife, Laura Luise Schultz, Martin Glaz Serup, Ada Smailbegivić, Catriona Strang, and Mia You. I had the good fortune to have excellent graduate student research assistants who facilitated and atttended these workshops, prepared bibiographies, hunted down performance and production information, and managed the website and social media for the project. Many thanks to Rebecca Dodd, Andrew McEwen, Carmel Ohman, Madeline Reddon, and Thomas Weideman.

The project composers also attended these workshops. As someone who thinks with and about music, but has very little capacity for playing or making it, I have found it to be a deeply rewarding, altogether fascinating pleasure to work with a handful of contemporary composers. I knew some of them from previous work and play together (Sam Shalabi, Olive Chokroun), some I was introduced to through friends (Daniel Thomas Davis, Dan Warner, Samuel Vriezen), and one was a colleague whom I approached cold (Dorothy Chang). All were willing to sit down with me and, in an open-ended series of conversations, walks, meals, and back-and-forths over email, phone, and in person, gradually develop the wherewithal to move from Stein's play text to completed performance or recording. I am impossibly grateful for their participation, and only wish to find ways to keep pursuing the form of radio melodrama with them and others. (I'll note here, with regret, the missed opportunities, the few composers with whom I began to discuss the project but that didn't work out for scheduling, funding, or other reasons: Emily Doolittle, Jesse Karlsberg, Stephin Merritt, and Cassandra Miller.)

I appreciate the chance to have worked with the enormously talented directors and stage designers Doug Fitch, Adam Henderson, and Jimmy Tait, who helped to realize several of Stein's plays in performance. American Opera Projects played a central role in bringing the New York show to life. Parker McLean designed the project website, which has held up remarkably well over ten years. And a big heartfelt thanks to all the actors and musicians who were involved. It's your voices I hear speaking and singing Stein's lines in my head.

The writing in this book developed over several years of giving invited lectures and conference presentations. Sarah Posman invited me to share some of the earliest research for this project as a keynote address at the Study Centre for Experimental Literature at Ghent University in 2015, and Saadi Lahlou invited me to share some thoughts in a roundtable event held at the IEA de Paris in 2019. Many thanks to them for these opportunities, as well as to organizers of other conferences, research groups, and workshops for invitations to present my work: Daniel Katz, Abigail Laing, Nicholas Manning, Isabelle Moindrot, and Mia You. Thanks to panel organizers and audiences at meetings of the American Comparative Literature Association, the Modern Language Association, and the Modernist Studies Association for their engagement with my work. Particular thanks to Lars Bernaerts and the other organizers of the conference "Tuning into the Neo-Avant-Garde" (Ghent University) for a chance to write about Glenn Gould and meet an engaging group of radio studies scholars.

I am grateful to Steven Meyer, whose research has oriented my thinking about Stein's poetics and who introduced me to a group of European researchers, especially Sarah Posman, Laura Luise Schultz, and Samuel Vriezen. These introductions kicked off the European part of the Radio Free Stein adventure. My collaboration with Samuel led me to the Ensemble Dedalus and to a sabbatical year in residence at the IEA de Paris. Many thanks to Isabelle Alfandary for supporting my application and to Antoine Cazé for responding so generously to my seminar presentation at the Institute. Antoine introduced me to a lively network of French researchers in American literature (and offered insightful explanations of the intricacies and challenges of the French academic system). I thank my fellow Institute colleagues for their great company over many lunches and seminar meetings, especially Michael Jonik, Andrew Kahn, Sahar Sadjadi, and Denis Walsh. Extra thanks to Gretty Mirdal and Simon Luck for their remarkable hosptitality, good humor, and warmth.

The work of archivists and librarians was particularly helpful in my research on Stein's radio interview. Thanks to Mark Bailey for locating the recording at Yale University's collection of Historical Sound Recording at the Irving S. Gilmore Music Library, and to Jonathan Manton for making it available to me in digital form. I am grateful to the work of librarians at the Library of Congress for help tracking down references to William Lundell.

Essay 3 and part of Essay 1 appeared in a special issue of *Textual Practice* 36, no. 12 (December 2022), titled "Feeling in Time: Radio Free Stein." The Estate of Gertrude Stein, through its literary executor Mr. Stanford Gann Jr., of Levin & Gann, P.A., has been generous throughout this project in granting permission to work with Stein's plays and other materials. Big thanks to Corinna Hagel, who came down from the heavens to handle permissions and fine-tune the illustrations for this book.

Jill Frank, Marcie Frank, Michael Moon, and Ned Schantz read earlier drafts of the essays in this book. I'm grateful to them, as well as to two anonymous readers for the press, for substantive feedback. Thinking about readers' comments during the revision process helped me to clarify my arguments and their stakes. And working with my editor at Northwestern University Press, Faith Wilson Stein (ideally named, for this project!), has been a genuine pleasure.

A handful of good friends have been vitally supportive of this project from the beginning. My Vancouver comrades in poetry include Jenny Penberthy, Marguerite Pigeon, and Peter and Meredith Quartermain. In Paris, Fred Collay and Anne-Laure Paumont were staunch companions and keen to perform an enjoyable experiment in group translation of Stein's play *What Happened* into French. Michael Moon has been consistently engaged with and supportive of this project with notes, observations, queries, as both host of and participant in workshops, and often as a first reader of my conference papers and essay drafts. Michael also introduced me to two of the project's composers. His ongoing presence in my life (we're counting decades now) has helped to form my thinking habits, tastes, and sensibilities. With Michael, Marcie, and others, I have been mourning the loss of Jonathan Goldberg, who passed away last year and whose deep commitment to musical and critical expression helped me to imagine what this project could be.

The workbook that contains my initial notes on "melodramatic stein" is dated the same month and year that Marguerite Pigeon's and my first child was born, and the grant that made the project actual was announced right around the birth of our second one. These two, Merle and Lewis, have kept us very good company over the years, everyone growing and changing, together and apart, in altogether unpredictable ways. Staying in touch with the reality of their changing needs, and Marguerite's, has somehow meant staying in touch with my own. It has also meant sticking with the needs of this project, which has both taken me away and given us opportunities for new experiences together (a week in New York, a year in Paris). For all the ways that Merle and Lewis have made me live for real, I dedicate this book to them.

APPENDIX

RECORDING AND PERFORMANCE NOTES

Between 2012 and 2019 I collaborated on Radio Free Stein with many others to render nine Gertrude Stein plays as works of radio and music theater. Streaming audio recordings, video recordings of live performances, and full information about production history and broadcasts can be found on the project website (radiofreestein.com).

This appendix includes credits for the recordings and performances as well as selected composer's notes on musical settings. It also includes visual material (photographs and posters) associated with the project. Readers wishing to know more about the music can listen to an archived YouTube series called RADIO FREE RADIO, a biweekly discussion (held during fall 2020) with most of the project's composers. Episodes can be located through the "broadcasts" page on the project website.

What Happened: A Five Act Play (1913)

Audio link [https://radiofreestein.com/plays/what-happened/]
Full audio [https://soundcloud.com/samuel-vriezen/what-happened-plays]
A concert staging of *What Happened | Plays* was held at the Hôtel de Lauzun in Paris on June 26, 2019.

CREDITS:

Composer: Samuel Vriezen
Libretto/radio script: Adam Frank
Music director: Didier Aschour
Sound engineer: Benjamin Maumus

Aurélie Nyirabikali Lierman (voice) as W, the Writer
Ensemble Dedalus:
Didier Aschour (guitar)
Amélie Berson (flute) as the Qualifier
Cyprien Busolini (viola)
Thierry Madiot (trombone) as the Negator
Pierre-Stéphane Meugé (saxophone) as the Splitter of Hairs
Fabrice Villard (clarinet) as the Seeker of Definitions
Deborah Walker (cello) as A, the Imagined Audience

The recorded performance was supported by: Dedalus Ensemble, the GMEA—National Center of Musical Creation of Albi-Tarn, the Paris Institute for Advanced Study, and a grant from the Social Sciences and Humanities Research Council of Canada (File 435-2013-1684).

RADIO FREE RADIO link to episode with Samuel Vriezen [https://www.youtube.com/watch?v=zy2fzPH61Ow]

White Wines: Three Acts (1913)

Audio link [https://radiofreestein.com/plays/white-wines/]
This play was recorded at the VSO School of Music, June 17–24, 2015. A concert staging (in conjunction with *He Said It*) took place at the Vancouver East Cultural Centre on June 4 and 5, 2016.

CREDITS (RECORDING):

Composer: Dorothy Chang
Scenario: Adam Frank
Musical Director: Marguerite Witvoet
Sound Engineer: Don Harder

Jenny Andersen as Therese
Mia Harris as Sylvia
Camille Hesketh as Jane
Kristin Hoff as Harriet
Katie Rife on percussion

ADDITIONAL CREDITS (PERFORMANCE):

Director: James Fagan Tate
Stage Manager: Adam Henderson
Video: Tim Matheson

Performance and recording made possible by a grant from the Social Sciences and Humanities Research Council of Canada (File 435-2013-1684).

Composer notes by Dorothy Chang (from the performance program)

When Adam and I began our collaboration to adapt Gertrude Stein's *White Wines* as a radio play, we had no precise concept of what we hoped to create, other than an exploration of various ways in which words and music might intersect within the context of Stein's work. We did have a list of what it would not be: not opera, not singspiel, not musical theater, not a song cycle, and not a theatrical play with incidental music. Through many hours of discussion, sharing of sketches, and workshops with the talented group premiering the semi-staged version, we collaboratively developed a work that borrows elements from all of the above genres.

The treatment of the text includes natural speech, contrapuntal layers of speech, rhythmic speech, recitative, chanting, and song. Being a play, the intelligibility of the text was of paramount importance, thus the delivery of the words is mostly straightforward even when sung. The percussionist, serving as the fifth character, is given material that contributes to the conversation in both spoken and musical form. To reflect a sense of yesteryear (*White Wines* was written in 1913), the musical language is largely modal and the textures transparent. It is my hope that the music helps to provide further definition to our adaptation of Stein's play, and that it underscores the charm, wit, drama, and poetic introspection in her work.

He Said It: Monologue (1915)

Audio link [https://radiofreestein.com/plays/said/]

This play was recorded at the VSO School of Music, April 12–24, 2015. A concert staging (in conjunction with *White Wines*) took place at the Vancouver East Cultural Centre on June 4 and 5, 2016.

CREDITS (RECORDING):

Composer: Olive (Dave) Chokroun
Scenario: Adam Frank and Ada Smailbegović
Director: Adam Henderson
Sound Engineer: Josh Stevenson

Lucia Frangione as Speaker
Leanna Brodie as Hearer
Olive (Dave) Chokroun as Narrator, on piano

CREDITS (PERFORMANCE):

Composer: Olive (Dave) Chokroun
Scenario: Adam Frank and Ada Smailbegović
Director: James Fagan Tate
Stage Manager: Adam Henderson
Video: Tim Matheson

Sarah May Redmond as Speaker
Leanna Brodie as Hearer
Olive (Dave) Chokroun as Narrator, on piano

Performance and recording made possible by a grant from the Social Sciences and Humanities Research Council of Canada (File 435-2013-1684).

Composer notes by Olive (Dave) Chokroun

"Serial-ish": This piece—like most of my scored music—used a few serial processes in its early stages. For me, the processes are for creating constraints on the choice of materials: pitches, rhythmic patterns, registration, and so on. Process and constraint create a constellation of problems to solve, which provides a pathway through the work. But this is essentially a starting point; as the work progresses I'll edit and adjust the generated material to make it expressive in the way I want.

For *He Said It*, I spent a lot of time speaking the text and trying to absorb the cadence of the spoken words—not for the purpose of transcription but to try to capture the affect of the text. This is, maybe, another way of taking an existing, generated source and adjusting and smooshing it. (What James Tenney is reported to have said to Steve Reich: If there's nothing but process in the music "then the composer isn't privy to anything." Also, Orwell: Break any of these rules rather than say anything barbarous.)

Influences: I'll take the description "post-Cagean," sure. I've always felt an affinity for the composers loosely known as "American mavericks," including Cage but especially James Tenney, Robert Ashley, Gordon Mumma, and Frederic Rzewski. What I read into them, and try to create in my own way, is a criticality of the apparatus of production and performance.

I am very influenced by Cage's idea that music is a container of time that you put things into, as heard in "Indeterminacy" (1959). Of course, that's also a work for a speaking voice and piano (and noise), and it really is one of my foundational pieces. I've done quite a lot of work incorporating instruments and a speaking voice. I see that as a really clear way of stating that music is text as well as sound: creating work where text and sound are equal partners. (Ashley and Rzewski's works with voice have been huge influences in that respect, though I don't know that they would describe that exactly the same way.) In *He Said It*, that led to the decision of giving voice and music separate sections for almost the entire piece. Our discussions about the history of melodrama—monologue with accompaniment—were also illuminating: in this piece, I don't see the music as "interludes" as much as restatements of the words that have been heard. And sometimes the restatements happen before the statements. As I said in the program notes—"the piano is just another person in the room."

The other particular influence on *He Said It* is Erik Satie—as seen through a Cagean lens—in the use of collage and repetition.

Improvisation: *He Said It* is completely scored but incorporates a few indeterminate sections, bars or gestures that are written out but arranged and repeated ad lib by the performer. In this piece that's done using box notation, as seen in Cage, Feldman, and onward in contemporary music. In my opinion, though, that's interpretation, not improvisation. By the numbers, I've worked more in improvisation than scored composition. I do think that there's no composition without improvisation, but that's not to say that there's a hierarchy between the two: that composition is more sophisticated, or that improvisation is more authentic. Improvisation isn't a privileged activity, it's a condition of being in the world.

Contemporaneity: One of the problems of working with a text from 1915 is that one doesn't want it to inevitably sound like music from 1915—that's too easy. However, we had quite a few discussions about the biographical details around the creation of Stein's text, and that gave me ideas about where this music was situated. It's the idea that the music could be something that could be played on a piano in a hotel in Mallorca in 1915, in an intimate setting; not a recital, but the sound of someone in a lounge fooling around. So—back to point 1 about serialism—there are quite a lot of gestures of turn-of-the-century classical and light music there, filtered through process-based decisions about structure and through an affective interpretation of the words. It was my best process to try and match the oblique, comic, and emotive things that I read in Stein's text.

RADIO FREE RADIO link to episode with Olive (Dave) Chokroun [https://www.youtube.com/watch?v=sS88z86ibpU]

Figure 10. Promotional poster for the Radio Free Stein production of *"He Said It" and "White Wines": A Concert Staging of Two Plays by Gertrude Stein*. Vancouver East Cutural Centre, June 4 and 5, 2016.

APPENDIX · 167

For the Country Entirely: A Play in Letters (1916)

Audio link [https://radiofreestein.com/plays/for-the-country-entirely/]

This play was recorded at the UBC School of Music and Otic Sound in December 2012. A semi-staged concert took place at the Western Front, Vancouver, Canada, on May 3, 2013.

CREDITS:

Composer: Dorothy Chang
Scenario: Adam Frank
Director: Adam Henderson
Sound Engineers: Brian Garbet and Ryan Noakes (UBC), Josh Stevenson (Otic Sound)

Cara McDowell as Ava
Lucia Frangione as Bella
Alan Marriott as Walter
Kurt Evans as William Cook

Mark Ferris on violin
Domagoj Ivanovic on violin

Marcus Takizawa on viola
Peggy Lee on cello (replaced by Rebecca Wenham in performance)

The recording was made possible by a grant from the Hampton Foundation at the University of British Columbia. The performance was supported by UBC's Peter Wall Institute for Advanced Study.

Dorothy Chang's "Composition and Collaboration: Music for Stein's 'For the Country Entirely: A Play in Letters' (1916)" can be found in *The Capilano Review* 3, no. 22 (2014): 71–72. My scenario adaptation of this play and a short introduction to the project appear in the same issue.

Figure 11. Lucia Frangione and Cara McDowell in the Radio Free Stein production of *For the Country Entirely*. Western Front, Vancouver, May 3, 2013. Photograph by Elizabeth Wilson.

An Exercise in Analysis (1917)

Audio link [https://radiofreestein.com/plays/an-exercise-in-analysis/]

Full audio [https://soundcloud.com/user-934067047/an-exercise-in-analysis/s-xOfqM]

This play was recorded at Dick and Roger's Sound Studio, Vancouver, Canada, on June 26, 2017.

CREDITS:

Composer and electronics: Dan Warner
Scenario: Adam Frank
Director: James Fagan Tait
Sound Engineer: Don Harder

Patti Allan as Part *x*
Emelia Symington Fedy as Act II
Evan Frayne as Act III
Kevin MacDonald as Act IV

Produced with the cooperation of the Union of B.C. Performers. This recording was supported by a grant from the Social Sciences and Humanities Research Council of Canada (File 435-2013-1684).

RADIO FREE RADIO link to episode with Dan Warner [https://www.youtube.com/watch?v=YxD_rQvHIVk]

SIX. TWENTY. OUTRAGEOUS.

Photograph: A Play in Five Acts (1920)

Audio link [https://radiofreestein.com/plays/photograph/]

Captain Walter Arnold (1916)

Audio link [https://radiofreestein.com/plays/captain-walter-arnold/]

The Psychology of Nations, or What Are You Looking At (1920)

Audio link [https://radiofreestein.com/plays/psychology-nations-looking/]

SIX. TWENTY. OUTRAGEOUS. Three Gertrude Stein Plays in the Shape of an Opera, a chamber opera production of these plays, was held at Symphony Space in New York City, February 9–11, 2018.

CREDITS:

Composer: Daniel Thomas Davis
Libretto: Adam Frank with the composer
Director/Designer: Doug Fitch
Musical Director: David Bloom
Choreographer: Kate Elswit
Sound Engineer: Ben Manley
Production Manager: Matt Grey

Jacqueline Horner-Kwiatek as V
Andrew Fuchs as ME
Ariadne Greif as THREE
Joseph Atkins as WE

Dimitri Dover, piano

MOMENTA QUARTET:

Emilie-Anne Gendron, violin

Alex Shiozaki, violin

Stephanie Griffin, viola

Michael Haas, cello

Coproduced by American Opera Projects and Symphony Space, the recorded performances were made possible by a grant from the Social Sciences and Humanities Research Council of Canada (File 435-2013-1684).

Trailer link [https://www.youtube.com/watch?v=6Y_ca-qWpII]

RADIO FREE RADIO link to episode with Daniel Thomas Davis [https://www.youtube.com/watch?v=wGwzokZhTic]

Figure 13. Jacqueline Horner-Kwiatek, Andrew Fuchs, Michael Haas, and Alex Shiozaki in the Radio Free Stein production of *Photograph* from *SIX. TWENTY. OUTRAGEOUS. Three Gertrude Stein Plays in the Shape of an Opera*. Symphony Space, New York City, 2018. Steven Pisano Photography.

Figure 12. Promotional card designed by Doug Fitch for the Radio Free Stein production *SIX. TWENTY. OUTRAGEOUS. Three Gertrude Stein Plays in the Shape of an Opera*. Symphony Space, New York City, 2018.

Figure 14. Ariadne Greif in the Radio Free Stein production of *Captain Walter Arnold* from *SIX. TWENTY. OUTRAGEOUS. Three Gertrude Stein Plays in the Shape of an Opera*. Symphony Space, New York City, 2018. Steven Pisano Photography.

Short Sentences (1932)

Audio link [https://radiofreestein.com/plays/short-sentences/]
This play was recorded at Breakglass Studios in Montréal, October 2017.

CREDITS:

Composer: Sam Shalabi
Scenario/Libretto: Adam Frank
Choir Director: Dina Cindric
Sound Engineer: Jace Lasek
Recorded and mixed at Breakglass Studio, Montréal
Audio mastered by Harris Newman/Grey Market Mastering

VOCALISTS:

Sarah Albu
Mark Andrew Hamilton
Kate Bevan-Baker
Katherine Black
Nils Brown
Emma Elbourne
Isak Goldschneider
Elizabeth Lima
Marie-Clair Saindon
Jake Smith
and The Monday Night Choir

INSTRUMENTALISTS:

Patrick Conan, drums
Jonah Fortune, bass
Guido Del Fabbro, violin
Jean-Christophe Lizotte, cello
Sarah Page, harp
Giulia Pozzi, viola
Sam Shalabi, electronics

The recording was made possible by a grant from the Social Sciences and Humanities Research Council of Canada (File 435-2013-1684).

RADIO FREE RADIO link to episode with Sam Shalabi [https://www.youtube.com/watch?v=2HUHKW70Mvs]

Figure 15. Gertrude Stein, manuscript notebook used for *Short Sentences. A Play* (1932). Gertrude Stein and Alice B. Toklas Papers, Yale Collection of American Literature. Beinecke Rare Book and Manuscript Library. Estate of Gertrude Stein.

NOTES

PROLOGUE

1. Major support for the Radio Free Stein project came from a Social Sciences and Humanities Research Council of Canada Insight Grant (2013–19) (File 435-2013-1684). Radio Free Stein has been funded as "research-creation" in the Canadian granting context, similar to practice-based or artistic research in other national contexts. For meditations on questions that arise from such arts-based research methods, see Loveless, *How to Make Art at the End of the World*, and Turner, *Feminist Speculation and the Practice of Research-Creation*.

2. Stein, *Lectures in America*, 174.

3. The number depends on how you count. See the appendices to the three major book-length studies of Stein's theater: Betsy Alayne Ryan's *Gertrude Stein's Theatre of the Absolute*, Jane Palatini Bowers's *"They Watch Me as They Watch This": Gertrude Stein's Metadrama*, and Sarah Bay-Cheng's *Mama Dada: Gertrude Stein's Avant-Garde Theater*. Using somewhat different criteria for identifying Stein's plays, Ryan counts seventy-seven, Bowers 103, while Bay-Cheng's tally of 110 includes the works on both these lists.

4. See Bay-Cheng's Appendix B ("A Chronological List of Professional Productions") and Appendix C ("A Chronological List of Dramatic Adaptations"), which include productions up to 2004. For a survey and analysis of some major performances, see Durham. The Radio Free Stein website includes links to various recordings, such as "Shutters Shut," the Nederlands Danz Theater interpretation of Stein's second portrait of Picasso ("If I Told Him"). See also Alain Longuet's *What About Ida*, a short film created for the French television network La Sept and adapted from a dance piece choreographed by Mark Tompkins based on Stein's novel *Ida* (available for viewing at the Bibliotheque nationale de France). Mark Tompkins and Alain Longuet, directors, *What About Ida?* France: Lieurac productions, 1990.

5. For one set of examples of the anxiety around Stein's politics and protection under the Vichy regime in France during the Second World War, see a number of the panelists' comments in Rosten and, by contrast, the more nuanced remarks by Catherine Stimpson, Al Carmines, and Charles Bernstein. See Will for one historical treatment of Stein's wartime experience. For a definitive response to claims about Stein's politics and war experiences, see Bernstein's dossier in *Jacket 2*.

6. See Meyer's *Irresistible Dictation*, especially chapter 5, "Writing Psychology Over: Toward a More Radical Empiricism." Other critics who have explored Stein's relation to Emerson and the pragmatist tradition include Joan Richardson and Ross Posnock.

7. Puchner, *Stage Fright*, 101. See Salvato for a helpful queer theoretical transformation of the term "closet drama." The Stein quotation is from Burns, *The Letters of Gertrude Stein and Carl Van Vechten*, 21.

8. Bay-Cheng, *Mama Dada*, 35.

9. Jarcho, *Writing and the Modern Stage*, 50.

10. Jarcho, 60.

11. Bottoms, *Playing Underground*, viii–ix and 148–54.

12. Fuchs and Chaudhuri, *Land/Scape/Theater*, 11; Lehmann, *Postdramatic Theatre*, 63.

13. For example, Marc Robinson asserts that "Stein was the first American dramatist to infuse the basic materials of dramatic art with independent life, making them noteworthy in themselves" (*The Other American Drama*, 2), while Bonnie Marranca claims that "the performance art and new opera/music theater lines begin with the influence of her work for the stage" (*Last Operas and Plays*, xxi).

14. Bowers, *They Watch Me,* 132.

15. Stein, *Lectures in America*, 93. Hereafter cited parenthetically in the text.

16. Frank, "Loose Coordinations."

17. Stein scholars have long observed the emergence of her plays from the portraits that preceded them and attempts to portray groups. See especially Steiner (105, 173–74) and Bowers (*They Watch Me,* 9–11).

18. For more on Bion's work and Stein's theater see my *Transferential Poetics* and "The Expansion of Setting."

19. The Radio Free Stein project has focused on the plays from the 1910s that Bowers calls conversation plays (*They Watch Me,* 8–24) and that Linda Voris calls voice plays (*Composition of Sense*, 10), not on the landscape plays of the 1920s. My choice to call these early works parlor plays is intended to capture their foregrounding of speech in domestic space, as I explore in some detail in Essay 2. I am persuaded by Voris's meticulous approach to Stein's "landscape homology" and her argument about a distinctive writing method that emerges in the plays of the early 1920s, and share with her a critical commitment to Stein's radical compositional epistemology (see Voris, *The Composition of Sense in Gertrude Stein's Landscape Writing*). But I believe that there is justification for my use of the term *landscape* as a general figure for a space of loose affective coordination that competes with narrative in both the early and later plays. Consider that terms associated with landscape, such as *country*, *ground*, *background*, *land*, *geography*, appear in Stein's plays and letters of the 1910s as she begins to experiment with theatrical form.

20. Traditionally in opera, a scenario is a sketch, outline, or synopsis that indicates how the source material will be (or has been) adapted into a full libretto, and may contain descriptions of characters, staging, and the plot or action of the opera. Grosser prepared his scenario for *Four Saints* after Stein wrote the libretto and Virgil Thomson (his partner) composed the music. In it he imagined the opera's staging as a sequence of vignettes and describes these in detail for use by a director, set designer, and so on. As Alice Toklas apparently said after reading Grosser's scenario, "It not only sounds like an opera but it looks like an opera" (Watson, *Prepare for Saints*, 134). I take up the question of seeing versus hearing Stein's plays later in this prologue and in Essay 1.

21. Grosser's script, as well as a letter from Stein to Henry Dunham and a signed agreement between them, can be found in the Maurice Grosser Papers. Dunham was intending to produce Grosser's script but was not able to raise the funds. Stein writes: "I have always felt that Maurice could do something with my plays" (Grosser, *Ladies Voices and What Happened*, n.p.). For more information about this film project, see Burns, *The Letters of Gertrude Stein and Carl Van Vechten*, 483–84.

22. Kim, "John Cage in Separate Togetherness with Jazz."

23. See Pondrom, "Gertrude Stein, Minimalism, and Modern Opera"; Weideman, " 'Without Too Much Anxiety.' "

24. For one approach, see Moon, "Taking a Chance on Love"; for another, see Wallace, *Improvisation*.

25. Stein, *Everybody's Autobiography*, 200.

26. Quoted in McCaffrey, " 'Any of Mine Without Music to Help Them,' " 28.

27. Quoted in McCaffrey, 28.

28. Meyer, *Irresistible Dictation*, 302. See also J. Frank, "Resonating Bodies," and Pound, "The Difference Sound Makes."

29. Like Radio Free Stein, Erik Belgum's Softpalate project (on Ubuweb: Sound) offers sonic treatments of Stein's early plays, primarily with the involvement of sound artists.

30. Chang, "Composition and Collaboration," 71.

31. Sutherland, *Gertrude Stein*, 103.

32. Stein, *Lectures*, 111.

33. Stein, *Everybody's Autobiography*, 199.

34. "Gertrude Stein Interviewed by William Lundell," audio recording, 3:06–3:48.

ESSAY 1

1. Wollaeger, *Modernism, Media, and Propaganda*, xiv.

2. Consider that the privileged status once accorded to film as the exemplary representational technology associated with modernism has been extended to typewriter, gramophone, telephone, wireless, radio, newsprint, halftone lithography, and others. See, for just a few examples, Armstrong, *Modernism, Technology and the Body*; Trotter, *Literature in the First Media Age*; Goble, *Broadcasting Circuits*; Murphet, *Multimedia Modernism*; and Lewis, *Dynamic Form*. For more on modernism and the field of public relations, see North, *Reading 1922*, and Wientzen, *Automatic*.

3. Major early publications on radio and literary modernism include Kahn and Whitehead, *Wireless Imagination*; and Strauss, *Radiotext(e)*. Others since then include Cohen, Coyle, and Lewty, *Broadcasting Modernism*; Murphet, Groth, and Hone, *Sounding Modernism*; others cited below. For a helpful overview, see Whittington, "Radio Studies and Twentieth-Century Literature."

4. On Stein and celebrity see Glass, *Authors Inc.*; Leick, *Gertrude Stein and the Making of an American Celebrity*; Kirsch, "Gertrude Stein Delivers"; and Jaillant, "Shucks we've got glamour girls too!,'" among others. On Stein and film see Bay-Cheng, *Mama Dada*, and McCabe, *Cinematic Modernism*, among others. The most important contribution on the topic of Stein and radio is Wilson, "Gertrude Stein and the Radio." My work particpates in the recent approach to Stein as a transmedial artist. See the collection edited by Posman and Schultz, *Gertrude Stein in Europe*, and Daugaard, "Collaborating with Gertrude Stein."

5. See Richardson, *A Natural History of Pragmatism*.

6. Peters, *Speaking into the Air*, 225.

7. Peters, 21–22.

8. "Gertrude Stein Interviewed by William Lundell." The archival recording I listened to drops audio at 4:30 and 9:43 but seems otherwise complete. It is a digitized copy of the CD located at Yale University's collection of Historical Sound Recording at the Irving S. Gilmore Music Library. This CD was copied from a reel-to-reel recording also located in the collection. The broadcast would have initially been recorded on electrical transcription discs. Please note, the date of October 12, 1934, that is ascribed to this recording appears to be an error (see the following note).

9. "Gertrude Stein Interviewed by William Lundell." The folder describes this item as a transcript, but this is unlikely since there are significant discrepancies between it and the audio recording. In addition, the script's last page includes the typists' initials and date, "kh/vh/11/10/34," two days before the broadcast on November 12. I believe this item is a copy of the prepared script that Lundell and Stein used as a basis for the broadcast. Steven Meyer has published a version of the interview that takes into account aspects of both script and audio recording ("Gertrude Stein: A Radio Interview").

10. *Radio Announcers*, 10.

11. Arnheim, *Radio*, 211.

12. Arnheim, 220, 218.

13. Stein, "I Came and Here I Am," 168.

14. Stein, "I Came and Here I Am," 168.

15. For a thorough historical account and itinerary of Stein's visit to the United States, see Rice, "Gertrude Stein's American Lecture Tour." For other writing on the lecture tour, see especially Kirsch, "Gertrude Stein Delivers," and Volpicelli, *Transatlantic Modernism*.

16. Stein, "I Came and Here I Am," 168. Hereafter cited parenthetically in the text.

17. "Gertrude Stein Interviewed by William Lundell," audio recording, 1:13–1:34.

18. For Stein, a key element of the phantasmatic quality of America pertains to the figure of the "red Indian." At the end of both the radio interview and her article she describes the movements of college football players as "a real Indian dance" (168), assimilating American national sport to Indigenous ritual in a prototypical colonial identification that Benedict Anderson has described as one basis for nationalism in *Imagined Communities*. On Stein's writing in the specific context of the Indian Reorganization Act of 1934, see Nyerges, "Styling Sovereignty." For a more general account of Stein's participation in tropes of geography and climate as determinants of national character, see Boyd, "Gertrude Stein's Geographical History of Literature."

19. Stein, "Meditations on Being About to Visit My Native Land," 255.

20. Stein, *Lectures*, 170. On her use of the term *essence* in relation to fuel, see D. Watson, *Gertrude Stein and the Essence of What Happens*, 66, and Lorange, *How Reading Is Written*, 167–68. See also Steiner's gloss on talking and listening at the same time: "One thinks of someone talking into a microphone connected to earphones which he himself is wearing" (*Exact Resemblance*, 44). I read this in the specific terms of radio audience, as will soon be clear. (Performances of some of Robert Ashley's operas involve a version of the apparatus that Steiner describes.)

21. Stein, "I Came and Here I Am," 168.

22. See Verma, *Theater of the Mind*, for an approach to radio drama that combines careful historical contextualization with aesthetic-phenomenological listening strategies.

23. Cerf, *At Random*, 103.

24. Stein, *Everybody's Autobiography*, 283–84. Hereafter cited parenthetically in the text.

25. A similar wish can be found in George Orwell's "Poetry and the Microphone" (1945), where he contrasts the potentially hostile audience at "That grisly thing, a 'poetry reading'" with radio broadcasting in which "the poet *feels* that he is addressing people to whom poetry means something" (Strauss, *Radiotext(e)*, 167). For a longer discussion of these protective aspects of radio in the context of Glenn Gould as a radio artist, see my "Studio Audience."

26. "Gertrude Stein Interviewed by William Lundell," audio recording, 03:06–03:48.

27. Harries and Rosenthal, introduction to "Comparative Radios," 1.

28. Adorno, *Current of Music*, 44. Hereafter cited parenthetically in the text.

29. Douglas, *Listening In*, 125.

30. Kane, "Phenomenology, Physiognomy, and the 'Radio Voice,'" 100.

31. Kane, "Phenomenology," 107.

32. Adorno, *Current*, 46.

33. Adorno cites Bernfeld's 1937 essay, whose title in English would be "The Revision of Bioanalysis." For more information on Bernfeld, see Ekstein, "Siegfried Bernfeld: Sisyphus or the Boundaries of Education."

34. See "The Biological Unconscious" in Wilson, *Gut Feminism*.

35. More generally, the history of technology that emerges from Adorno's radio writings resembles that of Raymond Williams in its rejection of either top-down or bottom-up linear determinism (see *Television*). Unlike Williams, however, Adorno rejects intention as a main driver of technological change: "It would be fallacious and a bad simplification to say that radio is a product of monopoly capitalism . . . The tendencies which associate it with the present social conditions have nothing to do with the consciousness of the originators of radio. These tendencies are being realized over their heads" (94 fn).

36. Hinshelwood, *Dictionary*, 32.

37. Mowitt, *Radio*, 37.

38. Curiously enough, Stein's radio interview shows up in *The Medium Is the Massage* (1967), McLuhan's collaboration with the graphic designer Quentin Fiore. In its opening pages we read the phrase "and how!" in large white letters on ink-black background floating above a quotation attributed to A. N. Whitehead ("The major advances in civilization are processes that all but wreck the societies in which they occur" [6–7]). Thirty years earlier, in her radio broadcast, Stein asserts that "the most vigorous expression in modern [American] speech is that composed of two words—'And how.' It is full of emotion and it says everything that needs to be said" ("Stein and Lundell" 08:56–09:05). *And how*, for Stein, is an emphatic echo, an insistence that amplifies difference-in-repetition to create an affective circuit that makes language lively. For McLuhan and Fiore, "And how!" insists that the reader qua listener has read and heard the book's title correctly, that it does indeed repeat McLuhan's popular mantra "the medium is the message" but with the difference of a single letter that leads to a new assertion, that "all media work us over completely" (26). Fiore designed the "and how!" graphics to represent the acoustic space that, McLuhan claims, accompanies electric technology, the particular "advance in civilization" we are being alerted to. For McLuhan, Stein's writing (like James Joyce's) is an index to the transformations wrought by radio and phonograph, a return to acoustic space.

39. We have already glimpsed the role that music plays in discussions of radio speech in Arnheim's analogy of the radio script to a musical score. In the 1930s, radio's words are cast as dependent on or guided by musical *techne* (scores, orchestrations, cf. Milton Kaplan's observation in *Radio and Poetry* [1949] that writers of radio verse such as Norman Corwin should best be thought of as orchestrators of words and sounds [150]). Arnheim argues that, in broadcasting, the sonic quality of spoken words renders them both contiguous and continuous with musical sounds and sound effects, a phenomenon of contiguity that he called "the acoustic bridge" (*Radio*, 195). Adorno is similarly attuned to the radio voice as an experience of sound (not only speech), and both are inheritors of the nineteenth-century German aesthetic theory that places so-called pure, allegedly nonrepresentational instrumental music at the top of a hierarchy of expressive forms. They are both aware that this aesthetic hierarchy becomes untenable when phonograph

40. Cerf, *At Random*, 104.

41. On switching off the radio see Benjamin, *Radio Benjamin*, 363–64. Contrast with Adorno, *Current*, 112.

42. On the acousmatic see Kane, *Sound Unseen*.

43. Arnheim, *Radio*, 220.

44. Quoted in Meyer, "Gertrude Stein: A Radio Interview," 86.

45. Stein, *Lectures*, 174. See Steiner, *Exact Resemblance*, for a definitve treatment of Stein's portrait techniques.

46. "Gertrude Stein Interviewed by William Lundell," 5. I quote here from the interview script. There is a brief gap in the audio recording that corresponds with this passage in the script, which then resumes.

47. "Gertrude Stein Interviewed by William Lundell," audio recording, 05:45–06:00.

48. See appendices in Ryan and Bay-Cheng.

49. Stein, *A Stein Reader*, 345. Hereafter cited parenthetically in the text.

50. Dydo, *Gertrude Stein: The Language That Rises*, 16.

51. The text as published in *Last Operas and Plays* has a typographical error and reads "if each one of them is reproduces." The composer chose to keep this error in his score for musical reasons.

52. Dydo, *Language*, 17. Hereafter cited parenthetically in the text.

53. Bay-Cheng, *Mama Dada*, 36.

54. *Stein Reader*, 328. Stein may be referring to this experience in *The Autobiography* when the narrator recalls "the photograph where Gertrude Stein and I were in the front row and had our portraits taken there accidentally" (205).

55. Bion, "Imaginary Twin," in *The Complete Works of W. R. Bion* 6:56. Hereafter cited parenthetically in the text.

56. Stein, *Autobiography*, 66.

57. This workshop was held at Emory University, February 10, 2014.

58. For a fascinating discussion of the role of "inner speech" in the theories of Bakhtin and other Russian formalists, see Caryl Emerson, "The Outer Word and Inner Speech."

59. Bridgman, *Gertrude Stein in Pieces*, 160.

60. Stein, *Geography and Plays*, 416. Hereafter cited parenthetically in the text.

61. Adorno, *Current*, 87.

62. See Chun, "Afterword."

ESSAY 2

1. For a lucid, helpful overview of the term and its associated concepts, see Loxley, *Performativity*. For a genealogy of the distinct meanings of the term, see J. Hillis Miller, who concludes that "these various forms of performativity, different as they are from one another, have a family resemblance, in the Wittgensteinian sense" ("Performativity as Performance / Performativity as Speech Act," 233).

2. J. L. Austin, *How to Do Things with Words*, 5. Hereafter *How*, cited parenthetically in the text.

3. For their initial, enormously influential analysis of the performativity of gender, see Butler, *Gender Trouble*. I will be turning to Sedgwick's use of the concept below. See Nealon, *Fates of the Performative*, for a recent genealogy of the different paths or uptakes of performativity in the theoretical humanities. Foucault mentions Austin in an unpublished lecture "Structuralisme et analyse littéraire" (*Society Must Be Defended*, ix).

4. Specifically, I do not accept Derrida's blunt critique of intention in Austin. For a very good discussion see Loxley, 85–87.

5. See Austin's *Sense and Sensibilia* for the clearest statements of his methodological commitments to phenomenological experience and his critique of dualist ontologies.

6. Sedgwick, *Touching Feeling*, 6.

7. This phrase appears in a long paragraph in *Touching Feeling* (7) that offers a remarkably compressed survey of performativity in the work of several prominent theorists (Jean-François Lyotard, Paul de Man, and J. Hillis Miller), a paragraph that appears verbatim in previous essays that Sedgwick published ("Queer Performativity," 2, and *Performativity and Performance*, 2–3). I read this self-citation in three distinct contexts as it both supports Derrida's argument about citationality but bends toward a more Austinian project.

8. See Moi, *Revolution of the Ordinary*, for a recent intervention into literary studies from a perspective associated

with ordinary language philosophy. But I wonder whether Moi's contrast between Wittgensteinian and Saussurean conceptions of language is too starkly oppositional. See Perloff, *Wittgenstein's Ladder*, for another approach to Stein and Wittgenstein.

9. The notion of performativity is itself an example of such an ongoing consequential resonance initiated by Austin's own lecture performances. *How to Do Things with Words* is based not only on his substantial lecture notes but also on a number of recordings, as well as notes taken by audience members who attended the lectures. See Andersen, "Any Search for an Origin Is Hysterical," for a discussion of Austin's Gothenburg recording and the theory of performativity "between orality and technologies of writing" (196).

10. Euripides, *Hippolytus*, translated by Gilbert Murray, l. 649. Here is David Grene's more recent translation: "My tongue swore, but my mind was quite unpledged" (l. 612).

11. In his foreword to Friedrich Kittler's *Discourse Networks, 1800/1900*, David Wellbery describes the "presupposition of exteriority" characteristic of poststructuralist thinkers (xii–xiii), a presupposition that may help to explain Austin's otherwise unlikely appeal to Derrida, Foucault, and those of us who have inherited an eclectic mix of English and Continental theoretical approaches to language, discourse, and media.

12. Readers have asked me to consider cases of deception (such as making a promise while crossing one's fingers) or changes of mind. A promiser who crosses their fingers may consider their promise void in the moment of its utterance. However, if the promisee is aware of the crossed fingers, they would treat it as hollow and insist that the promiser uncross them before repeating it. According to Wikipedia, to cross one's fingers is to make the sign of the cross in order to ward off evil. The gesture implies that the promiser is aware of their intention to deceive and crosses their fingers, not to void their promise but to ward off the satanic consequences of their hollow deception. I will take up relations between performative utterances and commitment below.

13. On various uptakes of Butler, see Nealon, *Fates of the Performative*, 50–55. On performative utterances in institutional contexts that claim to establish official antiracist policies, see Ahmed, "The Nonperformativity of Antiracism."

14. Barish, *The Antitheatrical Prejudice*, is the classic survey of this discourse.

15. Weber, *Theatricality as Medium*, 27.

16. Weber, 371.

17. Sedgwick, *Touching Feeling*, 90.

18. Cavell introduces the category of passionate utterance in his foreword to Felman and elaborates it further in "Passionate and Performative Utterance."

19. For a helpful overview of this concept, see Joseph, "Transference: The Total Situation."

20. See my *Transferential Poetics*, 19.

21. Cavell, *Pitch of Philosophy*, 101.

22. See de Vries for a reading of Cavell, Austin, and Euripides vis-à-vis sincerity.

23. See Kokkini for historical context.

24. I am in substantive agreement with Julia Jarcho's recent critical assessment of the consistent return to antitheatrical readings of Stein (*Writing and the Modern Stage*, 48–51). Jarcho analyzes Stein's "negative theatrics" by way of Adorno and the dispersive qualities of her theater: "For Stein . . . theater's essential operation is not the interposition of disruption and disparity *between* drama and its others but, instead, the cultivation of difference *within* an already-decentralized perceptual field" (55–56). This description foregrounds the structural hollowness of theater (as Sam Weber identifies it) and resembles Austin's use of theater as a figure for a differentiated psychical space in which multiple agencies or capacities move on and off the stage of consciousness.

25. Bowers, "They Watch Me," 4.

26. "They Watch Me," 130–33. See also Bowers, "The Composition That All the World Can See," for an analysis of Stein's landscape theater poetics as spatialized compositional form.

27. Ryan, *Gertrude Stein's Theatre of the Absolute*, 60.

28. Benveniste, *Problems in General Linguistics*, 236.

29. Benveniste, 238.

30. Felman, *Scandal*, 53.

31. Stein, *Geography*, 267.

32. This workshop was held August 21, 2014, at Green College at the University of British Columbia, Vancouver.

33. Rebecca Ariel Porte, in "Long Dull Poems," makes a similar point when she argues, about *Stanzas in Meditation*, that "Stein's text is not a-referential but *multiply referential* and really ought to be read through those layers of reference. In order to do so, we have to accept that the tactics of a purely affective reading are not, by themselves, sufficient for helping us to understand the operations of the poem as a whole" (83).

34. For a close reading of *For the Country Entirely* along these lines, see my essay "Radio Free Stein: Rendering Queen and Country."

35. *Stein Reader*, 268.

36. In her reading, Dana Watson proposes that the numbers may be names of characters (*Gertrude Stein*, 69).

37. See Schultz, "A Combination and Not a Contradiction."

38. Meyer, *Irresistible*, 281.

39. For a different approach to Stein's orientation toward counting and the paragraph as a bounded whole, see Ashton, "Gertrude Stein for Anyone."

40. For a discussion of Williams from the perspective of theater studies, see Worthen, *Drama*, 48–49. For his criticism of Sedgwick's approach to performativity, see Worthen "Drama, Performativity, Performance."

41. Williams, *Drama*, 13.

42. Matthews, "Change and Theory," 191.

43. Burke, "Words as Deeds," 155.

44. Loxley, *Performativity*, 104.

45. Gertrude Stein and Alice B. Toklas Papers, Yale Collection of American Literature, Beinecke Rare Book and Manuscript Library, Yale University YCAL MSS 76 Series 1, box 82, folder 1515. Reproductions of these ms. pages can be found on the Radio Free Stein website.

46. The workshop was held June 5, 2014, at Green College at the University of British Columbia, Vancouver.

47. Note, Bowers does not include Stein's earliest plays, *What Happened* and *White Wines*, in this category because they do not emphasize dialogue. I hesitate over this formal delineation (like other critics, for example, Dana Watson [*Gertrude Stein*, 62]), and propose instead to foreground the salience of domestic space.

48. For documentation about this back-and-forth between Stein and various supporters, see *The Letters of Gertrude Stein and Carl Van Vechten,* 16, 20–21, 23.

49. *White Wines* is not included in Ryan, Appendix C. See Smedman, "'Cousin to Cooning,'" for reference to a staged reading. For remarks on Drew Pisarra's production at St. Mark's in New York in July 2010, see Joelle Zigman, "White Wine and Post-Modernism," http://www.newmusicbox.org/articles/White-Wine-and-PostModernism.

50. Stein, *Geographical History of America*, 68, 108.

51. Bridgman, *Gertrude Stein in Pieces*, 137.

52. Ogden, "On Holding and Containing," 1359.

53. Bion, "Catastrophic Change," *The Complete Works of W. R. Bion*, vol. 6.

54. Hinshelwood, *Dictionary*, 251.

55. Hinshelwood, 252.

56. Burke, "Words as Deeds," 160.

ESSAY 3

This essay is dedicated to Sarah Posman.

1. By contrast, if you simply slow down or speed up playback of a recorded sound to make it longer or shorter, you will also alter its pitch content—slowed-down voices sound lower, sped-up ones higher, as anybody who has ever toyed with tape or played records at the wrong rotational speed should know.

2. Not having any deep knowledge of any musical tradition outside of the Western classical one in which I was educated, I did on occasion have the fortune of insightful conversations and collaborations with musicians working in other traditions. For instance it was fascinating for me to learn how in Arabic music traditions a mode is not just a scale—a collection of pitches as a theoretical construct and resource—but involves characteristic melodic formulas, articulations, ornamentations, and nuances of intonation, all living in fields of variability that allow for quasi-improvised expression, of which theories certainly exist but which are generally learned by ear and which may differ in subtle ways from region to region. Clearly, notes here are not just notes but part of very elaborate systems of musical motion, and knowing these well is what allows for richly expressive ways of playing together semi-improvisationally.

BIBLIOGRAPHY

Adorno, Theodor W. *Current of Music: Elements of a Radio Theory*. Edited and with an introduction by Robert Hullot-Kentor. Cambridge, Eng.: Polity Press, 2009.

Ahmed, Sara. "The Nonperformativity of Antiracism." *Meridians* 7, no. 1 (2006): 104–26.

Andersen, Tawny. "'Any Search for an Origin Is Hysterical': Summoning the Ghost of J. L. Austin." *Performance Philosophy* 2, no. 2 (2017): 189–205.

Anderson, Benedict. *Imagined Communities: Reflections on the Origin and Spread of Nationalism*. London: Verso, 2006.

Armstrong, Tim. *Modernism, Technology and the Body: A Cultural Study*. Cambridge: Cambridge University Press, 1998.

Arnheim, Rudolf. *Radio: An Art of Sound*. Translated by Margaret Ludwig and Herbert Read. New York: Da Capo Press, 1972.

Ashton, Jennifer. "Gertrude Stein for Anyone." *ELH* 64, no. 1 (1997): 289–331. Project MUSE, doi:10.1353/elh.1997.0001.

Austin, J. L. *How to Do Things with Words*. Cambridge, MA: Harvard University Press, 1962.

———. *Sense and Sensibilia*. Oxford: Oxford University Press, 1962.

Barish, Jonas. *The Antitheatrical Prejudice*. Berkeley: University of California Press, 1981.

Barthes, Roland. *Camera Lucida: Reflections on Photography*. New York: Hill & Wang, 1981.

Bay-Cheng, Sarah. *Mama Dada: Gertrude Stein's Avant-Garde Theater*. New York: Routledge, 2004.

Benjamin, Walter. "Little History of Photography." In *Walter Benjamin: Selected Writings, 2: 1931–1934*, edited by Howard Eiland and Gary Smith, 507–30. Cambridge, MA: Harvard University Press, 2005.

———. "The Work of Art in the Age of Its Technological Reproducibility." In *Walter Benjamin: Selected Writings, 3: 1935–1938*, edited by Howard Eiland and Michael W. Jennings, 101–33. Cambridge, MA: Harvard University Press, 2006.

———. *Radio Benjamin*. Edited by Lecia Rosenthal, translated by Jonathan Lutes with Lisa Harries Schumann and Diana K. Reese. London, New York: Verso, 2014.

Benveniste, Émile. *Problems in General Linguistics*. Coral Gables, FL: University of Miami Press, 1971.

Bernstein, Charles, ed. "Gertrude Stein's War Years: Setting the Record Straight: A Dossier." *Jacket 2*. May 9, 2012. https://jacket2.org/feature/gertrude-steins-war-years-setting-record-straight.

Bion, W. R. *The Complete Works of W. R. Bion*. Edited by Chris Mawson. 16 vols. London: Karnac Books, 2014.

Bottoms, Stephen J. *Playing Underground: A Critical History of the 1960s Off-Off-Broadway Movement*. Ann Arbor: University of Michigan, 2004.

Bowers, Jane Palatini. *"They Watch Me as They Watch This": Gertrude Stein's Metadrama*. Philadelphia: University of Pennsylvania Press, 1991.

———. "The Composition That All the World Can See: Gertrude Stein's Theater Landscapes." In *Land/Scape/Theater,* edited by Elinor Fuchs and Una Chaudhuri, 121–44. Ann Arbor: University of Michigan Press, 2002.

Boyd, Janet. "Gertrude Stein's Geographical History of Literature." In *Primary Stein: Returning to the Writing of Gertrude Stein*, edited by Janet Boyd and Sharon J. Kirsch, 199–214. Lanham, MD: Rowan & Littlefield, 2014.

Bridgman, Richard. *Gertrude Stein in Pieces*. New York: Oxford University Press, 1970.

Burke, Kenneth. "Words as Deeds." *Centrum* 3, no. 2 (Fall 1975): 147–68.

Burns, Edward, ed. *The Letters of Gertrude Stein and Carl Van Vechten, 2 vols.* New York: Columbia University Press, 1986.

Butler, Judith. *Gender Trouble: Feminism and the Subversion of Identity*. New York: Routledge, 1990.

Cantril, Hadley, and Gordon Allport. *The Psychology of Radio*. New York, London: Harper & Brothers, 1935.

Cavell, Stanley. *A Pitch of Philosophy*. Cambridge, MA: Harvard University Press, 1994.

———. "Passionate and Performative Utterance: Morals of Encounter." In *Contending with Stanley Cavell*, edited by Russell B. Goodman, 177–98. New York: Oxford University Press, 2005.

Cerf, Bennett. *At Random: The Reminiscences of Bennett Cerf*. Edited by Phyllis Cerf Wagner and Albert Eskine. New York: Random House, 1977.

Chang, Dorothy. "Composition and Collaboration: Music for Stein's 'For the Country Entirely: A Play in Letters' (1916)." *Capilano Review* 3, no. 22 (2014): 71–72.

Chun, Wendy Hui Kyong. "Afterword: After McLuhan." In *Re-Understanding Media: Feminist Extensions of Marshall McLuhan*, edited by Sarah Sharma and Rianka Singh, 225–32. Durham, NC: Duke University Press, 2022.

Cohen, Debra Rae, Michael Coyle, and Jane Lewty, eds. *Broadcasting Modernism*. Gainesville: University Press of Florida, 2009.

Cohen, Debra Rae, and Michael Coyle, eds. *Modernist Cultures* 10, no. 1 (2015).

Daugaard, Solveig. "Collaborating with Gertrude Stein: Media Ecologies, Reception, Poetics." PhD diss., Linköping University, 2018.

Derrida, Jacques. "Signature Event Context." In *Limited Inc*, translated by Samuel Weber and Jeffrey Mehlman. Evanston, IL: Northwestern University Press, 1988.

———. "Declarations of Independence." In *Negotiations: Interventions and Interviews, 1971–2001*, edited, translated, and with an introduction by Elizabeth Rottenberg, 46–54. Stanford, CA: Stanford University Press, 2002.

de Vries, Hent. "Must We (NOT) Mean What We Say? Seriousness and Sincerity in the Work of J. L. Austin and Stanley Cavell." In *The Rhetoric of Sincerity*, edited by Ernst van Alpen, Mieke Bal, and Carel Smith. Stanford, CA: Stanford University Press, 2009.

Douglas, Susan. *Listening In: Radio and the American Imagination*. New York: Random House, 1999.

Durham, Leslie Atkins. *Staging Gertrude Stein: Absence, Culture, and the Landscape of American Alternative Theatre*. New York: Palgrave Macmillan, 2005.

Dydo, Ulla, with William Rice. *Gertrude Stein: The Language That Rises, 1923–1934*. Evanston, IL: Northwestern University Press, 2003.

Ekstein, Rudolf. "Siegfried Bernfeld: Sisyphus or the Boundaries of Education." In *Psychoanalytic Pioneers*, edited by Franz Alexander, Samuel Eisenstein, and Martin Grotjahn, 415–29. New York: Basic Books, 1966.

Emerson, Caryl. "The Outer Word and Inner Speech: Bakhtin, Vygotsky, and the Internalization of Language." *Critical Inquiry* 10, no. 2 (1983): 245–64.

Empson, William. *Seven Types of Ambiguity*. New York: New Directions, 1966.

Esdale, Logan. "Gertrude Stein's Twin." *Textual Practice* 25, no. 6 (2011): 989–1014.

Euripides. *Hippolytus*. Translated by Gilbert Murray. Part 7 in *The Harvard Classics, Vol. VIII*. New York: P. F. Collier & Son, 1909.

———. *Hippolytus*. In *Euripides I*, edited by David Grene and Richard Lattimore, translated by David Grene, 185–251. Chicago: University of Chicago Press, 2013.

Felman, Shoshana. *The Scandal of the Speaking Body: Don Juan with J. L. Austin, or Seduction in Two Languages*. Stanford, CA: Stanford University Press, 2003.

Flatley, Jonathan. *Like Andy Warhol*. Chicago: University of Chicago Press, 2017.

Foucault, Michel. *Society Must Be Defended: Lectures at the Collège de France, 1975–1976*. Edited by Mauro Bertani and Alessandro Fontana, translated by David Macey, with an introduction by Arnold I. Davidson. New York: Picador, 2003.

Frank, Adam. "Loose Coordinations: Theater and Thinking in Gertrude Stein." In Frank, *Transferential Poetics, from Poe to Warhol*, 96–118.

———. "The Expansion of Setting in Gertrude Stein's Landscape Theater." *Modernism/modernity PRINTPLUS* 3, no. 1 (March 5, 2018). https://doi.org/10.26597/mod.0042.

———. "Exercises in Group Analysis: Sounding Out Stein's Plays." In *Approaches to Teaching the Works of Gertrude Stein*, edited by Logan Esdale and Deborah Mix, 151–57. New York: MLA, 2019.

———. "Studio Audience: Glenn Gould's Contrapuntal Radio." In *Tuning into the Neo-Avant-Garde: Experimental Radio Plays in the Postwar Period*, edited by Inge Arteel, Lars Bernaerts, Siebe Bluijs, and Pim Verhulst, 236–53. Manchester, Eng.: Manchester University Press, 2021.

———. "Radio Free Stein: Rendering Queen and Country." In *Primary Stein: Returning to the Writing of Gertrude Stein*, edited by Janet Boyd and Sharon Kirsch, 145–62. Lanham, MD: Lexington Books, 2014.

———. *Transferential Poetics, from Poe to Warhol*. New York: Fordham University Press, 2015.

Frank, Johanna. "Resonating Bodies and the Poetics of Aurality; Or; Gertrude Stein's Theatre." *Modern Drama* 51, no. 4 (2008): 501–27.

Fuchs, Elinor, and Una Chaudhuri, eds. *Land/Scape/Theater*. Ann Arbor: University of Michigan Press, 2002.

Glass, Loren. *Authors Inc.: Literary Celebrity in the United States, 1880–1980*. New York: NYU Press, 2004.

Goble, Mark. *Broadcasting Circuits: Modernism and the Mediated Life*. New York: Columbia University Press, 2010.

Grosser, Maurice. *Ladies Voices and What Happened*. 1936. Maurice Grosser Papers, Reel D285, Smithsonian Archives of American Art.

Harries, Martin, and Lecia Rosenthal, eds. "Comparative Radios." *Cultural Critique* 91, no. 1 (Fall 2015): 1–13.

Hinshelwood, R. D. *A Dictionary of Kleinian Thought*. London: Free Association Books, 1989.

Jaillant, Lise. "Shucks we've got glamour girls too! Gertrude Stein, Bennett Cerf and the Culture of Celebrity." *Journal of Modern Literature* 39, no. 1 (2015): 149–69.

Jarcho, Julia. *Writing and the Modern Stage*. Cambridge: Cambridge University Press, 2017.

Joseph, Betty. "Transference: The Total Situation." *International Journal of Psychoanalysis* 66, no. 4 (1985): 447–54.

Kahn, Douglas, and Gregory Whitehead, eds. *Wireless Imagination: Sound, Radio, and the Avant-Garde*. Cambridge, MA: MIT Press, 1992.

Kane, Brian. "Phenomenology, Physiognomy, and the 'Radio Voice.'" *New German Critique* 43, no. 3 (2016): 91–112.

———. *Sound Unseen: Acousmatic Sound in Theory and Practice*. New York: Oxford University Press, 2014.

Kaplan, Milton. *Radio and Poetry*. New York: Columbia University Press, 1949.

Kim, Rebecca Y. "John Cage in Separate Togetherness with Jazz." *Contemporary Music Review* 31, no. 1 (February 2012): 63–89.

Kirsch, Sharon J. "Gertrude Stein Delivers." *Rhetoric Review* 31, no. 3 (2012): 254–70.

Kittler, Friedrich A. *Discourse Networks, 1800/1900*. Translated by Michael Metteer, with Chris Cullens. Stanford, CA: Stanford University Press, 1990.

Knarp, Anne. "The Sound of Home? Some Thoughts on How the Radio Voice Anchors, Contains and Sometimes Pierces." *The Radio Journal—International Studies in Broadcast & Audio Media* 11, no. 1 (2013): 59–73.

Kokkini, Dimitra. "The Rejection of Erotic Passion by Euripides' Hippolytos." In *Éros and the Polis: Love in Context*, edited by Ed Sanders, 67–84. London: University of London Press, 2013.

Kostelanetz, Richard, ed. *Gertrude Stein Advanced*. Jefferson, NC: McFarland & Co., 1990.

Lehmann, Hans-Thies. *Postdramatic Theatre*. Translated and with an introduction by Karen Jürs-Munby. London, New York: Routledge, 2006.

Leick, Karen. *Gertrude Stein and the Making of an American Celebrity*. New York: Routledge, 2009.

Lewis, Cara L. *Dynamic Form: How Intermediality Made Modernism*. Ithaca, NY: Cornell University Press, 2020.

Lorange, Astrid. *How Reading Is Written: A Brief Index to Gertrude Stein*. Middletown, CT: Wesleyan University Press, 2014.

Loveless, Natalie. *How to Make Art at the End of the World*. Durham, NC: Duke University Press, 2019.

Loxley, James. *Performativity*. New York: Routledge, 2007.

Marranca, Bonnie. "Introduction." In *Last Operas and Plays*, vii–xxix. Baltimore: Johns Hopkins University Press, 1995.

Matthews, Sean. "Change and Theory in Raymond Williams' Structure of Feeling." *Pretexts: Literary and Cultural Studies* 10, no. 2 (2001): 179–94.

McCabe, Susan. *Cinematic Modernism: Modernist Poetry and Film*. Cambridge: Cambridge University Press, 2009.

McCaffrey, John. "'Any of Mine without Music to Help Them': The Operas and Plays of Gertrude Stein." *Yale/Theatre* 4, no. 3 (1973): 27–39.

McLuhan, Marshall. *Understanding Media: The Extensions of Man*. Introduction by Lewis Lapham. Cambridge, MA: MIT Press, 1994.

McLuhan, Marshall, and Quentin Fiore. *The Medium Is the Massage: An Inventory of Effects*. Toronto: Penguin Books, 2003.

Meyer, Steven J. *Irresistible Dictation: Gertrude Stein and the Correlations of Writing and Science*. Stanford, CA: Stanford University Press, 2001.

———, ed. "Gertrude Stein: A Radio Interview." *Paris Review* 116, no. 1 (Fall 1990): 85–97.

Miller, J. Hillis. "Performativity as Performance / Performativity as Speech Act: Derrida's Special Theory of Performativity." *South Atlantic Quarterly* 106, no. 2 (2007): 219–35.

Moi, Toril. *Revolution of the Ordinary: Literary Studies after Wittgenstein, Austin, and Cavell*. Chicago: University of Chicago Press, 2017.

Moon, Michael. "Taking a Chance on Love: Scenes, Scripts, and Affects in *Four Saints in Three Acts* and Jazz-Cabaret Songs and Performances of the 1930s." *Textual Practice* 36, no. 12 (2022): 2060–77.

Mowitt, John. *Radio: Essays in Bad Reception*. Berkeley: University of California Press, 2011.

Murphet, Julian. *Multimedia Modernism: Literature and the Anglo-American Avant-Garde*. Cambridge: Cambridge University Press, 2009.

Murphet, Julian, Helen Groth, and Penelope Hone, eds. *Sounding Modernism: Rhythm and Sonic Mediation in Modern Literature and Film*. Edinburgh: Edinburgh University Press, 2017.

Nealon, Jeffrey T. *Fates of the Performative: From the Linguistic Turn to the New Materialism*. Minneapolis: University of Minnesota Press, 2021.

North, Michael. *Reading 1922: A Return to the Scene of the Modern*. New York: Oxford University Press, 1999.

Nyerges, Aaron. "Styling Sovereignty: Gertrude Stein's Epideictic Constitution of the USA." *Textual Practice* 31, no. 1 (2017): 59–79.

Nyman, Michael. *Experimental Music: Cage and Beyond*. New York: Cambridge University Press, 1999.

Ogden, Thomas H. "On Holding and Containing, Being and Dreaming." *The International Journal of Psychoanalysis* 85, no. 6 (2004): 1349–64.

Orwell, George. "Poetry and the Microphone." In *Radiotext(e)*, edited by Neil Strauss, 167. New York: Semiotext(e), 1993.

Parker, Andrew, and Eve Kosofsky Sedgwick. "Introduction: Performativity and Performance." In *Performativity and Performance*, edited by Andrew Parker and Eve Kosofsky Sedgwick, 1–18. New York: Routledge, 1995.

Perloff, Marjorie. *Wittgenstein's Ladder: Poetic Language and the Strangeness of the Ordinary*. Chicago: University of Chicago Press, 1996.

Peters, John Durham. *Speaking into the Air: A History of the Idea of Communication*. Chicago: University of Chicago Press, 2000.

Pondrom, Cyrena N. "Gertrude Stein, Minimalism, and Modern Opera." In *Modernism and Opera*, edited by Richard Begam and Matthew Wilson Smith. Baltimore: Johns Hopkins University Press, 2016.

Porte, Rebecca Ariel. "Long Dull Poems: Stein's *Stanzas in Meditation* and Wordsworth's *The Prelude*." In *Primary Stein: Returning to the Writing of Gertrude Stein*, edited by Janet Boyd and Sharon Kirsch. Lanham, MD: Lexington Books, 2014.

Posman, Sarah, and Laura Luise Schultz, eds. *Gertrude Stein in Europe: Reconfigurations Across Media, Disciplines, and Traditions*. London: Bloomsbury Press, 2015.

Posnock, Ross. *The Trial of Curiosity: Henry James, William James, and the Challenge of Modernity*. New York: Oxford University Press, 1991.

Pound, Scott. "The Difference Sound Makes: Gertrude Stein and the Poetics of Intonation." *English Studies in Canada* 33, no. 4 (2007): 25–35.

Puchner, Martin. *Stage Fright: Modernism, Anti-Theatricality, and Drama*. Baltimore: Johns Hopkins University Press, 2002.

Radio Announcers. Providence, RI: C. De Witt White Co., 1934. https://worldradiohistory.com/Archive-Station-Albums/Networks/Radio-Announcers-1934-NBC.pdf.

Rice, William. "Gertrude Stein's American Lecture Tour." In *The Letters of Gertrude Stein and Thornton Wilder*, edited by Edward M. Burns and Ulla A. Dydo. New Haven, CT: Yale University Press, 1996.

Richardson, Joan. *A Natural History of Pragmatism: The Fact of Feeling from Jonathan Edwards to Gertrude Stein*. New York: Cambridge University Press, 2006.

Robinson, Marc. *The Other American Drama*. Cambridge: Cambridge University Press, 1994.

Rosten, Bevya, et al. "A Play to Be Performed: Excerpts from the Gertrude Stein Symposium at New York University." *Theater* 32, no. 2 (2002): 3–25.

Ryan, Betsy Alayne. *Gertrude Stein's Theatre of the Absolute*. Ann Arbor: UMI Research Press, 1984.

Salvato, Nicholas. *Uncloseting Drama: American Modernism and Queer Performance*. New Haven, CT: Yale University Press, 2010.

Schultz, Laura Luise. "A Combination and Not a Contradiction. Gertrude Stein's Performative Aesthetics." In *Performative Realism: Interdisciplinary Studies in Art and Media*, edited by Rune Gade and Anne Jerslev. Copenhagen: Museum Tusculanum Press University of Copenhagen, 2005.

Sedgwick, Eve Kosofsky. *Touching Feeling: Affect, Performativity, Pedagogy*. Durham, NC: Duke University Press, 2003.

———. "Queer Performativity: Henry James's *The Art of the Novel*." *GLQ* 1, no. 1 (1993): 1–16.

Smedman, Lorna J. "'Cousin to Cooning': Relation, Difference, and Racialized Language in Stein's Nonrepresentational Texts." *Modern Fiction Studies* 42, no. 3 (1996): 569–88.

Sontag, Susan. *On Photography*. Picador, 2001.

Stein, Gertrude. *The Autobiography of Alice B. Toklas*. New York: Vintage Books, 1990. Originally published 1933.

———. *Everybody's Autobiography*. Exact Change, 1993. Originally published 1937.

———. *The Geographical History of America; or, the Relation of Human Nature to the Human Mind*. Introduction by William H. Gass. Baltimore: Johns Hopkins University Press, 1995. Originally published 1936.

———. *Geography and Plays*. With an introduction by Cyrena N. Pondrom. Madison: University of Wisconsin Press, 1993. Originally published 1922.

———. "Gertrude Stein Interviewed by William Lundell." Recorded October 12, 1934, on NBC. YCAL MSS 77, Series IX, box HSR, CD. no. 36, Gertrude and Alice B. Toklas Collection, Beinecke Rare Book and Manuscript Library, Yale University. Audio recording.

———. "Gertrude Stein Interviewed by William Lundell." YCAL MSS 76, box 140, folder 3293, Gertrude and Alice B. Toklas Papers, Beinecke Rare Book and Manuscript Library, Yale University. Described as a transcription of the interview, but likely a prepared script.

———. "I Came and Here I Am." *Hearst's International-Cosmopolitan* (February 1935): 18–19, cont'd 167–68.

———. *Ida: A Novel*. Edited by Logan Esdale. New Haven, CT: Yale University Press in association with the Beinecke Rare Book and Manuscript Library, 2012. Originally published 1941.

———. *Last Operas and Plays*. Edited by Carl van Vechten, with an introduction by Bonnie Marranca. Baltimore: Johns Hopkins University Press, 1994. Originally published 1949.

———. *Lectures in America*. Reprint, with an introduction by Wendy Steiner. Boston: Beacon Press, 1985. Originally published 1935.

———. "Meditations on Being About to Visit My Native Land." In *Painted Lace and Other Pieces (1914–1937)*, 254–56. New Haven, CT: Yale University Press, 1955.

———. *Operas and Plays*. Barrytown, NY: Station Hill Press, 1998. Originally published 1932.

———. *A Stein Reader*. Edited by Ulla Dydo. Evanston, IL: Northwestern University Press, 1993.

Stein, Gertrude, and Virgil Thomson. *Four Saints in Three Acts: An Opera by Gertrude Stein and Virgil Thomson. Scenario by Maurice Grosser*. New York: Music Press, 1948.

———. *The Mother of Us All: An Opera by Gertrude Stein and Virgil Thomson, together with the scenario by Maurice Grosser*. New York: Music Press, 1947.

Steiner, Wendy. *Exact Resemblance to Exact Resemblance: The Literary Portraiture of Gertrude Stein*. New Haven, CT: Yale University Press, 1978.

Strauss, Neil, ed. *Radiotext(e)*. New York: Semiotext(e), 1993.

Sutherland, Donald. *Gertrude Stein: A Biography of Her Work*. New Haven, CT: Yale University Press, 1951.

Trotter, David. *Literature in the First Media Age: Britain between the Wars*. Cambridge, MA: Harvard University Press, 2013.

Turner, Sarah. *Feminist Speculation and the Practice of Research-Creation*. New York: Routledge, 2021.

Verma, Neil. *Theater of the Mind: Imagination, Aesthetics, and American Radio Drama*. Chicago: University of Chicago Press, 2012.

Volpicelli, Robert. *Transatlantic Modernism and the U.S. Lecture Tour*. Oxford: Oxford University Press, 2021.

Voris, Linda. *The Composition of Sense in Gertrude Stein's Landscape Writing*. London: Palgrave Macmillan, 2016.

Wallace, Rob. *Improvisation and the Making of American Literary Modernism*. New York: Continuum Press, 2010.

Watson, Dana Cairns. *Gertrude Stein and the Essence of What Happens*. Nashville, TN: Vanderbilt University Press, 2005.

Watson, Steven. *Prepare for Saints: Gertrude Stein, Virgil Thomson, and the Mainstreaming of American Modernism*. Berkeley: University of California Press, 2000.

Weber, Samuel. *Theatricality as Medium*. New York: Fordham University Press, 2004.

Weideman, Thomas. "'Without Too Much Anxiety': Re-Reading Cage and Feldman through Gertrude Stein's Theatre Poetics." *Textual Practice* 36, no. 12 (2022): 2078–97.

Whittington, Ian. "Radio Studies and Twentieth-Century Literature: Ethics, Aesthetics, and Remediation." *Literary Compass* 11, no. 9 (2014): 634–48.

Wientzen, Timothy. *Automatic: Literary Modernism and the Politics of Reflex*. Baltimore: Johns Hopkins University Press, 2021.

Will, Barbara. *Unlikely Collaborations: Gertrude Stein, Bernard Faÿ, and the Vichy Dilemma*. New York: Columbia University Press, 2011.

Williams, Raymond. *Drama from Ibsen to Brecht*. London: Hogarth Press, 1973.

———. *Television: Technology and Cultural Form*. Middletown, CT: Wesleyan University Press, 1993.

Wilson, Elizabeth A. *Gut Feminism*. Durham, NC: Duke University Press, 2015.

Wilson, Sarah. "Gertrude Stein and the Radio." *Modernism/modernity* 11, no. 2 (April 2004): 261–78.

Wineapple, Brenda. *Sister Brother: Gertrude and Leo Stein*. Baltimore: Johns Hopkins University Press, 1996.

Wollaeger, Mark. *Modernism, Media, and Propaganda: British Narrative from 1900 to 1945*. Princeton, NJ: Princeton University Press, 2008.

Worthen, W. B. *Drama between Poetry and Performance*. Malden, MA: Wiley-Blackwell, 2010.

———. "Drama, Performativity, and Performance." *PMLA* 113, no. 5 (October 1998): 1093–1107.

INDEX

Adorno, Theodor, on radio, 20, 23, 24, 32, 34–40, 52, 175n35, 175n39
affect theory, 7, 10–11, 14–15, 100
Anderson, Laurie, 18
Aristophanes, 102
Arnheim, Rudolf, 27, 41, 175n39
Artaud, Antonin, 104
Aschour, Didier, 156
Ashley, Robert, 17, 31, 39, 157, 167, 174n20
Austin, J. L., 21, 93–104, 107, 112–13, 121, 177n9, 177n11; use of scare quotes by, 94, 97, 102. *See also* illocutionary acts; performativity; speech acts
Autobiography of Alice B. Toklas, The (Stein), 8, 27, 46

Barthes, Roland, 28, 45
Bay-Cheng, Sarah, 10, 44
Beach, Sylvia, 115
Beckett, Samuel, 13, 45, 104, 120, 121
Beethoven, Ludwig van, 17
Belgum, Erik, 173n29
Benjamin, Walter, 25, 38, 40, 44, 45
Benveniste, Émile, 104
Berg, Alban, 17

Berners, Gerald, 16
Bernfeld, Siegfried, 36
Bion, Wilfred, 13–14, 15, 24, 31, 45–46, 47, 57, 115, 120
Bottoms, Stephen J., 10
Bowers, Jane Palatini, 10, 103–5, 117, 178n47
boxed sets, appeal of, 7–8
Brecht, Bertolt, 13, 112, 120
Brentano, Franz, 36
Bridgman, Richard, 49, 119
Burke, Kenneth, 113–14, 121
Butler, Judith, 93, 99

Cage, John, 16, 18, 38, 166–67
Cantril, Hadley, 36
Can You See the Name (Stein), 104–5
Captain Walter Arnold (Stein), 18, 49, 169–70
Carmines, Al, 16
Cavell, Stanley, 96, 99, 100–101, 102
Cerf, Bennett, 31, 32, 39
Chang, Dorothy, 18, 115, 165–66
Chaudhuri, Una, 10
Chekhov, Anton, 111, 112, 120
Chokroun, Olive (Dave), 17, 18, 166–67
Circular Play, A (Stein), 45, 47
containers, 119–20

Daugaard, Solveig, 56, 156
Davis, Daniel Thomas, 15, 16, 18, 19, 43, 47, 48, 51–52
de Man, Paul, 95
Derrida, Jacques, 94–95, 99, 100, 114
Doctor Faustus Lights the Lights (Stein), 8
domesticity, 21, 118–20
Dydo, Ulla, 43–44, 47, 108

Ehrman, Theresa, 115
Ellul, Jacques, 24
Emerson, Ralph Waldo, 9, 22
Empson, William, 34
Esdale, Logan, 45
etiolation, 94, 96
Euripides, 96, 97–98, 100–102
Evans, Donald, 117
Everybody's Autobiography (Stein), 17, 31, 32, 39, 40, 41, 42, 52
Exercise in Analysis, An (Stein), 18, 169

fantasy, 24, 30–31, 103. *See also* phantasy
feeling: structures of, 111–12; value of, 9, 11, 12–13, 21, 25
Feldman, Morton, 16
Felman, Shoshana, 95, 104

Ferenczi, Sandor, 36–37, 38, 42
Fiore, Quentin, 175n38
Fitch, Doug, 16, 48
Flatley, Jonathan, 55
For the Country Entirely (Stein), 18, 107, 168
Foucault, Michel, 38, 93
Fourier transforms, 151–52
Four Saints in Three Acts (Stein), 8, 10, 15, 27, 34, 173n20
Frederiksen, Lene Asp, 56, 156
Frege, Gottlob, 93
Freud, Sigmund, 14, 31, 36–37, 45
Fuchs, Elinor, 10

Geographical History of America, The (Stein), 119
Geography and Plays (Stein), 10, 49, 108, 117
Gibb, Harry Phelan, 108
Grosser, Maurice, 15–16, 173nn20–21
group therapy, 13–14

Harries, Martin, 34
Hegel, Georg Wilhelm Friedrich, 103
He Said It (Stein), 18, 21, 97, 105–8

Hinshelwood, Robert, 120
Hopkins, Miriam, 31, 39
Horkheimer, Max, 35, 38
Houseman, John, 10
How to Write (Stein), 58, 109
Husserl, Edmund, 35–36

Ibsen, Henrik, 96, 111, 120
"I Came and Here I Am" (Stein article), 24, 27–31
Ida (Stein), 31, 45, 172n4
illocutionary acts, 21, 94, 96, 98, 107, 113–14
improvisation, 16, 167

James, Henry, 98, 100
James, William, 9, 34, 109
Jarcho, Julia, 10, 177n24

Kane, Brian, 35–36
Kittler, Friedrich, 24, 37
Klein, Melanie, 11, 14, 24, 31, 37, 45; on transference, 96–97, 100
Kornfeld, Lawrence, 20

Ladies' Voices (Stein), 16
landscape figure, 10, 12, 17, 82–83, 107, 173n19
Last Operas and Plays (Stein), 10, 42
Laville, Claire, 48
Lazarsfeld, Paul, 35, 38
Lehmann, Hans-Thies, 10
Levy, Harriet, 115

"libretto" term, 15
Lierman, Aurélie Nyirabikali, 156, 159
Loxley, James, 114
Lucier, Alvin, 39
Lundell, William, interview with Stein by, 21, 24, 25–28, 31–34, 42, 174n9, 175n38; nonpayment for, 39

Making of Americans, The (Stein), 30, 119
Marranca, Bonnie, 172n13
Matthews, Sean, 111
McLuhan, Marshall, 36, 37, 52, 175n38
"Meditations on Being About to Visit My Native Land" (Stein essay), 30
"melodrama" term, 17
Meyer, Steven, 9, 17, 56, 109, 156
modernist literature, 9, 13, 17, 23–24, 49
Moi, Toril, 176n8
Moon, Michael, 47
Mother of Us All, The (Stein), 8, 15
Mowitt, John, 37

Nietzsche, Friedrich, 96, 99

object relations theory, 7, 10–11, 13–14, 24, 31, 100
Ogden, Thomas, 120
Operas and Plays (Stein), 10
Orwell, George, 166, 175n25

"parlor" term, 117
performativity, 21, 92–103, 112–13, 120, 176n1, 176n7; hollowness in, 21, 94, 96–100, 102, 103, 107, 177n12, 177n24; performative utterances: *see* Austin, J. L.
Peters, John Durham, 25
Peterson, Jane, 115
phantasy, 11, 24, 31, 32, 36, 39, 103, 115; America as, 28, 174n18; regressive, 15; unconscious, 37
phenomenology, 9, 12, 21, 31, 32, 35–36, 52, 95
Photograph (Stein), 18, 20, 25, 40, 42–49, 117
Pirandello, Luigi, 111, 120
Plato, 102
Play Called Not and Now, A (Stein), 31
"Plays" (Stein lecture), 10, 11–12, 40, 57, 108, 109, 110, 155, 157
Please Do Not Suffer (Stein), 107
podcasting, 23, 39
"Poetry and Grammar" (Stein essay), 153
"Portraits and Repetition" (Stein lecture), 12, 155
Porte, Rebecca Ariel, 178n33
pragmatism, 9, 25, 93, 96
propaganda, 23, 25, 40, 52
Psychology of Nations, The (Stein), 18, 20, 25, 40, 49, 51–52
Puchner, Martin, 9–10

Quartermain, Peter, 105
queer theater, 10, 98
queer theory, 92, 93

radio: scripted aspect of, 27, 30; Stein's concept of audience, 24, 27, 30–32, 34; term usage, 18, 20. *See also* Adorno, Theodor
Radio Free Stein project, 6–9, 11, 12, 14–21, 23–25, 40, 97, 100, 103, 173n19; renditions by: *He Said It*, 97, 105–8, 117, 166–67; *Photograph*, 42–43, 47–50, 169; *The Psychology of Nations*, 51–52, 169–70; *What Happened*, 56–91, 97, 108–10, 112, 122–49, 150–60, 164–65; *White Wines*, 97, 115, 117, 118, 165
"radio free" term, 22–23
"rendering" term, 7
Robinson, Marc, 172n13
Roosevelt, Franklin, 39
Rorem, Ned, 16
Rosenthal, Lecia, 34
Rousseau, Jean-Jacques, 13, 17
Russell, Bertrand, 93
Ryan, Betsy Alayne, 104

"scenario" term, 15–16, 173n20
Schultz, Laura, 56, 109, 156
Sedgwick, Eve, 93, 95, 96, 98, 99, 100, 120
Serup, Martin Glaz, 56, 156
Shakespeare, William, 94, 96
Shalabi, Sam, 17, 18
Short Sentences (Stein), 18, 171
SIX. TWENTY. OUTRAGEOUS. (Stein), 15, 16, 19, 25, 40, 43, 50, 169–70
Smailbegović, Ada, 105
Sontag, Susan, 45

speech acts, 100, 101, 104, 113, 121
Spinoza, Baruch, 25
sprechstimme, 17
Stanzas in Meditation (Stein), 178n33
Stein, Daniel and Solomon, 46
Stein, Gertrude: "difficulty" ascribed to, 8–9; on "emotional syncopation," 12, 13, 14, 40, 41, 59; influence on theater by, 10; lecture tour of, 25, 27, 28, 30, 32, 41; on machines, 52–53; music and, 17–18; paragraphs and, 109–10, 112, 115; patriotism of, 22; on photography, 44–45; playwrighting approach by, 8, 9–10, 12–13, 14, 20, 42, 103, 117, 120, 177n24; portraiture and, 8, 12, 13, 14, 34, 41–42, 81, 104; publicity reactions by, 27–28, 30, 32, 45; "red Indian" figure in, 174n18; stageability of plays by, 9–10, 104; on understanding as enjoyment, 21, 34
Stein, Leo, 32, 40–41, 46, 115, 117, 119
Stein, Michael and Sarah, 44
Sutherland, Donald, 20

Tender Buttons (Stein), 42, 117
theatrical conventions, 8, 21, 96, 103, 110, 111–13, 117
Thomson, Virgil, 10, 16, 17, 173n20
Toklas, Alice B., 27, 31, 32, 33, 41, 43, 45, 105, 107, 117, 119; on *Four Saints*, 173n20; moves in with Stein, 47, 115, 117
transference, 10–11, 12, 14, 35, 42, 52; group, 15; Klein on, 96–97, 100; transferential poetics, 25, 34

Van Vechten, Carl, 10, 11, 117
Voris, Linda, 173n19
Vriezen, Samuel, 18, 21, 56, 111, 122

Walker, Deborah, 159
Warhol, Andy, 53
Warner, Dan, 18
Weber, Samuel, 96, 99, 100
Weill, Kurt, 17
Welles, Orson, 36
What Happened (Stein), 10, 16, 18, 21, 56–91, 97, 108–12, 115, 119, 122, 150–60; original text of, 54–55, 151; time in 150–51, 152, 155
Whitehead, Alfred North, 93, 175n38
White Wines (Stein), 18, 21, 97, 115–19
Williams, Raymond, 24, 111–12, 175n35
Wilson, Elizabeth, 36–37
Wilson, Robert, 20
Wineapple, Brenda, 46–47, 117
Winslow, Robert, 16
Wittgenstein, Ludwig, 21, 93, 95, 99, 109
Wollaeger, Mark, 23, 24

Zappa, Frank, 18